ART START

FUNDAMENTALS OF THE STUDIO

A GUIDEBOOK FOR STUDENTS IN THE VISUAL ARTS

DENNIS LICK

Middlesex College • Edison, New Jersey

Kendall Hunt
publishing company

ART START

FUNDAMENTALS OF THE STUDIO

A GUIDEBOOK FOR STUDENTS IN THE VISUAL ARTS

Kendall Hunt
publishing company

DENNIS LICK
Middlesex College • Edison, New Jersey

Front cover art: Dennis Lick, *Night Sky*, collage on paper, 8 x 10", 2015 & 2019
Inside front cover art: Dennis Lick, *Compass in Cosmos*, acrylic and collage on paper, 10 x 7", 2015
Back cover art: Dennis Lick, *Full Moon*, collage on paper, 9.5 x 5.5", 2009
Inside back cover art: Dennis Lick, *Strategy for a Finite Planet*, acrylic and collage on paper, 10.5 x 7.5", 2020.

www.kendallhunt.com
Send all inquiries to:
4050 Westmark Drive
Dubuque, IA 52004-1840

ISBN 978-1-7924-8035-5

Published in the United States of America

DEDICATION

This book is dedicated to my students who know the difference that art makes.

CONTENTS

Section IV – Taking the Dive: Actions Speak Louder Than Words.. 113

Section V – Knowing Your Place: Understanding the Big Picture .. 125

Section VI – Putting It Altogether (Or, Getting the Hang of It)....... 161

Section VII – Art Making with Direction 197

Section VIII – Speaking of Art: The Verbal and the Visual.............. 247

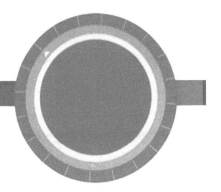

LIST OF ILLUSTRATIONS
BY JERRY ZINSER

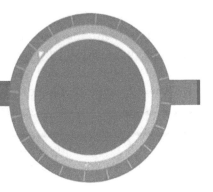

ACKNOWLEDGMENTS

I express my thanks to all whose encouragement and support have aided the efforts to bring this book to reality. I am fortunate to have continuing decades of support from friends, colleagues, artists, teachers, and family who have been mentors in shaping my life in the visual arts.

Thank you to Kendall Hunt, and specifically to Sheri Hosek and Sue Saad for their attentive support, patience, and guidance through the publishing process. I heartily thank Kendall Hunt's graphic designer, Suzanne Millius, for the compelling and unabashedly colorful cover design of the book.

I am greatly indebted to Kay Tsurumi for her enduring, enthusiastic, and expert editing on both grammar and content. Her many suggestions have been reliably wise and cogent. The book would not be in its current form without her active involvement. Jerry Zinser, a close friend and fellow artist since our graduate school days at Rutgers University, has been indispensable for designing the illustrations. He was able to interpret my crude sketches into clear and concise images. In countless ways Jerry's tech savvy often got me through rough patches of uncertainty. He also enhanced the photographic quality of the collages reproduced in the book.

My sister Nancy, artist and teacher, and her able husband, Pat Phillips, a professional editor, have contributed greatly in both editing and encouragement. Many thanks and hugs go to Marion Munk, long time friend and fellow artist-teacher, for her tireless support and enthusiasm in all respects, including this book.

Thank you to my many friends and colleagues at Middlesex County College. Thanks to Susan Altman for her unwavering support on many fronts, including our exchanges on teaching strategies and content, which contributed considerably to the topics in the book. Many thanks are due to Bryan Weitz, our jack-of-all-trades studio coordinator, for his reliability and expertise in assisting me in all manner of requests, including organizing teaching supplies, printing parts of the book before publishing, and adept proofreading at a moment's notice.

Thank you Annie Hogan, Chair of our department, for her enthusiastic support of teaching, art making, and writing. I must also thank Jay Siegfried, retired chair of our department, who was the first person I asked about the advisability of writing this book. His immediate enthusiasm for the project helped convince me to start scratching out ideas and typing them into intelligible form. Deep thanks return to 1974 when Jerry Vis hired me as an adjunct at Middlesex. His friendship, shared ideas on a vast range of subjects, and his roles as both artist and published writer has meant much to my own inclinations.

Finally, many thanks to the countless, talented students I have taught whose ideas and opinions influenced my own. The classroom studio is never a one-way street. Teaching and learning are interchangeable.

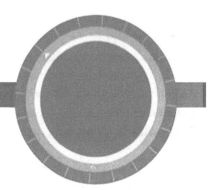

INTRODUCTION:
HOW TO USE THIS BOOK

After teaching for more than forty years, I have accumulated a considerable storehouse of visual ideas, artistic strategies, technical knowledge, and critical advice aimed at the optimistic task of improving the lot of art students. These methods and practices are derived from my experiences as an artist in the studio. What I do in my art becomes the basis of my attempt to guide students. The cross-currents between artist and teacher are, for me, empathetic rather than polarizing. I decided soon after graduate school that the way to keep my life unified was to be an artist who teaches, and to meld the dual roles as much as possible. I have never wanted to compartmentalize, as if my day job was a distinct necessity to support my artistic ambitions. When I am teaching, I am also explaining art to myself. Thus, in addition to artist and teacher I have a third role: I am the First Student.

I discovered early in my development that the intellectual, sensory, technical, and philosophical bases of creativity are common to all artists. What the artist/teacher can offer students in the classroom is no less than the benefit derived from this commitment. However, with the constraints of time and place imposed by academic calendars, a lot of loose threads go unexamined or discarded. One purpose of this book is to try to highlight some of those threads and bring them to the worthy attention of students—or to the attention of worthy students. If a student who peruses my musings gets just one good idea or insight from these pages, then my effort will be rewarded. A more modest, but equally worthy, goal is that the student looks at these pages and concludes, "Yes, I knew that, but now the idea is more apparent and I can act more confidently because my insight is confirmed."

If an artist's skills become second nature, that will serve him well in developing mature work. The artist with good work habits and discipline is in a position to provide useful guidance for students whose inexperience can leave them struggling to know how to begin. What a teacher asks students to do must have the whiff of authenticity. However, that advice may not have immediate meaning to students. Like artists, the way students understand is to *do*, to make essential ideas *their* experiences. My intention is that what I have to say, whether in the classroom or in this book, has already withstood the test of trial and error in the studio of *my* experience.

As an undergraduate at Miami University (Ohio), I discussed with my professors as to whether—of all things!—it was possible to teach art. As a naive student, I was taken aback by some of the answers—that, bluntly, art cannot be taught. To be more accurate, the full answer is, "You cannot teach someone to become an artist." I do not disagree. To become an artist is a personal decision involving great commitment complicated by compromises and sacrifices. The artist walks an arduous path of financial instability, creative angst, and diminished social rewards in a broader culture mostly indifferent to the fine arts. You become an artist because it is your only choice. It is a disease to which you willingly surrender.

If we as instructors fall short of the intended goal of bestowing artistic destiny on our students due to social, political, economic, and/or various unforeseen conditions, should we still teach art? The answer is a resounding yes. The broader skills acquired from earning a degree in the arts may be more significant than whether we are training practicing artists. Visual and verbal skills coincide in our field in a unique way. The ability to harness these skills for effective communication and the articulation of ideas will serve the student well in his adult life of career and leisure. The fact that the student's *visual* intelligence is honed to a higher degree than that of his compatriots will give him a leg up in many career choices, not just in the arts. We think in pictures as much as in words, and our dependence on electronic technology demands that we especially understand two-dimensional images and their implications in three dimensions. Visual literacy is as important as verbal literacy.

Despite the likelihood that many fine arts graduates will choose to work in unrelated fields, those individuals will both contribute socially and benefit personally as a result of their art educations. Since much of our contact with and understanding of the world is visual, those who have educated their *eyes* are in a position to experience it with greater depth and appreciation. While the art elements of color and form are available in great profusion in galleries and museums everywhere, they are also fully developed in nature. The enrichment that visual education provides to students throughout their lives is incalculable. At the same time, as art students develop their sensitivities to visual forms, they are more likely to support the arts in their communities.

But art often goes beyond art. An art education tends to nurture an aesthetic taste in consumer choices, ethical values in sympathy with a green consideration of resources in the environment, and a sophisticated understanding of the beauty and organization of both natural and human-made forms. The benefits are personal, social, and global. While the manifestations of connecting all these dots may not be apparent in a given art studio course, or even in several consecutive courses, invariably art students develop these values as they gain new perspectives, sometimes well after they have earned their academic degrees. One purpose of my book is to propose topics that will stimulate thought on a range of comprehensive matters both aesthetic and worldly—because art and life intersect. I have the immodest goal to raise consciousness on a host of practical and philosophical issues.

Not to dodge the question, what can we teach our students in an art program? We can provide a working knowledge of the *tools* by which students can *choose* to become artists. Technical skills, art fundamentals, conceptual understanding, critical thinking, knowledge of art history, and insight about personal development can all be enhanced by teaching. A self-directed art education would be a daunting task fraught with blind alleys and dead ends. I recall one professor at Miami who proclaimed that an art education provides a series of useful shortcuts that speed the process of an individual's development. You can get there faster with instruction, bypassing obstacles and detours that might otherwise waste time and undermine motivation. It is my hope that a few shortcuts are provided by this book.

I have another reason to write. From years of teaching and experimenting with various methods in the studio, I have come to appreciate that what I say, that is, the quality of what is conveyed verbally, has a great effect on what students are able to do with that information. I have witnessed how language can stimulate greater effort and deeper understanding. This makes me neither an accomplished orator nor a master teacher. Rather, I have learned three key principles in teaching: (1) say it clearly and thoroughly and you will be understood, (2) describe what you know from your own experience and it will have the ring of truth, and (3) when students know their task well from the first two approaches, they do their best work. My discovery has made me smitten with language. Now I cannot resist the idea that the oral word of the classroom might be reinforced by the written word.

The topics addressed in this book are meant to be supplemental and reaffirming to the studio classroom experience of art students. My remarks are especially aimed at first- and second-year students enrolled in an art program at a community college or four-year institution. The writing here does not replace classroom instruction and this book is in no way a how-to in any of the visual arts disciplines. The topics described and the issues raised are meant to give the student pause for thought. Their purpose is to stimulate thinking *outside* the classroom. At the same time, all the subjects, regardless of how they may circumnavigate the waters of creativity, are meant to support the practice of the visual arts.

I have deliberately chosen some topics—such as the chapters on art history, formalism, drawing, and painting—that are covered in the college classroom. These areas are of such importance to an art education that any repetition is worth bearing for the sake of confirmation or review—or reexperiencing in a new perspective. Other issues may have a tendency to be given scant coverage or avoided altogether in teaching because they don't fit the course objectives. By writing about these less-familiar topics (such as contemporary art), I want to shed light on worthy considerations that deserve greater attention.

The manner in which topics are addressed in written form necessarily differs from that of the classroom. Students and professors alike are aware of the value of various learning styles. It is also difficult, if not impossible, to pinpoint when and how you learn something. Sometimes that light bulb doesn't turn on until an idea is revealed in several contexts. If you missed learning a concept one way, you might pick it up another way. Only a few seeds take root, so you have to sow more than you think you need.

As a child, I recall working on a mural with others my age and feeling disheartened that their drawing abilities were so, well, childish. Classmates wanted to know how I *did* that. How did I draw so well? It was the first time I had to think about explaining what I could do that most others could not. It was a double revelation—that I could do something well and it might be possible to explain so others might know too. What I said then I am not sure I have been able to improve! I said that I could *see* the object in my mind's eye as I drew. My visual curiosity had been the motivation by which to *memorize* the appearance of many subjects in my environment. Starting from those early years, it has always mattered to me how the *forms* of things *looked*. Furthermore, understanding the *look* of a subject is also the first key to manipulating it creatively—that is, beyond the imitation of its appearance. But *seeing* remains the first essential step in making art. It is not the subject as much as the act of seeing the subject that matters. The world is a panorama of visual abundance. We use words as a catalyst to explain the experiences of our sensory world and to aid transformation of those realities into art. Words make images. See as you read.

To benefit the most from reading this book (or any text), here are a few suggestions. First, to gain a sense of a chapter's range of content, skim through the pages, noting especially the headings to know what information is covered. Then, read carefully word for word as you try to connect the meaning in the writing to how you experience making your art. Later, read again. You will understand the material better after more than one reading.

Please read the chapters when assigned since they will have a direct bearing on the projects that take place in class. At the same time, feel free to dip into any chapter at any time that it addresses what you are confronting in your artwork. The book is also meant as a ready reference in which you can turn to any page for help. The table of contents can direct you to the most relevant topics. Use the book as much as possible since the practical advice that fills its pages are meant to have an immediate impact as you advance your skills and understanding of the art process. Since it is your book, you can also write and draw all over its pages!

SECTION I

GREAT EXPECTATIONS: LOOKING, THINKING, AND KNOWING

chapter 1

LOOKING AT ART

"LOOKING IS HARDER THAN IT LOOKS," said the mid-twentieth century American abstract painter Ad Reinhardt. I have that quote posted on my office window. Nothing causes more consternation or fascination than the search for meaning in the visual arts. A work of art exists as a concrete object, but its meaning is intangible, abstract, multifaceted, and, often by intent, ambiguous and mysterious. To complicate matters, these qualities resist translation into words since art, after all, is a visual medium. But, we must use language if we are to understand and share each other's responses and confirm that we have gotten a greater rather than a lesser experience of the art.

WHAT MUST THE VIEWER CONSIDER WHEN LOOKING AT ART?

At first glance, subject matter is the most apparent. But identifying or understanding the subject matter is not the meaning. That would be too literal and very incomplete. The subject, represented as landscape, figure, still life, or abstraction, is really the *carrier* of meaning. *What* is only the beginning—the artist's excuse to make something. If you dwell mainly on the *what*—the representation—you will have only a superficial acquaintance with the subject, an anecdotal diversion. The *art* is *everything else.*

HOW THE SUBJECT IS EXPRESSED IS WHERE MEANING STARTS.

How does the artist express his subject? He has at his disposal:
- medium—his chosen materials,
- technique—the way tools affect materials,
- formalism—the visual elements and the principles of composition, and
- expression—the personal vision, the imagination with which all of the above are manipulated.

You have to get the meaning of the art out of these essential components. But meaning does not reside in any of these categories alone. They are woven together and interdependent in such a way that the whole effect of their melding is the meaning. Nevertheless, while it seems contradictory, it is useful to analyze them separately in order to understand the art. Why is a given figure depicted in an unlikely color? Why is this object so severely cropped? Why does the artist distort or exaggerate many forms? What does it mean when certain areas are rendered in rough, broken strokes? Why are some details obliterated and others highlighted? Questions are the road to meaning. These are clues, cues, and prompts that reveal multiple possibilities. Most of the questions you will ask have to do with the artist's unique manipulation of medium, technique, and formalism as he attempts to forge a vision of his subject matter.

Is one of these four components more critical than the others? While art could not exist without all of them, undoubtedly *expression* is the source of the artist's purpose and viewpoint. The expression of imagination is the heart of creativity.

Art is not about illustrating (not to be confused with the art of illustration) a thing or a message. It is not meant to be a stand-in for something else. Art is a complete entity with all the means necessary to arouse the viewer to contemplate its unique statement.

Because of the interactive complexities of the four variables above and the questions they provoke, it is not possible to reduce art to a single interpretation. As soon as you identify one idea, it becomes related to another. Then you have a visual conversation of comparisons and contrasts ricocheting off each other. The beauty is that thoughtful, considered analysis of the evidence conjures a rich variety of plausible interpretations. That is the art.

ART IS NOT IMITATION

Art would be utterly pointless as a mirror of the visible. The realities from which art derives its representations are never meant to be an imitation or an equivalent of nature. Art is either an *abstraction* of those realities or an object of its *own* reality. Instead of comparing art to a preexisting template, you must think psychologically from your experiential and philosophical bases. To find meaning, you must probe deeper than the visual description of what is seen on the surface. Everything you have experienced in the world—including your memory, emotional impressions, and the total of information and knowledge accumulated—you bring to bear in looking at art.

Art works in symbols and metaphors, subtleties, and subliminal implications. Nothing is as it seems on the surface. The surface is a camouflage. In that sense, looking at art is a transforming experience. I want to say transcendent because art takes you out of yourself to a new place. Art's concreteness as an object, the "suit" it wears in the physical world, is a means to an end, to a more universal statement or viewpoint.

The real materials of art, such as canvas, pigment, wood, plaster, and clay, are really a foil for the intangibility of experience and the transforming effects of emotional, psychological, philosophical, and lyrical content. To know art is to be transported to these other states of mind.

OPEN MINDEDNESS IS ESSENTIAL

To look for comfortable and familiar content is not an art experience. Art is not meant to confirm what you already know. If you approach art burdened with preconceptions and prejudices, you surely miss the point. If you bring too much subjectivity to the process of looking, you will eclipse the art. The hazard is that responding to art can become a simplistic mirror of your own biases rather than a thoughtful, sensitive search for meaning. The challenge is to see the art on *its own terms* and what you think the *artist* had in mind—a challenge because looking at art and getting something of value from the experience requires *effort*.

THE VIEWER'S ROLE, LIKE THAT OF THE ARTIST, IS TO BE A PARTICIPANT

Most pop culture that inundates our everyday world would have us remain passive recipients of simplistic messages. You must resist passivity. Viewing art for meaning requires a shift in awareness, a willingness to sift and filter the variables of subject, form, and materials the artist has handled in a particular way. The best art challenges our complacency by asking questions rather than providing answers.

You can and should propose plausible, thoughtful interpretations, but appreciate that there is *never a right* interpretation and *no single* viewpoint. In art, one size does not fit all. The viewer should arrive at his own conclusions, but these ought to share reasonable commonalities with the collective interpretations of those who have examined the evidence carefully. While there are always disagreements among the informed about meanings in art, there is also an established foundation of consensus.

EXPECT A NEW EXPERIENCE FROM ART

The new is the basis of all endeavors in art. Since the Enlightenment, we have pursued relentlessly the new, the secular, and the technological in every discipline. Art is a reliable barometer of our broader quests throughout history. The pursuit of the new is especially pronounced in modern art as the Industrial Revolution gathered steam in the early 1800s. This preoccupation is a testament to what we now value in the larger context of society, culture, and politics. Since art is continually expanding its horizons, the trends are now changing. There has been, in recent decades, a slight, but significant shift from the grander, more sweeping pursuit of the new to a focus on the private, and perhaps, more modest world of personal vision and reflection.

Whether practiced to foster the new or the private, expression resides in the quality of the artist's viewpoint and his intensity in rendering his unique vision. To achieve this, the artist manipulates his forms and materials in inventive and imaginative ways to cause us viewers to see *his* viewpoint, one that we embrace for its ability to impart to us *his* way—and thus, a *new* way—of knowing the world.

ART IS A REFLECTION OF WHO WE WERE, WHO WE ARE, AND WHO WE WOULD LIKE TO BECOME

The best art from all historic periods and global regions reflects a breathtaking range of variety, contrast, and purpose. It may be the best reminder of why it is that we are alive.

Bernard Berenson, a distinguished Renaissance art historian, said, "You see as much as you know." A reasonable knowledge of art history is a necessary foundation for the art major. Art is a language that needs to be learned and practiced to gain its richest insights. The sweeping grandeur and enormous range of that language is convincingly reflected in the great multiplicity of world cultures past and present.

If you wish to get more than a superficial, shallow glance from art, you will need to look thoughtfully, reflectively, lingeringly, and with unabashed pleasure at the art of your predecessors. The rewards can be handsomely enriching and, if you are committed to the arts, surely life changing.

chapter

HOW ART ENHANCES LIFE

If you look around, art is nearly everywhere. So much in our human-made environment is designed to be visually appealing, if not aesthetic. An advertisement in print or onscreen must be clear and well composed to attract attention. Graphic designers, trained in art schools or colleges, know they must design ads with compelling text and visual images. Objects we use, such as tools, clothing, cars, and buildings, are designed by art professionals and architects in collaboration with engineers and market specialists to be both functional and aesthetically pleasing. These two essential qualities of utility and design are closely linked and interdependent in order to attract the consumer with worthy performance and appearance. These attributes are many of the same components necessary in creating works of art. In that basic sense, art and life are connected.

On the other hand, there are consumer goods that are poorly designed or lack adequate performance. If we can distinguish good from indifferent to bad design, then art can help us become more discriminating consumers. The more sophisticated our understanding of visual art principles, the better we are in assessing the design, craft, and performance we acquire.

Making art and viewing good examples of art in history and contemporary practice increases an appreciation of all the visual properties that surround us. (Visit galleries and museums.) We have five senses, but our eyeball connection to the world is primary in our experience of its abundant form and color. Traveling in the landscape or walking in towns and cities of choice are ongoing occasions when we can appreciate (or denigrate) their visual formal qualities. In other words, the same ingredients in art—the formal elements of line, shape, color, light and dark, texture, and pattern to name some—also inform nature and the human-made environment.

Consider the visual richness of nature, its fauna and flora, the changes of the seasons, the greatly varied landscape throughout the world, or just that special moment of vivid light and color at dawn or dusk. In fact, nature is the best artist! For millennia, artists have derived their inspiration from the multitude of forms and colors in the natural world. Despite the formal innovations in art since ancient times to the present, all art has a counterpoint to something in nature. Nature invents, artists appropriate (or steal!).

To educate your eye, or more precisely, your mind's eye, is to expand your awareness and appreciation of the visual abundance everywhere. Most students enrolled in art courses will not become artists. However, the gain in developing an enhanced view of the world and a deeper understanding of its multifaceted richness is an enchantment to be valued for life.

With the educated eye comes a greater discernment of the relationship between humans and the natural world. Pollution, climate change, and excessive plundering of Earth's resources compromise the harmony, unity, and aesthetic qualities of life on the planet. This Big Picture is why artists throughout history have attempted and continue to create utopian refuges in their works in an otherwise imperfect world.

Thus, an encounter with art making and viewing art with its messages about the relationship between design and the splendors of the natural environment will make you a more sensitive and understanding citizen of the world. A philosopher once said "to know the world is to possess the world." If your encounter with art yields a broadened awareness of art and the world we inhabit, you will have all the riches you need. An education in art will surely give you that and more.

chapter 3

FORMALISM IS ALL IT IS CRACKED UP TO BE

Among the first-year requirements for art majors in a baccalaureate degree program are a pair of foundation courses known by a variety of titles including "Art Fundamentals: Two Dimensions" and "Art Fundamentals: Three Dimensions." Other colleges may include the words *foundation*, *art making*, and *design*. While titles vary, the course objectives are the same: To understand and to apply formalism in the practice of art. Formalism is the linchpin of an art education. It applies to all the fine, commercial, and applied arts, including specialties as various as architecture, industrial design, film, fashion, graphic design, illustration, painting, sculpture, and photography. Because formalism is the common bond among all these areas, the foundation courses are the art students' first encounter with art making. Traditionally, the 2D course precedes the 3D course, as in fall and spring semesters, but many students take them in reverse order as well.

Since the advent of the university system more than a century ago (one could argue since the apprentice-to-master system in the Renaissance), tradition mandates that mastering formalist principles is a priority in art education and a prerequisite for becoming an artist. Formalism is the organizational structure for all art, and its principles inform all styles, subjects, and historical periods.

Sometimes, less experienced students do not see the formal connections among all the visual arts. They are in great haste to practice their specialty before they have mastered basic skills and essential concepts. Art students must be prepared to spend the first two years of a four-year degree program learning and practicing the formalist principles in the foundation courses and in entry-level studio classes such as drawing, painting, and sculpture. Following the foundation program, specialization is concentrated in the third and fourth years.

If the purpose of art is to search for significant meaning, then *formalism* is the means of getting there. It is the grammar of the artist's language. Formalism is a complex system comprised of two parts: *Visual elements* and *composition* (sometimes called *design*). Its components are embedded in every successful work of art of every period and place. What are the components of formalism? From prior experience, you may recognize many of them already:

Visual Elements			
Line	Shape	Value (light and dark)	Color
Space	Texture	Volume/mass	Pattern
Composition			
Unity	Variety	Contrast	Repetition
Balance	Rhythm	Movement	
Emphasis (focal point)	Scale (size)	Proportion	

It may be useful to think of the visual elements as *things* and the parts of composition as *qualities*. (Note: When referring to both the visual elements and composition, it is common practice to use the single word *formalism* or the phrase *formalist principles*.)

The **visual elements** are the building blocks of art making. These elements are to the artist what ingredients are to the chef. The principles of **composition** are the directions for how to use these ingredients. In other words, the visual elements are *composed* to achieve coherent expression.

To compose is to organize all the components into a unified whole and a clearly defined expression. The importance of order in composition is not to be underestimated. Order is one of the most powerful ways we distinguish between

> Beauty and ugliness,
> Clarity and chaos,
> Randomness and purpose,
> Indifference and meaning,
> Casual and, well … formal.

Formalist principles and art content cannot be separated (though we do so to talk about them!) since they are inextricably woven together and interdependent. Line, shape, color, variety, contrast, and unity are the tools to enhance, clarify, and dramatize artistic expression. Think of formalism as the underlying structure that makes art visible. When we are making art or looking at it for pleasure, formalism may not be immediately apparent because our concerns may be focused on other matters ranging from technique to content. Formalism alone is not the art, but art is not possible without it.

Because visual elements and composition are learned through studio practice, the description given here of their essential traits will be brief. These terms are more thoroughly addressed in a variety of other studio textbooks. For more information, see the bibliography at the end of this book.

Line is the most basic tool of the artist. Line serves a variety of purposes, but the two most important ones are as follows: (1) it defines the edges that separate forms from each other, and (2) it conveys a wide range of descriptive functions, including emphasis, character, light and dark, detail, and emotional content. The first works of art that were discovered are over 30,000 years old and were made with lines depicting wildlife, and these are found on the walls of caves in Western Europe. Many modern artists, such as Henri Matisse,

Paul Klee, and Picasso, made expressive drawings in which lines exclusively define their images without sacrificing variety and richness.

Shape is line enclosed into a figure, object, or abstract form. Shapes are the closed boundaries that define forms. We see subjects as entities because of the encapsulating effects of shapes. Shapes invariably evoke references and associations. Everyone has gazed at the clouds or perused the patterns in polished marble to see all manner of figures and forms. The artist must be mindful of designing shapes specific to his intentions or else the art may degrade into a medium of self-reflection for the viewer. Shapes are essentially the underlying structures of composition and become the skeleton that supports all the other visual elements.

Value is the lightness or darkness of a surface. How values clarify, highlight, and cast form into relief with shadow is critical to art making. Sometimes, the word **light** is substituted for value. Highlight and shadow dramatize (actually, make *visible*) both subject matter and the space it occupies. Light and dark (called chiaroscuro) as a driving concept in painting was developed to great sophistication by Leonardo da Vinci, and into high theater by the Baroque painters Caravaggio and Rembrandt. The standard charge given to photographers—that light is the foremost subject matter—is appropriate to all artists.

Color is the mysterious bonus that nature bestows on vision. Since color is visible only in light, it is closely bound up with value. We are sensitive to the tints and shades of colors depending on the quality of light in which they are seen. But there is a dimension to color that is inexpressible. How do you define yellow? Red? Blue? Green? Answers are unsatisfying, including, for the artist, scientific explanations. Despite its elusive nature, color plays a monumental role in art with its descriptive, emotional, and symbolic undercurrents. Because color is one of the most expressive, but least understood, elements, I will address the issue in a separate chapter.

Space, **volume**, and **mass** are conveyed differently in two and three dimensions. In pictures, we employ devices called *conventions* to create the illusion of space on a flat surface—called the *picture plane*. These conventions include perspective and the concepts of overlapping, diminishing sizes, and tilting planes. Positive space is the subject matter, that is, the figures and objects that occupy volume and mass. Negative space is the "air" and surrounding background in between the subjects. Positive and negatives spaces must be designed with each other in mind for composition to be effective.

In three dimensions, we relate our bodies directly to the art because space, volume, and mass are real. Our relationship to sculpture is personal, one in which we easily navigate between the space we occupy and that of art. Of course we need to walk around the sculpture to see as many viewpoints as possible before the art can be fully appreciated.

Texture is the sensual connection we have with art. How does it feel? Surfaces can have any number of tactile qualities or illusionary textures. Artists exploit the properties of texture in order to enhance or dramatize expression. That smooth or rough sensation may be confirmed with our hands, but when unable to touch, we "feel" with our eyes. Contact with art as a concrete object and as an extension of our bodies is crucial to a fulfilling aesthetic experience that involves both body and mind, both the senses and the intellect.

Pattern is a cousin of texture if only because so many textures are visible as patterns. Pattern can be as straightforward as wallpaper: Arrange a motif in a repeating grid. Or pattern can become an artistic strategy involving multiple motifs, variations in overlapping, and complex geometrical sequences. At the same time, pattern can be understood as the less rigidly defined way that similar lines, shapes, and forms interact in recurring rhythms. **Repetition** is one of the principles by which patterns are made. Repetition's larger role is to repeat something (such as line, color, shape, or subject) for the purpose of emphasis, comparison, contrast, or unity.

Composition is the **unity** of all the visual elements into a cohesive whole, a singular statement. Unity is order and arrangement, organization and harmony. Order is fundamental to our ability to apprehend meanings in art. Without unity, chaos and confusion overwhelm expression.

Repetition may be the most accessible way to ensure unity, but when overused, it becomes dull and predictable. **Variety** and **contrast** provide differences and counterpoints, and surprises and riches that the mind craves. The adage (still worthy though a cliché), "variety is the spice of life," can be aptly applied to art as well.

Emphasis can direct the eye to specially developed areas in a work of art. **Focal points** are keys for how the viewer visually navigates the art to discover meanings, symbols, and content. Think of focal points as stepping stones that provide a "road map" for the viewer.

This road map facilitates identifying relationships among the visual elements interacting as **rhythms**. Rhythms spurred by repetition, emphasis, variety, and contrast are the means of releasing the illusion of **movement** in art. In a contemporary culture obsessed with the speed, bells, and whistles of technology, we must be mindful that the artist usually makes *still objects* and must create the suggestion of rhythm and movement.

Rhythm in art is commonly compared to the timed sequence of notes, chords, and pauses in music. The respective rhythms in both forms of expression help us understand how musical and visual elements form relationships to create coherent and unified statements.

Balance, **scale**, and **proportion** are closely related concepts. Where and how the visual elements are located in a work of art matters greatly. Placement and size must feel inevitable—that is, they must be *that way* in the art object. The red circle belongs exactly there in the painting. This sculpture must have a projecting form of a certain length and width at a precise angle. If you have the feeling that you can rearrange this or that, take something out, or put something into a composition without negative effect, then the art loses its effectiveness and coherence.

Balance is a matter of judging the placement of the visual elements in a composition. It is not a literal teeter–totter equivalence. Small forms can balance much larger forms depending on their differing characteristics. Contrasting elements have different "weights" and "measures," unique characteristics, that account for how an imbalanced balance, an asymmetrical harmony, may be one of the most effective strategies in composition.

Proportion has to do with comparative sizes among various parts in a work of art, especially shapes, objects, and figures. Successful composition is about thoughtfully adjusting the relationships of sizes to their optimum effect. Simply put, effective visual relationships among all the formal elements are what art is about.

Scale is how we relate the size of our bodies to the sizes of forms in art and nature. Scale as a concept is about how to adjust the sizes of subjects and their surrounding spaces to direct attention, create focal points, and dramatize expression.

THE PRACTICE OF FORMALISM

You will apply these principles in countless ways in a wide variety of projects and exercises you will do in your foundation and introductory studio courses. You will be asked to carry out many activities that are new to your experience, expanding your awareness of the possibilities of art and enhancing the versatility of your skills. Do not assume that those visual elements you have not practiced are inherent weaknesses to be avoided. With practice and guidance, you will find that all the elements and principles will have viable roles in your artistic repertoire.

During the process of working, you may not be thinking about formalism consciously, and certainly not collectively—that is, not about all the components at once. However, you should think about them before and after each working session. Planning and assessment are always part of your practice. Planning gives your work the best prospects for success, while assessment implies that you are learning from both successes and mistakes.

There may be times when you feel overwhelmed by too many variables. Focus on just one or two elements— line, shape, texture or value, or a combination. Imposed limitations will help you learn about those visual elements in depth. Focusing on a few will test your imagination and your ability to uncover the most out of the least. You may be surprised how much can be done with less. Many artists are able to build a career on one great idea involving the exploitation of a few selected variables.

Do not jump to the conclusion that formalism is a tedious, clinical approach to art making. If it seems that way, it is only from the temporary process of learning. Formalist principles serve to organize and clarify your personal expression. The artist wants to express his point of view, not imitate. If that expression is not put into the best form to communicate effectively, then it is lost. In short, your command of formalism will dramatize feeling and make your content seem to matter.

To enlarge your frame of reference about formalism, cultivate the habit of looking at other artworks. Seeing how the masters have employed these principles will inspire you to develop your own strategies. Art images today are easily available for viewing in books, on the internet, and, most desirably, in visits to galleries and museums. (Reproductions are always a distortion and can be misleading if not combined with seeing art "in-the-flesh.")

A good simple exercise is to find two reproductions of artworks created in different periods (or by two different artists in the same period) but of similar subject matter—still lifes of roughly similar objects, landscapes of a similar place or terrain, or abstractions with geometric forms. Ask questions:
• What visual elements (line, shape, space, color, and others) are most at play in each artwork?
• What role does each element serve in expressing mood or feeling?
• How do color choices affect the subject matter and the image?

- Do thick, heavy lines generate a different feeling from thin, delicate ones?
- If the artist distorts or exaggerates forms, does that intensify expression?
- Is the execution plodding and methodical, or spontaneous and gestural? How does that affect what the visual elements express?
- What is the overall impact of the work?
- What visual forms or compositional features account for that effect?
- What elements account most for the differences in these works?
- What similarities do they share?

Answering questions about what you are viewing is a good start at uncovering the not-so-obvious strategies artists employ to serve the purposes of their art. Look at your own work and apply these questions. Some answers may remain elusive or multifaceted, but discovering questions may be more important than conclusive answers. Once you make a habit of looking at art critically, you will steadily increase your understanding of what formalism can do to make your work effective.

chapter

THE STUDIO CRITIQUE

The studio class critique is the standard model in college art programs for educating the student artist. Constructive criticism is the tool of choice for acquiring the fundamentals of formalism and for developing the personal vision required for art making.

The main purpose of a critique is to help you identify what is effective in your work and why. Understanding what works successfully is crucial to making sound improvements and exploring new possibilities. At the same time, critiques will illuminate weaknesses and shortcomings. Yes, most artworks have these too! Once you know these weaknesses, you are in a position to be rid of them once and for all—no reason to repeat what does not work. As soon as you can discriminate between strengths and weaknesses, noticeable improvement should follow.

In a typical critique, the class is led in discussion by your professor about your artwork displayed in the studio on the due date of an assignment. This is not a lecture. The professor will keep the topics relevant and offer advice as appropriate, but each member of the class is expected to contribute comments and questions. The advantage of a group setting is that many solutions and insights are uncovered in the give and take of verbal discourse. Putting many heads together in the exchange of ideas can yield more possibilities for improvement and exploration than you could ever imagine on your own.

In addition, class critiques will help you develop the discipline of questioning and examining your choices, and, in the process, teach you the danger of becoming too easily satisfied. For example, if you are hurrying to finish a project rather than getting involved in a creative struggle, your work will fall short of its potential. You will not do your best work if you grasp the first solution that comes to mind and not consider the alternatives. Criticism encourages you to slow down, think, and ask questions. How can I generate ideas? How can I make good choices among alternatives? How do I decide what is effective? What is worth doing?

My experience in teaching is that the most critical, least satisfied students do the best and most ambitious work. To stop at just "good enough," to be content with mediocrity, is the kiss of death in art. Becoming critical is not an end in itself, but a means of insuring that you are getting to a better place and gradually expanding your artistic aspirations.

There are several types of critiques that are useful and valid. If you wish an in-depth response, you can request a one-to-one critique with your professor. For this type of critique, come prepared. Have questions and priorities you would like addressed. At the same time, be open to new areas of concern your professor may uncover and recommendations for how to handle them. Follow-up with more questions if there is anything you do not understand or about which you are unconvinced. Understanding is the tool to doing.

Another good method of critique is to get together informally with one or more classmates to analyze each other's work and share ideas. This peer-to-peer contact is especially useful during in-progress assignments—that is, before they are finished and when everyone is in a position to apply advice while there is time to make immediate revisions and improvements. Be choosy about the advice. Not all your classmates will have the same level of understanding about what you are doing.

More problematical are critiques solicited from outsiders. These may be friends, family members, and past teachers or mentors who may or may not have any art background and who likely will not fully understand the context of your assignment and its objectives. You might get useful advice, but you are just as likely to encounter an unwieldy contradiction of opinions, ranging from glib praise to utter bewilderment, and even irrelevance, quiet disdain, or outright condemnation. Be prepared for the gamut and take any criticism from outsiders with a healthy dose of skepticism.

Be critical of criticism. Always ask for reasons and evidence behind opinions and never accept "I like or don't like" without rationales or explanation. Ask yourself questions about any evaluator. What background or experience does he have? Is this person interested in art and does he have an open-minded nature? Does he understand the basic parameters of the assignment and what is attempted in the work? A viewer takes from an artwork what he brings to it—he sees as much as he knows.

There are three major areas of concern in a critique: (1) the handling of the formal elements including composition; (2) technical execution; and (3) the subject matter and content. It is usually easier to assess the first two concerns since these are issues that have reasonable consensus among professionals and informed viewers. Reinforced by critique, these practices of formalism and technique can be mastered during your art education.

Content is another matter. The interpretation of meaning can be the most challenging part of the viewing process since, of all historical periods, contemporary art embraces the greatest freedom of choice in subject matter and how it can be expressed. If styles and choices of content are as numerous as the individuals making art, then we have a daunting task in determining quality as viewers. Nevertheless, there is sufficient common ground among the most contrasting artistic endeavors, so we must not shrink from exercising our best judgments as we attempt to uncover meaning in art.

In a work of art, the cues about content are already in the formalism, style, and technical handling of materials. How these things are managed *expresses* the content. For example, if the brushwork in a painting is physical and gestural, if the shapes are angular and jagged, that may say something about the artist's intention to evoke aggression or dynamism. It is important to realize that all these attributes of a work of art—form, style, materials, and content—are essentially interdependent and woven together. As viewers, we separate them in order to unlock meaning. As long as you strive to find visual evidence and reasoning for your observations, you will be on solid ground.

The sticking points about content are its emotional undercurrents and the multiple possibilities for meaning. The validity of emotional responses and interpretations in art depend on informed and sensitive viewing—and not confusing the emotions of life with those in art. Good criticism comes from asking good questions and then looking carefully at the evidence in the work for sound answers. Whether you are in a gallery, museum, or classroom critique, ask the following questions:

- What is the initial impact, the overall impression the work has?
- What features or qualities in the art account for that impact? Color? Form? Style? Materials? Something else?
- Describe first what you see. What is concrete in the visual sense? Subject, medium, size, materials, form, and color?
- How do these concrete elements contribute to mood, feeling, and meaning?
- Go farther. How does the visual evidence suggest an interpretation or multiple interpretations?
- What are the work's strengths, those parts that most effectively support meaning?
- What are the weaknesses, areas that diminish or distract from meaning?
- What is there in the work that might have greater potential if explored with more awareness and concentration?
- What would you add? Change? Subtract?
- From what you know of art history and contemporary trends, how and where would you locate the work compared to other movements and styles?
- Does the work hold your attention and interest? Why or why not? What specific qualities account for that?
- How does this work compare to other works by the same artist?

Besides these issues, the nature of the assignment has much bearing on the criteria considered during a critique. Some of these might include:

- Acquiring technical skills.
- Focusing on certain formal elements such as line, shape, or color.
- Developing a given subject matter according to specifications or limitations.
- Expressing the tenets of a style or movement.
- Interpreting parameters and limits as creative problem-solving.
- Executing an idea or theme in planned stages of development.
- Responding to a subject in spontaneous, intuitive expression.
- Working in series or modular forms.
- Considering the time frame for the project in determining its appropriate scope and degree of involvement.

To be eligible for a studio critique, the requirements of an assignment must be met first.

Whether those parameters are stringent or liberal, the integrity of the project must be addressed before all the other issues of quality can be considered. For example, more might be expected of a project that took three weeks to complete compared to one that was allotted only three days. Similarly, we expect different results from a work executed spontaneously in a single studio session versus a project in which various planning stages are required before the work is executed. If the assignment emphasizes the practice of a technique or a material process more than the finished product, that changes greatly what is expected in the results. These "insider" conditions are why asking advice from outside observers can be misleading and less relevant.

Finally, there is never a "right" solution or only one best solution to an assigned project—or to any work of art for that matter. The assignment sets in motion a situation for you to learn through your own creative resources.

The success of a critique—that is, the value of the advice—depends not solely on the expertise of the professor but also on the active participation of the class members—with respect to both work submitted and verbal participation. In my experience of leading critiques, I have seen a predictable tendency for beginner students to hesitate in participating. There are likely a host of reasons for this, such as:
- Self-consciousness about speaking in a group—that common social affliction, shyness!
- Concern for offending fellow students whose work may have lapses or weaknesses.
- A fragile or overwrought ego caused by feelings of inadequacy or arrogance.
- The misguided notion that you do not know enough about art to make critical observations.
- The mistaken conclusion that your work does not need or cannot benefit from critique.
- Lack of involvement due to insufficient effort given to the project or not doing the assignment at all.

If you see yourself in any of the above categories, get over it! Please. You cannot make progress in your work if you resist participating in the critique process. I take the position that we are all in this Art Ship together. A good critique is exciting to lead because I learn too! The learning process never stops. You have more to gain and contribute than you may think.

I preface the first critique in class by stating emphatically that criticism is never aimed at the art maker but rather at the object or the effort. When you submit your work for critique, you must separate your worth as a *person* from that of your *artwork*. See your work in the eyes and mind of an *observer*. You are the viewer now rather than the artist. If necessary, *act* the role of viewer to jump-start the concept of getting outside of yourself. If you find you are reacting emotionally with anger or hurt from comments about your work, discuss it as soon as possible with your professor. Critiques must be a positive and supportive process to be effective. Use criticism to get better, not bitter.

During a critique of your work, have an *open mind*. Seriously consider all comments and suggestions gracefully, not defensively. You will have time later to assess which ones are relevant. The responses you receive—some new and some surprising—should be exciting to ponder as you calculate your next artistic move. I recommend that you take notes in your journal sketchbook of the best insights offered. In a good critique, there is so much information rebounding among participants that you need to write down the best of them before they vanish. The right suggestion or a particularly incisive observation can be game-changing to your work.

Of course, you are especially interested in the responses to *your* work during a critique. But understand that critiques must be interactive and reciprocal among people with similar goals. The attention in kind given to your artwork is dependent on your active participation in discussing your classmates' efforts. You will learn much about what you are doing in art by responding critically to the work of your fellow students. Furthermore, I will venture to say that you will learn as much from each other as from your professor!

How you understand your work will be different before and after a critique. Often, one is so close to the work that it can no longer be seen objectively. Your emotions can overwhelm your intellect. For example, you may consider that since you were able to carry out your goals and intentions, your work is successful. So, when you hear a critical remark, you may be tempted to say, "But I meant it that way!" Goals and plans can be misguided or poorly executed, and that successful result you assumed may not communicate as intended.

Such a reality check is one of the great benefits of critiques. You will begin to see your work as others do. Do not fret about illusions shattered or mistakes uncovered. That is when you are learning most. There is advantage in knowing the truth early in your development when you can readily do something about it. Take heart. Much about art remains under the radar until an audience responds. Art is, after all, a form of communication. You want others to see your work, warts and all.

Criticism is meant to be practical. Apply it! It should help you see possibilities and opportunities you might overlook otherwise. Finally, the critique format is an introduction to the established criticism in the media about professional art and design. You have a stake in knowing about the state of art in the world at large. With the perspective gained through practice, you will develop a greater appreciation of what you and your contemporaries can do as artists.

chapter

CHARACTER OF THE ARTIST

Do you have what it takes to become an artist? An artist's life requires versatility. Art is not just a skilled activity to produce objects and images. The content of art must be connected to an understanding of the cultural and social environment and how to respond as a global citizen. The integration between art and life makes our discipline challenging and complicated.

The rewards of a creative life can be fulfilling and satisfying in ways that other professions may offer but do not demand in order to be competent or successful. The artist has the privilege of dipping his brush into any field of interest if that content is relevant. Similar to the writer, the artist may research a countless range of subjects. Art is really a way to continue extending one's personal education.

The search to find desirable content requires that the artist be organized and set goals that are realistic. It is that and more. Below is a list of attributes that artists need. See if you measure up and how you may want to adjust to become more effective as an art maker. These are not in a particular order, though some have greater priority or importance. Furthermore, this list is not exclusive. You can decide what others to add and what matters most.

- A strong predisposition to working with your hands is a must. Whether digitally aided or workshop made or a combination, art is made visible by manual effort.
- Art is labor intensive and often takes more time to make than anticipated. A good work ethic is essential. The multifaceted chores in art making range from the exciting and pleasurable to the arduous and tedious. You must be able to complete your work regardless of these demands. I have received comments from viewers that they would not have the patience to do art in my style.
- Thus, a healthy dose of patience and tolerance to follow through is required. Once art making becomes a habit, tedious tasks often cease to seem tedious. Your skills will increase to the extent that what once seemed difficult becomes an efficient routine.
- Commitment to the long term is a challenge to every artist. It takes years to make art worthy of exhibition in a gallery or museum. Since your experiences inform your art, you need to live and work for the time it takes your art to mature.

- Risk taking—the willingness to both succeed and fail—is at the heart of creativity. Since we try to avoid unnecessary risk taking in life, doing so in art is a privilege. Extending your horizons is what makes art compelling. Cultivate an adventurous spirit. Because art dwells in the new, original, and personal, you must be willing to go out on a limb to explore form and content that others have neglected.
- The creative arts, more than most other disciplines, require a high degree of input and balance between the intellect and the emotions. Responses dependent on mere emotion are often knee-jerk reactionary and misguided. Those dependent only on the intellect can seem clinical and sterile. Art making can be especially rewarding as it calls upon all our best inner resources and human faculties.
- Innovators in all fields anticipate needs and desires through their awareness of history, politics, social trends, current events, and the ever-changing cultural environment. Be in touch with the temper of your times. Keep your radar tuned into the world and you will be assured of tracking relevant content.
- Artists use verbal language as a tool to understand visual language. Verbal skills are important as a medium to understand what you are doing. The how's, where's, why's, and what if's are questions that require clarification and focus to direct your art. Your goals are as meaningful as you can articulate in words.
- Good skills and working habits are necessary, but take advantage of luck and chance as well. Know when to take opportunity. Ask for what you want, consider all offers, and act with both reason and intuition with what comes your way.
- You will need a day job that may or may not have to do with art. Be flexible. Living double lives is another skill artists demonstrate. The vast majority of artists do not make a living showing and selling their work.
- Sincerity and honesty of purpose are mandatory. If you wish to please viewers or make art to satisfy the marketplace, you may find a career in the applied arts a more suitable vocation. However, if you are interested in art for its own sake, make it for yourself first. It can only matter to others if it matters to you.

SECTION II

GETTING ON WITH IT:
KEY STUDIO PRACTICES

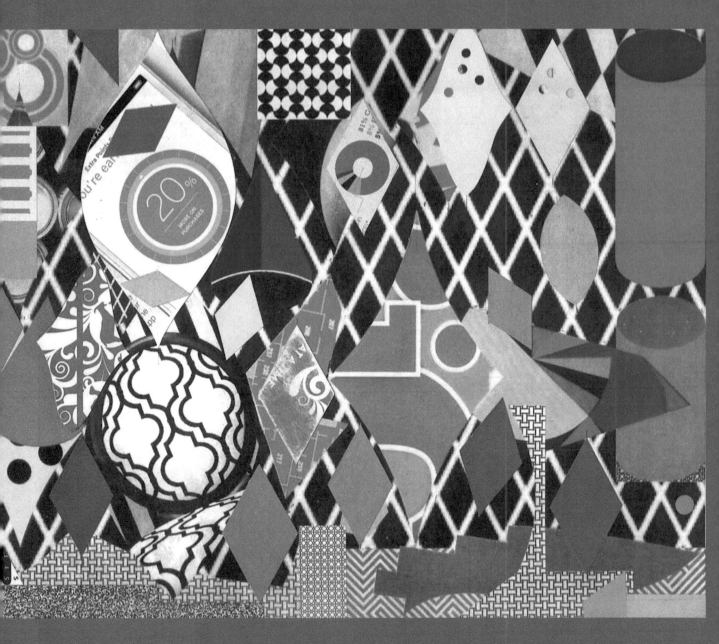

chapter 6

HOW TO MAKE GOOD TWO DIMENSIONAL ART

Successful picture making depends on what you know—what to do and what not to do. All the arts—visual, performing, poetry, and prose—depend on a combination of emotional and intellectual abilities combined with subjective and objective experiences during the creative process. That makes art making especially challenging since there is no scientific method to prove the merits of artworks.

Nonetheless, there is a general consensus among artists and professionals about the essential classic attributes that are necessary to execute effective art. These qualities are directed by the mind and less by the emotions. So, to that extent, these criteria are hard evidence. The dexterous hand by itself has no inherent skill. The hand takes orders from the brain. Contrary to popular conception, artistic ability does not come from divine intervention, lightening-like inspiration, or fall out of the sky as accomplished talent.

Rather, it takes actively applying the best principles and concepts to the drawing process. You must know and understand them first. In that interest, here is a list of what are the most important criteria that characterize the best two-dimensional art. These have stood the test of time and are true for both old and new masters and for the contemporary art of our time. Anyone who looks carefully at art will see the reasons and evidence for these criteria. If there is any secret (I'm sorry, there are no silver bullets or shortcuts) to making good art, the process starts with applying the list below to your working methods. Then, this must be followed by practice, practice, and, well, more practice. Be patient, Rome was not built in a day.

When you make good pictorial qualities a regular part of your practice, you will begin to experience art making with its rich, engaging, and beautiful forms in all its variety and visual glory. By the way, this list is not exclusive, that is, other principles can be added here, but these are an essential start to get you in the right direction now. Also, these principles apply to all subjects in drawing, including still life, landscape, figure, and abstraction.

1. **Lights and Darks.** The illusion of 3D form on a 2D surface depends greatly on how the subject is seen cast in light and shadow. These contrasts of highlight and shadow are called values, and the various tints and shades of lighter and darker grays and blacks describe objects in space.

2. **Composition.** This is the orderly and clear manner of how all the parts of the picture—subjects, objects, shapes, lines, etc.—are arranged in a beautiful and harmonious way. The relationships among all the subjects and forms, and then all of those in relation to the whole, is always infinitely more important than any one part or object. You must have the entire image in your mind's eye as you put individual components into your drawing. Order is its own kind of beauty, and it does sound simpler than it is.

3. **Positive and Negative Space.** Beginners usually understand what positive space is, the subjects, figures, or objects that are described in enclosed shapes. But equally important is the negative space, the open areas in between objects, the air around them—in short, the background. The negative space must be designed at the same time as the positive, and they must weave together into one seamless whole.

4. **Interpretation vs. Imitation.** Picture making is about interpretation, extracting some formal essence from the subject that speaks its lesser known or less considered qualities. These are qualities that give us a new experience of what the subject seems to be, a different viewpoints from one that is primarily factual, as in a photograph of the subject. If you only attempt to copy what you see, you might be better off using a camera. To interpret means to exercise your imagination, to see beyond surface appearances.

5. **Mark Making.** Each medium has unique physical features and can be exploited technically in inventive ways, that is, with texture, gestures, and other flourishes of line, tone, and value. The way you make lines, marks, textures, and move the medium across the surface is your artistic signature. Make a big deal out of that; celebrate the medium. In fact, the medium is the message, even more than the subject matter. *How you exploit your tools* is greater than what.

6. **Variety and Contrast.** These extra emphasis qualities are a way to exaggerate, to make scale, value, lights and darks, and other forms more important and visible. For example, white looks whiter next to black, and vice versa. Small looks especially so against something large. This is a way to improve on the ordinary.

7. **Impact.** We view pictures from a distance, hung on a wall. An image should carry its drama across 10-20 feet or more from the observer. Think of your picture as a dramatic stage. Make it important enough to invite the viewer, to draw her into your image. Specifically, make the image you have drawn stronger than the paper's surface. Working distance, 18-24 inches, is a distortion of how your picture works. At close range, you tend to see it in individual parts and passages. An essential habit while working is to set your picture against the wall and step away to look at its progress. It will reveal more of its overall impact and the quality of its composition, while approximating the manner in which pictures should be seen. Stop many times during your process to look at your work from greater distance.

8. **Description and Detail.** The cliché "the mind hungers for detail" is true. Be generous. Tell us a lot about what and how you are representing. Looking at art should be a leisurely and lingering process. It is likely that the more we see, the more we will respond to the image. Give the viewer, and yourself, something to chew on, to ponder, to take away, and to think about. Art should be about the complexity of looking, not easy signs or slogans or sound bites.

9. **Rhythm.** Pictures need movement to first draw us into the image and then to transport us around the picture so that all of its parts are revealed and feel connected. Give us a road map to circulate around your composition rather than a central spot that becomes as static as a target. Art is about traveling to new places and finding viewpoints different than our own.

10. **Make Art As If You Mean It!** A cardinal sin is to make art insincerely or merely out of duty or obligation. You communicate your state of mind and your attitudes when you make an image. The viewer will sense how you felt about the process, and this is an important part of the art's content.

chapter 7

DRAWING ON NECESSITY

Few blanket statements are as true as this: Drawing is the foundation of all disciplines in the visual arts. The first skill the beginner needs to develop and eventually master is drawing. Artists in both fine and applied arts draw frequently to explore possibilities, anticipate outcomes, test ideas, and communicate information. Drawing is the first tool of choice—the medium most immediate and easily available for the artist to bridge the gap between his idea of an image or object and the material form of its reality.

Drawing is indispensable as an expression to plan the development of an artwork. Drawing allows you to visually test ideas so that you can, by a process of elimination, avoid wasting time on unproductive approaches. For countless centuries, artists have drawn to illustrate for themselves and for clients their proposals for subject matter, composition, and content.

There are more reasons than ever to master the fine art of drawing. A growing trend in contemporary art is to recognize drawings as major works of art on their own terms. Today, many artists are committed to making drawings that are the equal, in scope and concept, of other major art forms. A drawing can now stand side by side with a painting or sculpture in size and ambition. Furthermore, drawing is often incorporated into the increasingly important practice of mixed media, seamlessly melding with paint, collage, found objects, and other materials.

Before you can effectively create art, you must see the visible world objectively. Seeing is the first step. Art is a language that must be learned. If you do not know the grammar or structure of a language, you cannot have thoughts that take the form of sentences and paragraphs through which you communicate with yourself and others. In a similar sense, drawing, as the *grammar* of the language of visual arts, is the most direct method of seeing and communicating your understanding of the world.

REQUIRED ART SUPPLIES

The following supply list is what I require in my drawing classes, but every instructor will likely require some variations. Purchase supplies at local art stores or from online websites.

- One or more 4B, 5B, or 6B graphite pencils: one graphite stick
- One or more hard, medium, or soft charcoal pencil; one compressed charcoal stick
- Conte crayons, black and white
- One white charcoal stick, or white pastel stick, or white conte crayon; one white charcoal pencil
- White vinyl, gum, or kneaded eraser
- Blending stump, any size
- Chalk pastels in twelve or twenty-four color set
- Aerosol spray fixative (hairspray may be substituted)
- Bottle of black India ink
- Penholder and fine steel drawing point; bamboo pen
- Watercolor brushes numbers 2, 4, 6, and up to 8, choose 3 or more sizes; or one bamboo style brush, fine or medium
- Watercolor set, cake or tubes
- Mixing tray with reservoirs for ink and watercolor
- White glue (such as Elmer's) or acrylic matte gel
- Utility knife (mat knife) or razor box cutter
- Sketchbook, hardcover or spiral binder, 8.5 × 11 inches or 9 × 12 inches
- Portfolio, envelope or zipper style., minimum size of 20 × 26 inches
- Drawing board at least 18 × 24 inches
- Metal straight edge 24 to 36 inches

SEEING VERSUS KNOWING

In your first-year drawing courses, you will work directly from the observation of a subject in your immediate surroundings that can be seen and referred to continuously during the drawing process. The subject, called nature, may be a still life arrangement, a human model posed in the studio, or a landscape observed outdoors. The point is that you are *there*—that is, you observe your subject simultaneously as you render it. To put it simply, each line, mark, or tone you put on paper should correspond to your having seen the subject that way in the moment of observation. In one sense you are translating appearances from one reality (nature) to another (art). The objective in drawing from observation is to maintain simultaneous connections between both art and nature (between drawing and subject) as you work. This is more difficult to do than it seems. Looking continuously at your subject as you draw may feel like an unnatural act, but it is an essential acquired discipline.

Many beginners become complacent or bored with the act of *seeing* in consistent concentration. They make assumptions about what something looks like and look only intermittently and casually at their subject. Big mistake! *Knowing an object is inferior to seeing it.* Memory is faulty: The moment after you have seen something you have already forgotten it. You must cultivate the habit of looking, then immediately put tool to paper to interpret what you just saw. Only then will you be able to represent nature with convincing objectivity and substance.

The practice of this new skill will seem unnatural, like a great effort at first. Once the habit of observation is mastered, however, seeing and drawing simultaneously will become second nature—not like work at all. If there is any secret or silver bullet about successful drawing, this is it: *see* with focus and understanding, then immediately *do*.

There is another wrinkle in this phenomenon of seeing. You must be able to see *priorities* in the structures of objects. Not all forms are obvious or clear in their three-dimensional qualities. For example, though the mass and volume of a tree may seem to be dominated by the leaves of its foliage, those leaves are not the essential forms that make a tree three-dimensional and stand in space. You must acknowledge and render the underlying structures of its trunk and branches first. Build from the inside out, from the foundation up. While the trunk and branches may seem to be largely obscured by foliage and leaves, those woody structures must be drawn convincingly to create the illusion of a tree in space.

Furthermore, individual leaves are trivial compared to how those leaves suggest clusters of shapes and then light-to-dark illusions of volume. Trunks, branches, clusters of foliage, lights, darks, and, finally, those pesky leaves all have their places in the hierarchy of drawing—that is, the artist *builds* a tree on a sheet of drawing paper. The same scenario follows for all objects in nature. The human figure is not just surface and skin, but, as a form with volume in space, a complex interaction of skeleton, muscles, and soft tissues. If you are drawing a traditional building, you become aware of its cube-like structures that make up its mass and volume more than its outer shell of brick, wood, steel, or glass. Represent the underlying, supporting structures of objects before you decorate its surface. *See with x-ray vision.*

The best way to improve your observational drawing skills is by regular practice. The more you draw the more keenly aware of your surroundings you become, even when you are not drawing. You will begin to notice objects and forms around you that will become more exciting due to their familiarity through the drawing process. A sketchbook is an excellent place to make informal, regular drawing from observed subjects a regular habit. See Chapter 11 for more information.

WHAT IS DRAWING? WHY DRAW?

If you are prepared to see, you are ready to start drawing. But, what is a drawing? The simplest questions are often the most complex. A drawing is an act of illusion like a magic trick. It is sleight of hand, the illusion of space on a flat surface, a universal given that we may easily take for granted. Too bad if we do, for we miss some of the magic! Here's the contradiction: A drawing is a flat, usually white surface on which the artist has intentionally placed marks, lines, tones, and textural effects with contrasting tools that describe a subject in a variety of grays, blacks, and colors. These marks are designed to coalesce into a coherent image of three-dimensional illusion, a mirror of a perceived reality. It's a strange activity when you think about it. Why are human beings concerned with the artful tooling of flat surfaces to represent illusions of various realities?

- Do we need souvenirs of our experiences?
- Does it help us understand our world and our place in it?
- Do we need to make our private realities/fantasies visible in order to communicate them?
- Do we have a curiosity to know other people's visions and to know how they differ from ours?

- Do we wish to pay homage to nature in its construction of form and beauty?
- Are we probing our inner selves to see what is there, if anything?
- Do we make images because we yearn for meaning?

Whatever the case, humans have made images for tens of thousands of years for these reasons and many others. These are all worthy and valid inducements for drawing specifically and making art generally. You should embrace these rationales and invent some of your own to derive the most from drawing. Remember that drawing is a form of communication and that art is an act of optimism that heightens the sense of being alive. Regardless of your level of skill and your reasons for making art, always draw as if you mean it.

HOW TO DRAW

My title here is deliberately tongue-in-cheek. You cannot learn how to draw by only reading a book. But I hope the ideas here are useful now and again, and that they may help jump-start the drawing process. The following topics describe in short summaries the concepts, procedures, and formal issues that underlie the drawing process. Most of these topics will be addressed in your drawing courses, but these descriptions can serve as a useful introduction and reminder of what it takes to make effective drawings. Of course, there may be other effective methods not described here, and you may find individual approaches to drawing that work for you. Since you must start somewhere, you can combine these suggestions and those you learn in class, refine and experiment as you see fit, and develop an effective routine from those various resources. Making art is never only one way or carved in stone. If one thing does not work, try something else.

COMPOSITION

Composition may be the single most important and least understood concept of good drawing. Consider the most basic components, the bare bones of a drawing or any picture. Handmade marks of a contrasting tonal material, such as graphite, charcoal, or pastel, are applied to a two-dimensional surface, a sheet of paper usually shaped as a rectangle, in order to represent the descriptive forms of a subject in a compelling and personal expression. *How you organize* your forms within the boundaries of that rectangle is what drawing and all pictures are about. Style, content, and expression are important, but composition is the first step. Art is unintelligible if its parts are arranged poorly. Organization is the lens through which everything else becomes visible. The reason is deceptively simple. In art, the totality, the ensemble, the Big Picture—composition—is always more significant than single items, individual passages, or particular details. Composition is closest to that mysterious thing we call art.

Your first consideration is how to *frame* the subject. How will those objects or figures that comprise your subject matter relate to each other and to the shape of the paper? As the great French painter Henri Matisse said, "It is not things that matter but the *relations* between things." Composing or framing the subject into an organized whole is often a stumbling block for beginners. Once a drawing is started, there is a misguided inclination to focus on how to represent one object at a time without the seeming burden of concern for its effect on everything else in the picture. But *you must be burdened* in the sense of holding in your imagination how each object will relate visually to all other objects in the drawing. As you are drawing an object, you are simultaneously adjusting its effect in the larger scheme of the picture's arrangement. The sense of order you *invent* from the subject matter becomes the path to perceiving drawing's artistic expression and formal beauty. Composition is the catalyst by which the viewer can see your intentions.

THE RENAISSANCE WINDOW AND THE MODERN VIEWPOINT

At the risk of oversimplifying modernism's approach to composition, it is useful to identify the two major methods of framing a subject in the last 500 years. During the Renaissance of the 1400s, artists developed a compositional tendency to fully reveal their subjects by centering them in a deep space of perspective. Backgrounds often occupied more pictorial space than the subjects, which were usually seen as part of their larger immediate surroundings. This manner of seeing events in a larger worldly context is called the *Renaissance window* and prevailed in pictorial art for centuries. Another way of thinking about this window is to imagine looking at the world through a keyhole. The subject matter is fully revealed, but it remains at a considerable distance from the viewer.

The invention of photography in the 1830s and the social/political upheavals of the nineteenth century changed everything. From the beginning of modernism, with the Industrial Revolution, composition tended to minimize background in order to thrust the subject matter forward into the viewer's space. This had a second effect of diminishing deep space and limiting perspective. Suddenly the viewer felt more a part of the picture's space and, thus, became a more active participant instead of a voyeur looking through a window or keyhole. Getting closer to the subject meant a more dramatic involvement with both the subject and the art as an object. The implications of these developments are still being felt today in art and in all images.

A significant consequence of getting closer to the subject is that much of that subject is going to get truncated at the frame of the picture. The interruption of the subject at the outer edges is called cropping. Everyone who has taken photographs knows about cropping when checking the image through a viewfinder or on the monitor of a digital camera. Compositional cropping is not superior to the Renaissance window. In fact, both options are open to the contemporary artist. However, the modern practice of cropping is a general tendency of our time both to dramatize the subject and to emphasize the material surface of the picture. How you frame your picture should be a product of understanding the differences between the Renaissance window and the modern viewpoint.

CROPPING: DRAWING WITH A VIEWFINDER

An important device to apply this concept of cropping is the viewfinder frame. This practical and efficient tool is a simple sheet of cardboard or rigid paper about 4" × 6" with a rectangular opening cut in the middle of about 1½" × 2" or 2" × 3". The opening or window of the viewfinder approximates the proportions of a standard sheet of drawing paper of 18" × 24". By holding this device in hand at arm's length and looking through the opening directly at the subject (with one eye closed to avoid seeing double), the drawer can easily see a miniaturized version of the composition—that is, which objects are to be visible within the picture and which objects will be cropped at the framing edge. In other words, a smaller version of the drawing will be seen occupying the opening of the viewfinder.

Beginners should hold the viewfinder with one hand and draw simultaneously with the other. Though this may feel awkward, it is helpful to persist until you understand the relationship between the image you see and the image you draw. As you gain experience you may rely upon the viewfinder less—often in the initial stages and then occasionally thereafter for reference.

It is simple and fast to make a viewfinder. Every drawing student should do so. You need a razor knife, a straight edge to measure and cut, and a sheet of cardboard or stiff paper. Cut with a razor against the straight edge according to the measurements above.

POSITIVE AND NEGATIVE SPACE

Positive and negative spaces are the complementary halves of pictorial space. Neither positive nor negative space can exist independently. Positive space is the shape and volume of an object or figure—essentially the subject matter. Negative space is everything else: the background, the *empty* space in between objects, the atmosphere around the subject. Beginners often assume that only positive space matters. Artists know that negative space matters as much. Since objects have shapes, then the *spaces in between* those objects have shapes too. These open spaces as shapes, that is, as palpable visual forms of design, may be less apparent than the objects' shapes, but negative shapes are critical to both the illusion of space and the effective organization of that space. Think of these two kinds of spaces as a series of puzzle parts that must interlock to reveal the picture. Consciously relating positive and negative spaces in drawing is the way the artist creates order, clarity, and unity.

PROPORTIONS AND SIGHTING

Judging proportions, or sighting, between objects relative to their lengths and widths and the spaces in-between them is an essential skill to good drawing. Learn to use your eye as a "measuring tape" to estimate the relative sizes of objects and their distances from each other. For example, compare the height and width of a vase with a box next to it. If the box is shorter in height, how many boxes would it take to be the same height as the vase? You can use mental arithmetic to estimate. Maybe the vase is 3 times as high or the box is 1/3 the height of the vase. Perhaps the distance between them is half the width of the vase.

Another method is to hold up a pencil at arm's length against any given length or width in your subjects (close one eye to not see double) and make a comparison based on the measurement you see along the pencil's shaft. Once you begin to make these estimations, it will automatically become easier to see objects and figures in their rightful proportions. With practice and habit, this skill should become second nature, and will improve the quality of how you observe nature.

Sometimes, a seasoned artist will deliberately distort or violate the proportions for the sake of expression. The artist can bend the rules to better dramatize his picture, but only after he has learned the basic principles of drawing.

THUMBNAIL DRAWING

Thumbnail drawing or preparatory sketching is an essential practice before attempting a sustained drawing, usually the larger and more finished product that is considered the work of art. (Sometimes, accomplished thumbnail drawings are considered works of art as well.) Thumbnails are usually small in size—roughly 4"× 6" or slightly larger—and executed on the spot in a few minutes. Their primary purpose is to efficiently research compositional solutions to find the most promising means to frame or organize the pictorial space with the subject matter involved. Rough sketching in this manner is a critical step to get oriented to the drawing so that you minimize guesswork in relation to cropping, describing positive and negative space, and the placement and proportions of your subjects in the composition. Thumbnail drawing is a common and established practice in the visual arts for beginners and professionals alike. If you have not already incorporated this into your practice, you will soon do so in your studio classes.

Three or four thumbnails are essential to identify your best choice of composition before starting a sustained drawing. Choose the most promising sketch as a model for reference on which to base your approach. In addition to composition, look for engaging formal qualities of line, shape, space, rhythm, variety, unity, and contrast. Do *not* use a thumbnail sketch as an image to copy. Copying from another sketch will make your drawing feel like a dull imitation—and you will feel bored doing it. The spirit of any drawing, whether thumbnail, gesture, or sustained, should be spontaneous, experimental, and *fresh*—as if its marks were only just put down in the previous moment. In drawing, we do not want to feel your pain.

Drawing thumbnails is a useful warm-up for the greater effort of a larger, more ambitious drawing. Think of quick sketching as the aerobics of art. Drawings executed in rapid succession have the advantage of not being precious since little time is invested in any one. With the pressure off, you can feel more creative, exploring possibilities you might not otherwise have considered. In addition, handling tools and materials as you look carefully at your subject will boost your interest and self-confidence. Thumbnails are good ice-breakers and provide the enthusiasm to get going with a project.

Please note that the following stages of drawing describe methods for both thumbnails and sustained drawing. Their applications are necessarily distinct for each type. While each has different purposes—thumbnails as quick takes on exploring possibilities, sustained drawings as deliberate and thoughtful development into works of art—the technical approaches for both are similar. Sustained drawing involves additional stages that are described later in this chapter.

Stage I: Blocking in—Thumbnail Drawing

Begin a drawing by lightly blocking-in the main contour lines of objects and figures. Keep your marks and lines *light* in the beginning to allow for quick changes and corrections with minimal erasures. Draw just the shapes of objects as they relate to the shapes of negative spaces. Resist for now the temptation to describe surfaces and details. Once you have established the linear framework or skeleton of objects and spaces on the paper, carefully check the proportions and locations of objects so that they are spatially convincing. Evaluate whether the composition is orderly and clear. Be critical and make changes as required.

Frame your subject matter so that no one object dominates the center at the expense of visual interest when moving to the sides, top, and bottom of the drawing. Too much centering or symmetry may create a static, repetitive effect, like a target or a black hole. You want to invite the eye to move to all areas of the drawing. Multiple points of interest are better than one.

Stage II: Lights and Darks—Thumbnail Drawing

Now you can move from the edges to the surfaces. Look for the light as it comes primarily from one direction. What surfaces on the objects are light and where are they in shadow? You should see a predictable pattern. If the light comes from the left, most objects will be highlighted on the left, and in varying degrees of shadow on the right. Since the highlights are going to be the white of the paper (a given convention in drawing), you will need to start with shadows. It is practical to do this in a systematic way. Look first for the locations of the deepest, darkest shadows. Make all of them as *black* as your medium is capable of marking—even though black may be an exaggeration. Then, render shadows of the next level of values, those that are slightly less dark. Continue drawing shadows of increasingly lighter values until you reach the highlights. If the value gradations of your shadows are convincing, the highlights will look like positive reflections moving forward in space—despite the fact that they are areas of paper left untouched.

Stage III: Description—Thumbnail Drawing

In this stage of the drawing process, you should strengthen or vary contours and lines to enhance clarity and three-dimensional effects. Create variations in line quality. Build up the thickness and darkness of lines where appropriate to important forms, especially in foreground areas, while rendering lighter, thinner lines to suggest lesser objects that should recede in space.

Once contours and values are established, your drawing may still look spare and may not suggest sufficiently whether the image is suitable for a sustained drawing. Add enough description to characterize your subject matter and to suggest the feeling you want to express.

GESTURE DRAWING

Gesture drawing is closely related to thumbnail drawing, except that size is less a consideration. These drawings can be any size convenient for the purpose of quickly recording a response to a subject. Gestures are even more speedily drawn than thumbnails. They are done, by definition, extra rapidly, in a matter of a minute or a few minutes to capture the spirit and "action" of a subject rather than its naturalism or detail. They are often practiced in multiple numbers, one after the other, as a warm-up introduction to the prospect of drawing more deliberately later.

The warming up exercises practiced by athletes are what gesture drawing is to the artist. Drawing in rapid response loosens tensions and activates the mood to begin art making. Process is greater than product. The act of drawing in this ad hoc way enlivens your awareness and manual dexterity. It is a kind of controlled scribbling, one that is not censored or erased, but appreciated for both its physical and psychic benefits. If you do ten to fifteen gesture drawings, one might be worthy to keep as a work of art.

Gesture drawing is an especially important component of figure drawing. Since the poses of a model generally suggest motion, or the implied effects of motion, gesture drawing is a natural embodiment that expresses both the subject and the action of how it is accomplished physically.

SUSTAINED DRAWING

While similar to the three stages of development in thumbnails, sustained drawing is a "slow burn" approached with greater planning, deliberation, and concentration. Sustained drawing is usually of such scope and involvement that the artist develops it during a number of sessions. In fact, the strategic advantage of working on a drawing for days is that each time you return to it you have a different perspective. You are a little smarter than yesterday and can make the drawing a little better each time you work. In the early twentieth century, psychologists concluded that the unconscious mind processes solutions to problems the conscious mind has not resolved. You will do a better drawing—and feel less overwhelmed—if you work on it during several shorter sessions rather than in one long sitting.

Stage I: Blocking in—Sustained Drawing

Since the need to change and revise will be a constant, begin a sustained drawing with a light touch. For example, if you start with graphite or charcoal, make your lines just visible. That way when you change anything, little or no erasing will be necessary. The first 30-45 minutes worth of lines and marks should be lightly rendered. If changes are easy to make because you have made them *light* enough, you will be more likely to make corrections as necessary.

When blocking in your subject matter, draw the basic forms in all parts of the paper before starting any light and dark patterns or descriptive detail. It is essential to comprehend—to apprehend the essential image in the mind's eye—the whole picture as soon as possible. A big mistake made by novices is that they tend to work on individual objects in an A- to- Z mode, finishing one, then the next, in a piecemeal approach. The vision of the whole is always greater than any of the parts. Think of the blocking-in stage as the construction of a roadmap for your drawing. You want to know where you are wherever you move on the paper. Try to keep all the parts of your drawing equally developed as you move freely around all the areas of your paper. Claude Monet, the great French Impressionist, said it is necessary to work on a painting (or drawing) "all over at once."

The spirit of play and experimentation that naturally characterizes thumbnails should continue in sustained drawings. Just because you are slowing down in the development of a longer drawing does not mean the process should become tedious or laborious. When drawing becomes too much like work, it loses the excitement of the moment and can then feel dull, leaden, and predictable—and worse, the art will look that way. Find a balance between work and play, challenge and amusement, as you draw. Both process and product will benefit greatly.

Seeing Critically From a Distance

After you have drawn the major forms of the blocking-in stage, step back and be critical. Literally! Move several feet back from your drawing to view it from a distance. You will see it in a new perspective. Assess the following:

- Are objects reasonably proportioned?
- Are positive and negative spaces adequately defined?
- Do forms divide the picture rectangle into interesting variations of size and direction?
- Do objects and figures relate spatially as they overlap, touch, and interact?
- Do objects recede and advance convincingly in space? In all areas of foreground, middle ground, and background?
- Is there too much or too little of anything?
- Are the static qualities of symmetry, centering, and repetition avoided?
- Does the composition seem unified and coherent?

Viewing your drawing from a distance should be done often during the process to check its progress. This should become a natural habit of continuous assessment and analysis. A drawing is meant to be seen from ten or twenty feet away or more while it is hung on a wall. You will understand your drawing better from a distance and be in a good position to know what to do next. Working over a drawing board with eyes one or two feet away is not how we *see* drawings.

Stage II: Developing Lights and Darks—Sustained Drawing

When you start the second stage of laying in the dark and light patterns, be prepared to return to all those areas several times. Work up the shadows gradually until you are confident of their values. It is much easier to make an area darker than to lighten something that got too dark—in wet media, it may be impossible. *Sneaking up* slowly on darks is a good general policy. In addition, the layers that result from multiple applications are often enriching and add depth and detail to surfaces.

While they are not built up to their deepest values until later, establish lights and darks *throughout* the drawing as *early* as possible. The sooner you can determine that those light and darks are doing the job of spatial illusion, the better. After the first layer of values is rendered, move away and assess again:

- Are the lights and darks giving weight and volume to objects and figures?
- Do those objects and figures seem related in space?
- Do the lights and darks enhance the illusion of pictorial depth?
- Which shadows and highlights will need more or less contrast?
- Are there any "holes" in the picture where values are greatly overstated or understated?
- Does the light seem to fall convincingly on the subject from a consistent direction?

When drawing shadows, be sure to notice that the area a given shadow occupies, that is, its surface, is rarely a uniform, flat value. Individual shadows are virtually always *gradations* from light to dark or dark to light in visible patterns. You must make the effort to record these changes of value in the shadows if your forms are to be convincing illusions of volume and depth. The process of rendering lights and darks effectively may be one of the most demanding requirements in the act of drawing. This is the point where seeing and knowing (or assuming) can be confused. If you can consciously match the values of what you see in the subject with those you render in the drawing, you will be making the right attempt. A helpful method in properly distinguishing a variety of values is to squint your eyes at the subject. Squinting eliminates the distractions of details and allows you to make easier comparisons among different lights and darks.

A good drawing should demonstrate about eight to ten values from highlight to deep shadow. You can easily count to see if you are approaching that. The fewer the values, the less convincing will be the illusion of space, depth, and volume. Mastering the rendering of lights and darks is the nuts and bolts of drawing—in fact, of all picture making. Give it the time it deserves.

Stage III: Description and Detail—Sustained Drawing

Contours, highlights, and shadows are not the whole story. Eventually, you must give your drawing specific features and individuality. Tell us what the object or figure is doing in space, how its weight feels, how it may interact with what is around it, how its surface is textured, and how the light may affect its role in the composition. It is not too farfetched to imagine rendering an object with "personality," temperament, or character. In a thumbnail sketch, you may not take time to address that much detail, but in a sustained drawing what is represented should invite us to linger, imagine, and contemplate. Remember, the mind's eye hungers for detail. Sustain us.

An important consideration in the later stages of all types of drawings is to reconcile the relationships between lines and surfaces. Frequently, beginners execute them as separate systems of representation, a consequence I call the Coloring Book Syndrome: lines are thick, uniform, and predominant, while highlights and shadows are more weakly indicated, playing a secondary role as they meagerly, that is, barely *fill* the shapes made by contours. If anything, the surfaces of lights and darks should be more aggressively drawn than lines and contours. Throughout the drawing process you should attempt to meld lines and surfaces so that in many places one is *lost* in the other. Edges and areas should seem unified as they describe form and space. For example, a very dark shadow might eventually merge into the same value as its adjacent contour line. Thus, the *shadow* defines the edge of the object instead of a line. Focusing on melding line and surface will express objects and forms with more convincing spatial relationships.

Stage IV: Revisions—Sustained Drawing

At most stages of its development, sustained drawing is a process of revising, reworking, then revising more. Few of us get it right the first stroke, the first attempt. By no means should that be a discouraging process. Each time you change something, you are likely to improve it. When you see that second efforts are rewarded, you will be more motivated to continue. Take heart: Mistakes are not really mistakes. They are important bits of information that help us to see a better road ahead. A cautionary message: Do not be too easily satisfied. A quotation by Picasso expresses a similar insight if somewhat differently:

> When you begin a picture, you often make some pretty discoveries. You must be on guard against these. Destroy the thing, do it over several times. In each destroying of a beautiful discovery, the artist does not really suppress it, but rather transforms it, condenses it, makes it more substantial.

Assessing your drawing's progress at each working session is critical to its development as art. Looking attentively at your work *before* and *after* the act of drawing is a habit that will reinforce confidence that revisions are productive. When approached this way, reworking a drawing is not just correcting mistakes. It is the greater goal of getting the work to a higher level of quality.

Revisions are especially critical in the latter stages of drawing. As more description and detail develop, the more there is to compare and assess as the relationships between areas become more complicated.

FINISHING THE DRAWING

The first two stages of drawing are a kind of container after which you develop a full and expressive characterization of your subject matter. The latter stages of *Description* and *Revisions* may be the least specific but they are the longest and most crucial part of the drawing process. Here you are personalizing and adding your creative imprint to your image. If you have adhered until now to your observation of nature, now is the time to *improve* on it. Your drawing should look better, be more visually enticing, than the reality of your model. Exaggeration, distortion, and creative alterations should be mixed into the drawing if the results are to be compelling, inventive, and dramatic—and if you understand that you are deliberately departing from observation for the purpose of artistic enhancement.

You can describe your subject as no one else can—and that makes your art original. Remember, in art the mind lavishes details. That is an opportunity. Think of your drawing as the arena for an event, a stage on which you are directing actors in a drama. In fact, art *is* drama. Take us to that fictional place. Art is about abandoning the mundane in favor of exploring our curiosities and fantasies. Art is traveling. We need to go places. Take us there!

chapter

8

FIGURE DRAWING:
THE MIRROR OF HUMANITY

Representing the human figure is the most difficult subject in art. Drawing the figure from a live model is one of the great challenges for the beginning art major. In one sense, it ought not be so. After all, each of us who draws possesses, no *is*, a human figure. We are, in fact, the same subjects that we attempt to draw! We assume that we know our bodies—not only how we look (via mirrors, photographs, and media technology), but what we are capable of physically, from sports to manual skills. Comprised of the same stock of anatomical inventory—flesh and skeleton—as our posed model counterparts, we ought to be able to draw figures with the relative ease that comes with familiarity. But, alas, artistic logic does not work this way! We are humbled by how little we really understand when putting to paper our first figures. Those initial scratchy efforts tend to be poorly shaped, ill proportioned, and possibly comically rendered figures in their utter lack of reasonable resemblance to human form. Take heart. It seems to be a universal experience. So, it is back to the drawing board.

If early difficulty with drawing the human form seems counterintuitive, consider the problem. The essential structures of the body's three-dimensional form—skeleton, muscles, and soft tissues—lie hidden beneath a continuously curving and nebulous surface of skin. In other words, the body's three-dimensional planes and edges seem diffused and undefined—visually elusive. The drawer must first understand and appreciate the nature of these concealed structures, that is, their functions of weight distribution and motion, and especially their consequent visual effects.

ANATOMY IS KEY

The figure drawer must understand the underlying structure of the human form in all its complexity and totality. Understanding basic anatomy is key. Interior systems of muscle, soft tissue, and skeleton are the structures in the body that express motion, tension, weight distribution, and angle of pose. For example, shifting weight to one leg when standing affects the angle of the hips and also the shoulders. The weighted leg will lift the hip on that side compared to the other. Thus, you have an angle rather than a horizontal line between both hips. The shoulders will be affected off the horizontal as well. The angle will depend on the rest of the pose and whether props are used.

All parts of the anatomy work in unison, that is, in response to each other. Although these shifts and tensions may seem subtle, they are crucial to expressing an effectively drawn figure. It can be the difference between the contrapposto of weight shift with its implied motion as in Greek or Roman figure sculptures or the rigid, static block figures of Ancient Egyptian art.

As soon as possible, I recommend a short pause for research. Go to the library to look at books on anatomy for the artist. There are many. The bible of anatomy for both science and art is *Gray's Anatomy*. Many art students and artists acquire copies early in their careers as lifetime references to the details of the human figure. It has been in print since 1901! Most how-to drawing books, especially those focused specifically on figure drawing, have chapters on introductory anatomy and illustrations of the skeleton and the major muscle groups of the human body. In addition, the internet has scores of websites where you can access information about this topic or purchase figure drawing books online. For example, Dover Publications makes an excellent line of anatomy books for the artist at reasonable prices. See illustration about body measurements at the end of this chapter.

Reading the text of your research is optional—this is visual research!—but study the illustrations with attention and interest. This is a case of "a picture is worth a thousand words". You do not need to memorize the technical names for bones, muscles, and tendons. However, a few of the major ones are likely to be familiar. How these bodily components function as an ensemble of movement and affect the appearance of the figure is what matters. You can soon start to connect these anatomical structures to reality by imagining how your own body (arms and legs in particular) moves—reaches, bends, lifts, stretches, leans, walks, and runs. You will come to appreciate the body's remarkable versatility of coordination, balance, and motion.

A final reason I advise every art student to pursue a basic study of anatomy is because figure drawing classes do not cover these issues in the same ways. For better or worse, there is no uniform syllabus for drawing and understanding the human form. A healthy curiosity about how the body works as a highly complex machine of intricate forms will pay dividends in developing your abilities to represent the figure in art. If nothing else, you will learn more about yourself!

THE MODEL AS MUSE

When you draw from a model—a live person posing, often in the nude—it is essential that you respect and identify with that individual. We are common humanity. We have much to learn from each other. When teaching, I am impressed by how often the model will show an interest in what we are drawing, sometimes making useful suggestions that the rest of us did not consider. Some models know instinctively what kinds of poses are most apt to a particular class without my having to specify. The positive give and take among professor, students, and model can be enriching and rewarding so long as you are open to these special circumstances.

Models provide invaluable visual opportunities for artistic practice. Despite our burgeoning and rapidly evolving technology, nothing can replace the centuries-old relationship between model and artist. Drawing from a live pose means that you are participating in an enduring tradition while simultaneously responding to a unique moment in contemporary life. Sometimes the drawings produced in those moments stand on their own as artistic documents of their time and place. Whether by an old master or a modern master, drawings made that way retain the spontaneity and urgency of artistic expression.

On the other hand, drawings from the model can serve an entirely different premise, as preliminary plans or points of departure for further development and exploration. A figure drawing may serve as a catalyst for a more sustained painting, sculpture, or other artistic endeavor that the artist will develop after the model has finished posing. So, drawing from the model can be a worthy end in itself or a means to an end, to a project the artist develops beyond the drawing studio.

STAGE I: THE STICK FIGURE

Are you ready? Always look first before doing. Pause and take a few deep breaths. Think about how you will place the figure on the paper, how it will be composed on the sheet. Use a viewfinder to see the pose as it relates to the rectangle it will inhabit. The most essential step in starting a sustained drawing from the model is to spend the initial minutes to indicate with light marks (for example, with graphite or charcoal) the form of the body's pose. Forget about details. Fingers, toes, eyes, and ears are irrelevant at the beginning. Focus on the whole effect. The devil may be in the details, but art is in the totality. Always think *big forms* first.

If you consider a roadmap as having key landmarks to guide your itinerary, the figure has them as well to plot its anatomy and proportions in space. Since the figure is a complex ensemble of interacting parts programmed to work together, to move in unison, then to eventually come to rest in balance, and always to repeat these patterns, it is essential to appreciate the dynamics of these relationships. A good metaphor is a symphony orchestra with its strings section, woodwinds, horns, percussion, solo piano, and conductor. All must work together in interdependent dialogues of sound and respond in kind to the music of each group. When you can appreciate the concept of complex interactions in the service of unity, you have the basis to begin drawing the figure.

So, what are the key landmarks in the human figure? The joints. Period. Know where each starts and ends. They are patently obvious when described: top of the head to neck, neck to shoulder, shoulders to elbows, elbows to wrists, wrists to fingers, shoulders to waist, waist to hips, hips to knees, knees to ankles, and ankles to toes. Become acquainted with the basic measurements among the joints. The total height of the body is seven to eight lengths of the head (top of head to chin). The torso, shoulders to waist, is the longest dimension and most central portion of the figure. The torso is about double in height to what it is in width. Each arm or leg is comprised of three parts: upper, lower, and hand or foot. Arm parts are shorter in length than leg parts. For example, an upper or lower arm is about three quarters in length to a corresponding upper or lower leg on the same model. Many books and professors will cite additional ratios and measurements. Commit those to memory that have the most meaning and usage to your way of drawing.

Once a pose is set, start your drawing by mapping a stick figure of the joints and the body parts relative to their lengths, widths, and directions. This is almost literally a system of connecting the dots with sticks. The cliché that declares, "All I can draw is a stick figure" is where you must start. Think of the joints with their bony ball-bearing-like structures as dots to be located proportionally on the drawing's paper and then to be connected to identify the location of the head, neck, torso, arms, hands, legs, and feet. Voila! The stick figure!

More easily said than done. Remember, at this point, you have a map of the body, not yet a drawing. But, you must get this map reasonably accurate or what follows will fall apart. It takes effort and experience to find the right locations and proportions to build a convincing figure. You must be willing to make many corrections (thus, the mandate to keep the marks light) and not accept too readily as accurate your first placements of joints and body parts.

In all drawing, but especially in figure drawing, every part is relative to every other part. If you are drawing an arm, you must see it peripherally, out of the corner of your eye, as you scan the rest of the figure—even as you are drawing one part, you are aware of the others. Ask yourself, does the size and location of that arm seem reasonable to the other arm, the torso, the legs, and the head? One of the best ways to judge the accuracy of proportions is to step back several feet from your drawing. At close range, when working at your board, you tend to consider only the part you are drawing. From a distance, you will see more readily the relationships among all the parts as your eye scans across, up and down, and diagonally throughout the picture. Good working proportion in the guise of your informed stick figure is an essential foundation before a more recognizable figure can be "fleshed" out with contour lines, light and dark patterns, and other details.

The Torso and the Egyptians

The center of the universe in figure drawing is the *torso*, essentially the anatomy between shoulders and hips. A common misconception is to assume the head as the primary focal point. That would be true if the intention is portraiture, but that is an art of a different species. Figure drawing is about the whole body and its expression in space.

As you begin your drawing of the model, consider what the pose is doing. The torso determines the pose in the sense that it is much like the hub of a wheel. Arms, hands, legs, feet, head, and neck all branch off this central trunk. As a metaphor, a tree (figure) has as its main structure, a trunk (torso), from which branches (arms) and roots (legs) all sprout. Once you think with these priorities in mind—a hierarchy of forms with the most important first, and so on down the line—your mission to draw the figure is a more orderly and comprehensible process. In short, focus first on what the torso is doing. The rest of the body branches out in various directions.

In all standing, sitting, and reclining poses, the torso will have greater or lesser curvature, depending on the model and the position. Sometimes it seems to resemble a "C" shape, other times an "S" shape, but never is the spine a plumb line or a straight arrow. Look at illustrations of the spine. You will see the "S" curve in any diagram. As you study a pose, try to imagine the curved line of the vertebral column as it supports the torso and helps determine the shape and weight shift of that part of the figure.

These curves and twists are often referred to as the *line of action*. This is the most dominant line that can be seen throughout the pose of a figure. That line often animates the length of the pose from head to foot. It is not the contours along the outer edges that create this action, but rather the feeling of the whole sweep of implied motion that the torso and limbs of the figure express.

When assessing the blocking in of your figure in its initial stages, be mindful not to have the direction of the torso, head, or limbs set in parallel vertical or horizontal alignment with the rectangle of the paper. Orienting key parts of the body parallel to the edges of the paper is a way to ensure that the figure will look rigid and static, like that of a statue or sculpture rather than a human being. Avoid the ancient Egyptian practice of drawing the human form in a perpendicular box! In fact, when lines in the body do appear to your eye to be parallels to the frame, set them deliberately at slight diagonals to ensure the sense of a natural pose. There are a few instances when it is wise to improve on what you see. If you understand why you are taking a departure from nature's appearance, the slightly altered figure may work better as art.

There are other arguments for the plentiful use of angles and diagonals. Lines that run counter to the perpendicular stability of the picture frame impart movement and dynamism. You want to encourage the eye to move around in the drawing. These implied rhythms create excitement and keep the mind interested. Take advantage whenever you can. The crouch of an arm or leg, the body bending, leaning, or just the simple weight shift to one hip can remind us that the figure is capable of motion and that it is a living entity. A figure drawn from a pose ought to evoke the impression that it has just arrived at its resting place or that it is momentarily about to move into space.

Before going further, reread Chapter 7 since many of the principles described there apply to figure drawing. Read especially the section with the subheading GESTURE DRAWING.

STAGE II: FLESHING OUT THE CONTOURS

When your stick figure is established in reasonable proportions, start to "flesh out" the figure with lightly drawn contour lines that give shape to the bulk of muscles and soft tissues that comprise the model's body. Laying in contour lines to form the body in drawing is akin to the sculptural technique of building clay onto the hard armature of a figure.

Those contours, when examined closely in the model, are complicated and highly descriptive in their sudden turns in space. Think simpler to complex, larger to smaller initially. As with your stick figures, keep your contours light in the beginning. Many corrections will need to follow. Lighter lines are easy to eliminate by quick erasure or, more efficiently, by overdrawing slightly darker with each correction.

Contours do not occur only at the outer edges. If you indicate lines only on the periphery, your drawing may look as flat as a silhouette. There are wrinkles, curves, dents, bony outlines, muscles, and bulges all around the interior of the figure. Be sure to spend time articulating the lines of those forms.

Bundle or Bungle

Drawing is a lot like educated guessing. It is a search for the best forms—and both the process and the finished drawing should reflect that. Because drawing is a search of discovery, make several passes of lines over a given contour with the intuitive impulse that each line placed on the paper is an improvement to the preceding attempts. Drawing this way is a little like shadow boxing. You hover above your drawing board, move your hand in tandem to the desired lines and make contact with the paper as your gestures feel true. As you do this, you will make bundles of lines instead of single lines. The accumulation of these lines as they are improved and built in succession will read to the eye as a series of defined, coalesced forms. Those line bundles will tend to meld into comprehensible shapes and body parts while also suggesting movement and animation by their visible multiplicity.

Bundling lines can also be thought of as the process of sketching. The word *sketching* implies a more informal, spontaneous, and rougher manner of drawing. Its goal is the approximate rather than the exact. Since these searching lines are tentative, subject to change and revision as the bearings of the composition are sought, keep all lines light at this stage. That way you do not have to spend unnecessary time erasing and correcting. As your confidence builds in how those contours describe the structure of your subject and composition, you can render them with greater emphasis. Those later lines will then be what become most visible to the eye, whereas the lighter lines before may either disappear or be retained as animated "ghost" lines that animate the more established forms of the drawing.

If you look at examples of both old and modern master figure drawings, you will see this tendency of line bundling. (No, to the informed eye it does not look like line *bungling*.) Learn to see and appreciate the melding effect and how the eye of the viewer tends, like that of the artist, to put the lines together in the mind. This multiple line approach is similar to how the Impressionists manipulated small patches of individual primary colors to appear mixed as secondary colors from a distance. A fringe benefit to this technique is that we as viewers get to see evidence of the artist's hand and thinking as he drew. In this way, artists and viewers communicate and develop empathy for both the making of the drawing and its finished product.

Pause to Assess

After fleshing out your figure in light, sketchy contours, step back and assess the progress. Ask these questions:
- Is the figure emerging as a convincing three-dimensional form in space?
- Are the proportions still convincing?
- Does the pose seem natural and relaxed?
- If a standing pose, how is the weight distributed? Is there a weight shift?
- How are the shoulders rotated in relation to the hips? Is one shoulder higher? One hip?
- Does the shape of the torso reflect the curvature of its spine?
- Are there any problems with foreshortening? (See Chapter 12, Perspective, page 82, Foreshortening.)
- Does the figure engage the paper in a satisfying, compositional way?
- Does the figure seem to be developing in all areas? Is anything neglected?
- If the figure is cropped, do the places where the figure meets the edge look graceful or awkward?
- What areas need the most work or revision?

Crop but Do not Multilate

To crop or not to crop is always a question in figure drawing. Neither is better than the other, but both choices have pitfalls. If you do not crop, be sure to make the figure large enough to dominate the visual field of the paper. Then, add background features that connect the figure to the spatial field of the drawing. If you crop, do not do so at any point near the joints or at the neck. In the former it will look like amputation, in the latter it will look like decapitation! It is acceptable to crop anywhere through the head from top to chin as well as directly through the hand or the foot, and at places in between the joints. As with so many other drawing issues, it is helpful to look at how the masters handled these choices.

STAGE III: LIGHTS AND DARKS

After Stage I of stick figure mapping and Stage II of fleshing out with contours, you are ready for Stage III, rendering with lights and darks. Light and shadow play a pivotal role in figure drawing since these are the primary means to create the illusion of three dimensions on a two-dimensional surface. The difficulty of articulating a figure in light lies in the fact that there are few definitive edges between planes in the body compared to inanimate objects. Think of a cube or box with six sharply defined planes of which we can see three in perspective bounded by no less than nine edges of contour lines. In the figure, these edges tend to be elusive or seemingly nonexistent as the body's gradually and continuously curving forms elude any starting or stopping points.

What's a body to do? Think of human anatomy as comprised of a series of cylinders, cones, and spheres—especially cylinders. In the studio where the model will usually be illuminated by light from one direction, you can see the effect of this light on an arm, leg, or torso as a continuous value gradation. If the right side of the arm (or cylinder) is in highlight because the light source is coming from the right, then the gradation to shadow will darken to the left. This will be consistent throughout all parts of the body in the same pose with light from the same direction. So, if you solve effectively the light and dark on one part of the body you can feel confident that you will see similar patterns throughout the figure. However, since no rule is ever foolproof in art and reality has a way of allowing various exceptions, you can never use one part as a template for another. Always look carefully before drawing.

Because of the body's predominantly rounded, cylinder-like architecture, most highlights will gradate to shadow so gradually and subtly that it can be difficult to see where highlights end and shadows begin. Then, there are those middling grays in between both light and shade. Whether brilliant highlight, reflected light, pale shadow, dark shadow, or cast shadow, they all play key roles in the three-dimensional illusion of the figure.

Rendering lights and darks is really a matter of matching up the values you see in the model to their corresponding areas in your drawn figure. My advice is to start laying in the darkest and largest shadows first. These will serve later as useful reference points to judge the values of succeeding shadows as the scale moves gradually from dark to middle range to light. Reserve the highlights as untouched paper. Then, you have two references at either ends of the value scale to make informed renderings of all the grays in between.

The darkest shadows should be as black as the medium (e.g., graphite, conte crayon, or charcoal) can mark—even if that is darker than the shadows appear. Exaggeration in drawing is an effective strategy. Then, in a systematic way, go to the next darkest shadows and draw wherever you see them. Continue to each consecutive level until you have rendered about eight to ten values of shadow. Blend and gradate as needed, but whenever you have an opportunity to define an edge or a sharp contrast in values, do so. The more you can dramatize three dimensions the better, the more convincing the weight and volume of the figure. Work attentively to match values in drawing to what you see in the model. It is too easy and tempting to improvise from assumptions, that is, to start guessing rather than seeing. Never assume you know without looking carefully first. This is one of the most challenging stages in figure drawing, but also one of the most satisfying since it is with the means of light and dark that your figure drawing will start to come to life. If you become complacent, you will compromise the quality of your work.

REVISING: THE DEVIL IS IN THE DETAILS

At frequent stages during the light and dark drawing process step back to assess what is working and what is not. Be prepared to make adjustments and changes as needed. Be prepared, too, that as your drawing becomes more visible, darker, and detailed, it will tend to look different at working range versus viewing distance. The whole of your drawing is what matters, so the parts must work in concert with each other. Revise those areas that demand too much attention—that seem to diminish other worthy areas in the figure. Work to get all the parts unified, related, and consistent.

A single figure on a sheet does not a composition make. Connect the figure to a plausible space, an environment, or setting that gives the figure purpose and context. It can be as simple as the stool the model sits on and the wall or furnishings in the immediate area. These background elements may be drawn with less detail and finish, but they do need to establish the figure's place in space. If we think of the figure and the sheet of paper separately when we look at a drawing, then the vital context of composition is missing.

When drawing from the model or any subjects from life, truth is stranger than fiction. How something looks when you study it intently is usually unique and more peculiar than you can imagine. It is important when drawing complicated and highly varied forms, such as the human body, to look carefully at each part of the subject as you draw. As details become more specific and the complexity of your drawing grows in the later stages of the process, refer to the model as frequently as possible. When the modeling session or class has ended, you will not have another opportunity to check your drawing with the original pose.

In the last stage of a figure drawing, you should do as much critical looking as doing. Make improvements whenever and wherever possible. Do not be too easily satisfied. You will miss a lot if you work in haste. Do not be afraid to dig in, build up, erase, make a mess, start again. The mind's eye hungers for details. Describe, describe, tell us a story in lines, marks, and tones. When in doubt, put it in. You can always eliminate when necessary. If you do not enjoy getting up to your elbows in materials and the drawing process, you are either doing something wrong or drawing is not meant for you. An artist is always tinkering with new ways to get to a better place in his work. The beauty is in the twilight zone between tradition and experimentation.

WHEN IS IT FINISHED?

When you think your drawing is done, live with it. Hang it on a wall at home and see whether it stands the test of repeated viewing. If you are listening, the drawing will eventually tell you what, if anything, it needs. After the model's pose is finished, feel free to add or subtract elements to the drawing from memory or creative need. Do not censor your impulses. Art is about freedom and expression.

So, when is your drawing finished? My own test is living with the work in my studio and looking at it frequently—usually for a few days, but sometimes for weeks. Whenever I have the urge to change something, I do. There is always some risk that you will destroy a quality that you cannot retrieve once you take action. But fear makes art and artists mediocre. If you feel the need to revise something, there is probably a reason for it. Sometimes you know the reason, and sometimes you do not. Go ahead in either case.

The drawing is finished when you feel that adding or subtracting anything would compromise it. The experience is complete when you can look at a drawing time and again and still feel the sense of excitement you had when you were working on it.

Many artists today create work in which the human figure is central. Perhaps it is a response to our curiosity about who we are and our place on this planet. For those who reject the human form in favor of other subjects, figurative art may seem too narcissistic, confining, or literal. Whether art contains representations of the figure or not, its presence is always felt. All art is about human experience. To that extent, figure drawing is a dramatic foundation in the education and career of the artist. If art is about our collective humanity, drawing the figure could not be more relevant.

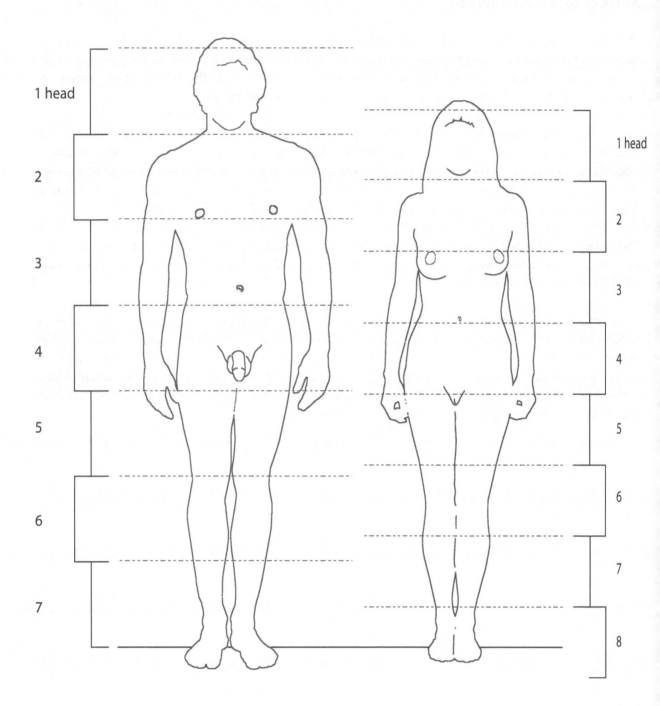

Human Figure Proportions

With the head as a unit of measure

Illustration contributed by Jerry Zinser. Copyright © Kendall Hunt Publishing Company

chapter 9

NOTES ON PAINTING

Painting is a wonderfully complex practice of manipulating colored pigments onto a flat surface to evoke an expressive image. Its directness of execution, immediacy of response, and intimacy between hand and material has had a far-ranging appeal across all geographic boundaries and cultures. At the same time, the subject matter and content of painting is as grand and inclusive as history itself. Because the parameters of art have expanded widely since the advent of modernism, whatever the mind can imagine is what painting can be about. Every student of art will do well to explore the potential of this universal medium.

An inexhaustible surplus of information and advice about painting can be gotten from books, the Internet, and other media sources. In fact, the beginning painter may easily feel overwhelmed while perusing a painting textbook, shopping for the necessary supplies, or confronting that first blank white canvas. A main purpose of this book is to bypass the barrage of information—often contradictory, repetitive, and confusing—and offer a condensed version of studio advice that will get you quickly and effectively engaged in the painting process. This chapter is neither comprehensive nor inclusive (that is, the guidelines described here are not the only way to paint), but is meant to be a useful, basic reference of what you need to know to get started.

A quick background is useful in understanding how painting has evolved in the Big Picture of Art and Culture. Painting has been an enduring language in virtually all civilizations throughout history. It may be the oldest art form of all if we consider that the earliest known artworks are cave paintings dating back 30,000 years or more and made with some of the same materials (minerals, oxides, and plant dyes) used to manufacture paints today. Furthermore, painting dominated the art world, from the illuminated manuscripts of the Middles Ages to the floridly saturated canvases of Neo-Expressionism of the 1980s. That is at least a one-thousand year run! Since Cubism and, later, Abstract Expressionism, painting has greatly influenced the development of the other fine arts (including sculpture and architecture) and applied arts (including graphic design and fashion design). The historical reach and cultural depth of painting is unparalleled. Thus, easel painting is an excellent entry point to art making. As a painting student, you are walking on one of the great paths in the history of art.

The reports in the art media—"Is Painting Dead?"—that have occasionally surfaced during the past few decades are grossly exaggerated. These provocations are irrelevant. Though many new art genres and burgeoning technological media now compete for our attention, there will always be the primeval need of artists to paint and viewers to look at paintings. In fact, one can argue that the proliferation of other visual media makes painting all the more unique, important, and desirable.

But what is painting? One can answer this question with the same philosophical arguments that try to answer, "What is art?" Philosophy aside, knowing some practical traits and parameters is helpful. Painting is a pictorial representation of illusionistic forms made with liquid, opaque pigments spread over a primed or unprimed panel or canvas surface. Drawing, by contrast, is done on sheets of paper with a variety of media designed for that purpose. However, these distinctions are not foolproof either. Paintings can be made on fine arts papers as well. To keep it simple, I will define easel painting as made with either of two major media regardless of the surfaces on which they are applied: oils and acrylic polymer paints.

When I teach painting, I give students the choice of either traditional oils (invented in the mid-1300s) or the more recently developed acrylics (late 1950s). Some instructors may insist on the use of oils since its history is a long and distinguished one and its technical handling may be somewhat more versatile and inclusive—especially as a precursor to acrylics and other paint media. Art majors should practice with both media, but not at the same time! Oils and acrylics are not compatible when mixed together.

Key differences should be noted before choosing either medium first. There are pros and cons with both—though some pros are also cons, and vice versa! The advantages of oils are: (1) the slow drying time, which allows the painter ample opportunity to manipulate blends and mixtures for representing gradations of lights and darks; (2) its paint films, especially thickly applied impastos, which can be easily removed entirely with the scraping of a palette knife; (3) the appearance of the paint, which once applied will not change from wet to dry states; and (4) its pigments and surfaces, which have a depth and luminosity unmatched by other media. In the case of #4, my observation is that the virtues of oil or acrylic surfaces depend more on the experience and skill of the painter rather than on the characteristics of the medium.

The disadvantages of oils are (1) its slow drying, which time can make handling or transport awkward or prone to damage; and (2) the thinning and clean up with turpentine that are required. These cons are minor considerations since managing drying time and using turpentine are easily made routine. It should be emphasized that neither of these characteristics add significant time or expense to the painting process.

Acrylic paints have the following advantages: (1) the fast drying time allows corrections and revisions (that is, repainting) to be made quickly and easily without the underlying layers affecting the newly applied ones; (2) paint films when dry are reasonably flexible to accommodate painting on various papers and unstretched canvas that may be rolled up for storage; (3) pigments are virtually color fast and resist fading in direct sunlight; and (4) cleanup is convenient, necessitating only ordinary hand soap and warm water.

The disadvantages of acrylics may be (1) the fast drying time, which may hinder slow painters who have difficulty manipulating blends and gradations before the paint dries, and (2) the colors that tend to dry slightly darker than when wet. Once understood via practice, neither of these characteristics is significant.

As you might conclude, the superiority of either oils or acrylics is a wash. If you have never used either, they may be arbitrary to assess. In that case, flip a coin or choose oils simply because there may be some sense to starting in chronological order.

SUPPLY LIST

The supply list below is what I require in my painting classes, but every instructor will have some variations. Unless noted otherwise, items are for both oils and acrylics.

Tube colors:
Titanium White or Zinc White
Mars Black or Ivory Black
Hansa Yellow or Cadmium Yellow Light (or Medium)
Pthalocyanine Blue or Ultramarine Blue
Napthol Red or Cadmium Red Light (or Medium)
Pthalocyanine Green or Permanent Green Light
Yellow Ocher or Yellow Oxide
These additional tube colors are optional but highly recommended:
Raw Sienna, Burnt Sienna, Raw Umber, Burnt Umber, Alizarin Crimson, any of the Magentas and Violets
Long-handled hogs' hair bristle brushes* (4 brushes minimum):
Flats preferred, Rounds optional
Choose #2 through #12—for example, 2, 4, 6, and 8 are most useful sizes
One 2" or 3" bristle or nylon house painting brush
*Acrylic painters may purchase nylon, polyester, or synthetic brushes instead of hogs' hair brushes
Palette knife or painting knife: The latter is preferred with a diamond-shaped flexible blade and cranked
    shaft
Palette: any rigid, nonporous panel of wood, Masonite, metal, glass, or Plexiglass in oval or rectangular
    shape, 10" × 12" or slightly larger. Seal wood or Masonite with varnish
For oil painters: two (2) jars with watertight lids
Odorless turpentine or odorless paint thinner, pint or larger
For acrylic painters: two (2) quart-sized plastic or metal containers
Several paint rags from old cotton sheets, linens, shirts, and the like
Hand-sized terrycloth towel and bar of soap
4B to 8B graphite drawing pencils or medium charcoal pencil and block eraser
Staple gun and staples, 36" metal straight edge, scissors, and razor knife
Optional for acrylic painters: small jar or tube of acrylic gel or acrylic medium, matte or gloss
Optional for oil painters: small bottle of linseed oil
Acrylic gesso or matte white house paint, quart or larger
Surfaces:
Cotton duck or linen canvas, 3 or more yards at 36" or wider
Several Masonite panels or smooth plywood at ¼" to ¾" thick, sizes from 18" × 24" and larger
Variety of canvas boards, canvas paper, or illustration boards, 12" × 18" and larger

NOTE ABOUT SAFETY: Handle paints with care since they are chemicals. Do not eat or smoke while painting. Use solvents, turpentines, paint thinners, and brush cleaners carefully and sparingly with proper ventilation. Do not pour solvents, thinners, or oil paint residues down the sink. Always reseal containers securely and as soon as possible after use. After each session, wash hands and tools thoroughly with soap and warm water.

STRETCHING CANVAS AND PREPARING SURFACES

Since most easel painting is done on stretched canvas, this is one of your first tasks. You will learn this simple skill in your first painting course. Since some of these procedures can be easily overlooked and result in a poorly made canvas, it is good to keep in mind a few essentials as reference.

You can make a stretcher in two ways. You can fasten together a frame of premilled stretcher strips with mitered, tongue-in-groove ends that fit together at right angles. They are designed to be tight enough to hold in place without glue or nails. Or, with fairly simple carpentry skills you can make your own frame from 1" × 2" or 1" × 3" pine planks cut at the ends to 45 degrees and attached at right angles with glue and nails. The advantages of the latter are that handmade frames are vastly cheaper and that different sizes and shapes can be made that are not possible with prefabricated stretchers.

Regardless of your chosen method of construction, check your corners with a carpenter's square to be sure each is an accurate 90 degrees. This means checking every corner several times during and after construction. Nothing looks more inferior and amateurish than a badly angled canvas.

Next, place the frame over a sheet of canvas resting on a flat surface (table or floor) closest to the edges and corner to minimize waste. Measure the canvas so that it is 3" larger in length and width than the frame. Make pencil marks on the canvas as a guide. Draw the outline of this rectangle directly on the canvas with a straight edge and pencil. Place the frame inside the pencil lines to confirm that it is 1½" smaller on all four sides. Cut the canvas with scissors along the pencil lines.

Lay the frame over the canvas so that its margins are equal (about 1½") at the four sides. At the center of one of the long sides, wrap the canvas around the frame and staple into the back of the wood strip. Go to the opposite side and do the same. Be sure to stretch the canvas taut (but not so taut that you distort the frame) before applying a staple. Do the same center stapling on the short sides. Return to the starting point and stretch the canvas from center to corner, applying staples every 2" or 3" apart and stopping short of the corner by about 3". You are first stapling just half of each side. Since there is little resistance at the other end at this point, do not apply much pressure in stretching. It is more important to keep the weave of the canvas in a straight line across the frame as you staple. Staple the diagonal opposite half on the other long side. Continue the halves on the shorter sides.

Go back to the starting side again and complete the stretching of the other half. This time, stretch the canvas tautly since the other side is now stapled. Use canvas pliers or just pull the canvas with your hands against the frame. Continue the process until all is stretched except the corners. Test the tautness by thumping your forefinger in the center of the canvas. It should have a spring to it similar to a musical drum. If the canvas is loose, remove staples on one long side and pull tighter as you apply new staples. Fold the corners over neatly to the back and staple firmly. Voila! You have made a canvas as Rembrandt or Picasso might have. You are ready to prime.

Since canvas is highly absorbent, the surface needs to be prepared with the application of at least two coats of acrylic gesso. Matte latex house paint is an alternative. Thin the gesso with water in another container to a commercial paint consistency, a ratio of about 2/3 gesso to 1/3 water. Mix well. Apply a coat thinly with a 2- or 3-inch house painting brush moving in all directions to completely fill the woven fibers of the canvas. Brush out the gesso vigorously and as flat as possible so as not to leave three-dimensional marks. When dry (about 20-30 minutes), sand lightly with fine sandpaper. The first coat will have sunk into the canvas "pores." Apply a second coat so the gesso becomes a barrier between canvas and paint.

Priming with gesso is the same for hard panels, such as Masonite or plywood. Apply two coats and sand after the first coat. You are almost ready to paint a picture.

SETTING UP AT AN EASEL AND OBSERVING THE SUBJECT

As in drawing, painting is learned best by representing subjects that the painter observes directly. In the classroom studio, you will paint from an easel and most likely begin in response to a still life arrangement. Position the easel at a 45-degree angle to your line of vision so that you can see the still life clearly without leaning your body or craning your neck. Set the canvas on the easel at about eye level to its center. There will be a crank on the support to adjust the height. Place your palette, paint tubes, and brushes within easy reach of your painting hand. Use a viewfinder as described in the drawing chapter to plan your composition. Be prepared to stand as you paint. This stance makes for a more proactive and alert state of mind as you work. Painting is both a mental and a *physical* act. You will tend to be more observant of the subject and your painting if you are standing rather than sitting. In the long term, this approach will make a better picture. Now you are ready.

THE STAGES OF PAINTING

The development of a painting as described here is meant to guide you through a multifaceted process and offer a way to understand a complex activity by breaking it down into steps. These stages are not meant to be fixed in precise chronology. The reality of painting is that the processes overlap. Some you may find more or less useful, and others you may invent yourself. You can certainly deviate as your needs, habits, and experiences evolve. Some of these stages are similar to the drawing process.

1. **Block-In of Linear Forms.** With the aid of a viewfinder (whether observing from still life, figure, or landscape) determine your composition by drawing with light pencil or charcoal strokes the contour lines of objects and/or figures, their shapes, and the critical relationships between positive and negative space. Make frequent corrections of forms and their proportions as necessary by erasing and redrawing. This "skeletal" sketch is your pictorial roadmap. Many painters start by immediately "drawing" in paint. Your instructor may require this method. Take a small quantity of yellow ocher or other light neutral color and thin to a wash consistency by diluting oils with turpentine or acrylics with water. With a #1 or #2 brush loaded with the wash paint, "draw" your lines and contours. Mistakes can be wiped away with a rag if they are still wet. If dry, repaint with a slightly stronger line or somewhat darker color. Step back

frequently and critically analyze from a distance whether proportions are accurate and composition is satisfying.

2. **Lay-In of Light and Dark Patterns.** Expand your palette by adding black, white, and earth colors such as Siennas and Umbers. Make washes of these colors by diluting with the appropriate water or turpentine. Find the deepest shadows. With a #6 to #8 brush apply your darkest washes to these areas wherever you see them in your subject—that is, in all the key areas of the painting. Paint those shadows that occupy the most space first. Next, lay in the next darkest shadows wherever they occur and throughout the picture. Do this systematically in sequential steps from darkest, darker, dark shadows, and then medium or middle values, to light, lighter, lightest highlights. Do not yet attempt to match color of paint to visible reality. Concentrate on establishing a foundation of accurate values with the monochromatic scales of the earth colors modified by black and white. Cover all areas of the white canvas with the appropriate values of your subject matter. As in Stage #1, assess frequently and critically from a distance. Make adjustments by repainting areas that seem off by comparison to surrounding lights and darks. After a time, you should have developed a convincing and illusionistic rendering of the light and dark structures of your subject matter.

3. **Direct Painting of Description and Detail.** Lay out on your palette a full color range that approximates what you will need to interpret your subject. Direct painting is applying the medium so that your colors have the identity, thickness, and textural effects that best express your intentions. Of course, what you intend at this early stage is still tentative and subject to frequent changes as you observe, compare, and readjust. While painting is a process of trial and error, you paint as if you mean it each time you apply a stroke. If this sounds contradictory, you will soon understand as you practice. Apply paint to tell the story of your subject's life—that is, its visual description, its many details, its colors in visible light, and its textures and patterns. While observing in reality is important, consider the subject's inner life, how the forms feel to you or what they suggest in addition to the visible. Meld the observed with the felt experience if you can take the imaginative leap into paint. Painting is not exclusively "eyeballing." You can exaggerate, distort, embellish, add, subtract, or otherwise change the painting until you can say "my picture is more exciting to view than the original subject matter."

4. **Corrections and Revisions.** This is not really the last step and is not meant to be chronological. The painting process from start to finish is always about corrections and revisions. Painting is about repainting. The opacity of easel paint is a great advantage. Any "disaster" on a canvas can be quickly and efficiently eliminated by applying a new layer of paint or gesso over that area. For painters this is a great comfort. No matter how bad a painting may seem, it can always be repainted in part or in full. Your goal in doing so is to improve the picture. This malleable quality implies that painting is a labor-intensive craft. It is! The best painter leaves one great painting on the surface while underneath may be 50 other pictures!

TECHNIQUES OF PAINT HANDLING

Some beginners have the misconception that if they know the "right" techniques, they will be able to make good paintings. Maybe they are misguided by too many TV painters and how-to manuals—both depend on strict imitation and conformity. In fact, techniques are essentially a catalog of applications: the various ways that paint can be manipulated. Selecting techniques to apply to specific subjects, forms, highlights, shadows, or to any other aspect of painting has no instruction manual. These choices are made by the painter according to his experience, ability, and originality. It takes practice for the painter to know how to handle paint. There are no magic bullets! But I can tell you what the techniques are. Then you can choose.

In addition, painters often invent new techniques that fit the needs of individual goals. In that sense, there are as many techniques as there are painters. For example, I often paint using, believe it or not, oven basters filled with diluted paint and applied into specially made reservoirs constructed to hold "lakes" of color on my paintings. What you do with techniques must be suitable to the art and to your intentions. Since painting is a kind of personal "signature" of how you track paint across a surface, it is important that you experiment with these techniques and use the ones that are most compelling to your individual manner of working.

1. BLENDING is one of the most common ways to apply paint. Mixing two or more wet colors on a surface so they gradate from dark to light or from one color to another is one of the basic methods to render the illusion of highlights and shadows. This technique is also called modulated color. A blended surface has three components: one color on the left, the other color on the right, and their mixture in between at a middle position. The colors may be smoothly graded or they may be broken and uneven with brush strokes visible.

2. OPTICAL BLENDING is the discovery of the Impressionists. A more precise and regimented system invented by Georges Seurat is called Pointillism. Many small dabs or spots of pure color are placed side-by-side but not physically mixed. From an optimum viewing distance, the eye mixes the colors to give the illusion of gradation or mixing.

3. WET-IN-WET is the application of a color over an existing wet color so that both colors "bleed" but retain some of their original hues. Wet-in-wet is distinct from blending since it does not attempt to make specific gradations. Instead, it is a way to enliven a surface with the sensation of depth, movement, and unpredictability.

4. GLAZING is placing a darker transparent color over a lighter one, which can still be seen through the top layer. For example, a transparent blue painted over a yellow base will filter through as a visible green. But the effect is much different than actually mixing blue and yellow to make green. The viewer still "senses" the individual colors even as they suggest a third color. The luminosity that results from glazing is unique to this technique. The second overlaid color is made transparent by mixing it with a medium such as gel for acrylics or linseed oil for oil paints.

5. SCUMBLING is nearly the opposite of glazing. It is usually accomplished by applying a light color over a dark. However, the light color is not as diluted and is applied as a broken color (that is, uneven in coverage) over the darker color.

6. DRY BRUSH is applying a brush nearly run out of paint over a surface so that the color is broken and randomly scattered in irregular patterns. The result can be unpredictable but highly expressive. This is also a technique frequently practiced in drawing using a brush with India ink or watercolor.

7. IMPASTO is laying on color straight from the tube with a palette knife, a coarse brush, or a squeegee. There is a physical, relief-like quality to the paint that can cast its own shadows and highlights as a result.

8. PALETTE KNIFE PAINTING or knife painting is applying paint with the edge or spatula portion of this tool. The knife creates textures and patterns distinctly different from brush marks. Knife painting is often employed where impasto is desired.

9. SGRAFFITO is "drawing" with a sharp tool into wet paint to reveal lines below the surface. The lines made are really negative spaces. It is a way to add detail and pattern.

10. GRISAILLE is painting strictly in values of black, white, and gray. It is a good method to understand that all colors in nature have their counterparts as light and dark values.

11. WIPING OUT is a method of applying a wet color over a dry and then with a finger or rag wiping out the wet color to reveal the layer of color below. It is similar to sgraffito, except more areas are revealed than lines.

12. STIPPLING involves applying tiny dots or fragments of color by taking a brush, holding it vertically, and hitting the surface repeatedly without lateral movement. It is similar to the Pointillist technique made famous by the Post-Impressionist Georges Seurat.
13. SPATTERING is taking a paint-loaded stiff brush, such as a toothbrush, and flexing its bristles toward the painting to deposit minute dots of color.
14. TONKING is applying a sheet of absorbent paper, such as newsprint, to a dense area of wet paint by tamping it down by hand or with weights. Then, the paper is lifted to reveal patterns and textures.

How you use these techniques is as important as the fact that painting is always about the way paint is applied. Since its physical and visual properties are unique, always bear in mind that *how* you manipulate paint is as important as, no, is more important than, *what* you are painting. How paint looks when it is deposited on a surface is the single greatest visual attribute of painting. Spend time understanding how to move it around.

PAINTING AND THE PALETTE

Some of the most practical advice I can offer involves using the palette. I have observed beginners spending exorbitant amounts of time fiddling and fussing with paint mixtures on a palette and then brooding about what to do with them. Marking place in this way is an anxiety-driven form of procrastination. Such fears hold you back and are a royal waste of time. Instead, think of your painting as the palette and get the paint on the canvas as soon as possible. Think of the palette as a launching pad for paint rather than a holding pattern or a clearinghouse. It is more productive (and fun!) to mix your paint directly on the picture. For example, if the color you are applying is too dark, quickly pick up some lighter color on your brush and continue. A lighter color will emerge as the brush moves the paint around on the canvas. The point is that how a color looks on the palette is different than how it looks on the painting. So get to the painting sooner rather than later.

Another useful trick is to keep two brushes going at once, one with lighter color and one with darker. Instead of fussing with frequent brush cleanings in water or turpentine, adjust your colors as needed by dipping your brushes into the colors you anticipate will mix to what you have in mind. With a little experience, you will be able to judge reasonably well how two separate colors on your brush will mix when applied to your painting. Remember, the action is in the picture and what you do there is what matters.

COLOR MIXING

Before attempting a painting, I recommend that you do some color mixing in the form of charts and gradations. What pigments will do when mixed is unpredictable to the novice. Some colors straight from the tube are opaque, some are transparent, and others are in between. A given yellow mixed with a given blue does not necessarily make the expected green. Minute amounts of black can quickly dull or darken a color, while small amounts of white mixed with a color may seem to change it hardly at all. Then there is the wide variation of how a color behaves when diluted with a medium. All of these qualities of mixing and variation need to be practiced before they can be anticipated and applied effectively to painting.

A good learning exercise is to execute a number of color scales. On a primed sheet of paper or board, draw with pencil and straight edge ten 1⊠ squares in consecutive, adjacent order. Apply pure white paint in the first square and black in the last. In the remaining eight squares mix various grays so that each mixture applied in a square is an equal step from the previous and the one ahead. You should be able to see a reasonable gradation of ten distinct and equidistant values from one end to the other. Do the same with two complementary colors (opposites on the color wheel), such as orange and blue or green and red. The middle color mixed will be a neutral brown.

Then do a series of ten shades by gradually adding black to any color. Do the same for tints by adding white to a color. Finally mix analogous colors (colors that are adjacent on the color wheel), such as yellow and red, to see the gradations move to orange in the middle of the scale. After completing these simple exercises, you will save much time because you will understand what to anticipate when mixing colors in your painting.

GOUACHE AND WATERCOLOR

These are not easel paints but are worthy of mention. Gouache and watercolor straddle the fence between drawing and painting. Because of a cultural bias, these media are considered minor and are given little or no instruction in college art departments. This neglect is a pity since these paints have a wondrous history and rich technical possibilities. As a student, you may have to take the initiative to explore their technical and expressive potential. Few colleges have separate courses for watercolor or gouache, and when they do appear in the curriculum, they are usually shoe-horned into an existing course.

Watercolor is a water-soluble, transparent paint medium with a gum arabic binder. Watercolor's hallmark effects rely on the vibrant interaction between the whiteness of the paper and the lush transparencies of its pigments. Since the medium tends to be watery in its application to paper (compared to the thick body of easel paints), colors tend to gather and dry in slightly uneven concentrations, yielding rich textures and tonal effects. These qualities naturally aid the illusion of light and dark gradations, as well as evoking complex details in their surfaces. The experienced watercolorist will exploit these tendencies to enhance expression.

Gouache is opaque watercolor, although the same effects of transparency can be easily gained by thinning with more water. Both media operate from the premise that more pigment means stronger, more vibrant colors, while more water added yields lighter and more transparent effects. Both gouache and watercolor are available in dry pan sets or tubes. When these media are dry, they easily reactivate as paint when mixed with water. Completely dried color squeezed from a tube can be mixed as paint again when water is added. Other advantages include virtually no waste and easy clean up with plain water. They require little material investment, are inexpensive compared to easel paints, but have all the creative challenges and rich possibilities of other art materials. They are so portable that you can paint at the kitchen table or in the corner of a room.

THE BIG PICTURE

Painting engages the full range of human capacities and abilities, including intellect, emotions, the senses, perceptions, intuition, imagination, and discipline. The opportunity to exercise both mind and body in a state of heightened awareness is its great appeal to painters and viewers alike. It is not as daunting as it sounds. Feeling more alive because the act of painting makes you feel more on the tips of your toes is not intimidation. Rather, it is freedom.

Though fixed when the artist declares it finished, a painting is remarkably malleable. A painting can stimulate various interpretations depending on an audience's time and place. A painting can seem to change—like a chameleon changing its colors—with each new generation. The painter may persuade us by the strength of his vision, but time and culture influence the way we see art. Despite the way a painting may seem to change outside the studio, the artist paints for himself—from his internal need—rather than for posterity.

Techniques, color theory, art history, skills, and practice are only part of the picture of a painter's quest. Anyone with average intelligence and diligent pursuit might become a good technician. But, technical facility is all for naught if painting is not about a greater mystery—that which is profound or provocative that only the painter knows. Painting is what can *only* be said with color and form.

So, when you paint, cast all else to the wind, including this chapter. Forget rules and guidelines. Focus on what you want to say. Get as close to your urges and desires as you can—with colored pigments as their equivalents. That may seem impossible or funny, but that's what artists do. Ignore ego, audience, teacher, classmates, friends, and family. How can you interpret what you know and feel at this time and place with these materials? Answer that in paint!

HOW TO STRETCH A CANVAS

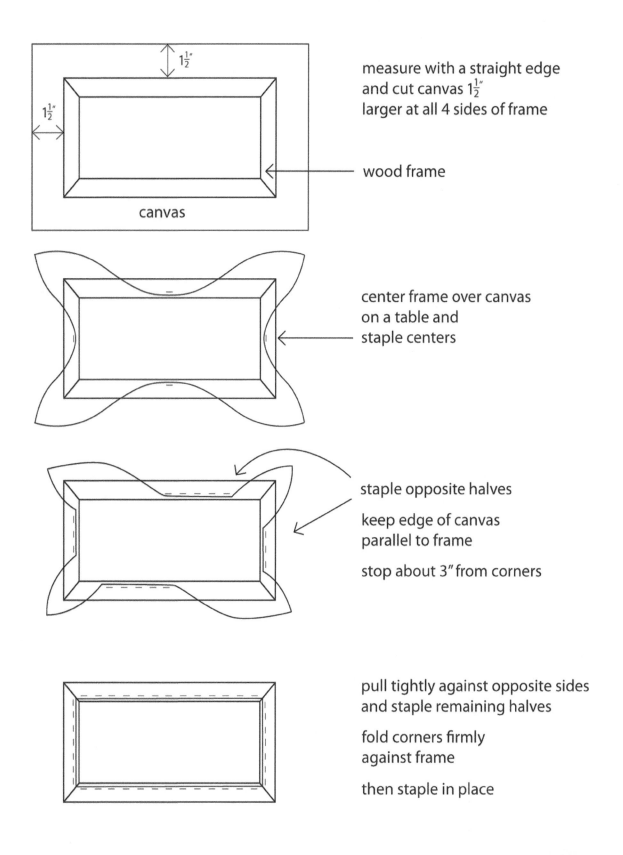

$1\frac{1}{2}''$

$1\frac{1}{2}''$

canvas

measure with a straight edge
and cut canvas $1\frac{1}{2}''$
larger at all 4 sides of frame

wood frame

center frame over canvas
on a table and
staple centers

staple opposite halves

keep edge of canvas
parallel to frame

stop about 3" from corners

pull tightly against opposite sides
and staple remaining halves

fold corners firmly
against frame

then staple in place

chapter

COLLAGE AND MIXED MEDIA

Collage and mixed media may be the least understood of the traditional art genres. Both disciplines involve a great variety of materials and techniques that may not be apparent to the general observer. By contrast, drawing and painting offer clear distinctions about the materials and properties of their making. A little background may be helpful.

Collage is one of the most recent inventions in art history, developing during the Cubist years as an offshoot of that movement. Picasso made the first collage in 1912 by attaching with glue to his canvas a piece of oilcloth with a pattern of chair caning printed on its surface. He further transformed his oval-shaped composition by wrapping a line of rope around the outer edge as both a frame for the picture and a definition of the painting as the shape of a tabletop. In the same year, Georges Braque made the first *papier colle* (paper collage) by attaching three pieces of decorative wood-grain paper to a drawing whereby they became the background wall of a charcoal still life.

These works began a revolution in mixed media. Collages by nearly all artists practicing Cubism soon followed. In 1918, the Dadaists invented photomontage by pasting together multiple photographic clippings into singular compositions of political and social satire. As Picasso leaped ahead by applying collage concepts in three dimensions with the invention of assemblage, the Constructivists began to make mixed media relief pictures fashioned from wood scraps, broken glass, wire, tin cans, and other discards of the street and household.

Late Cubist paintings, called Synthetic Cubism, tended to look like collages (though nothing was pasted to them) when artists painted wallpaper patterns, imitated wood-grain effects, mixed sand into their paint, and defined contrasting spatial areas with hard edges and shadows. The forerunner to Surrealism—Giorgio de Chirico—made paintings that looked like an illusionistic blend of collage and assemblage. In the 1920s, the Surrealists Max Ernst and Joan Miro took collage on a voyage of dream and fantasy as they broke away from the Cubists' preoccupation with still life subjects.

After Abstract Expressionism had had its run by the early 1950s, many American artists began to rediscover collage on a grand scale, befitting the post-war New World flexing its cultural and political muscle. The work of Robert Rauschenberg may be the single greatest contribution to the renewed interest in mixed media that has shaped American art from the late 1950s to the present day. In fact, one could argue that mixed media is the dominant form of expression, replacing easel painting and traditional sculpture as the most widely practiced genre in the twenty-first century.

MIXED MEDIA GENRES

Since there are a variety of forms and techniques practiced in mixed media, a few definitions of basic terms will help clarify their differences.

- COLLAGE is the art of pasting into a composition various materials not normally associated with one another. Materials may include printed matter from magazines, newspapers, and commercial packaging, but may also include nonpaper items such as cloth, wood, glass, plastic, or any other matter that can be attached with glue. The English use of the word *collage* derives from the French *colle*, to paste, and from *collage*, a pasting.
- PHOTOMONTAGE (sometimes shortened to MONTAGE) is a specific type of collage made from joining photographs and cutout portions of photographs. These may be original photographs or those reproduced in magazines and other printed media. Photocopies and rephotographed images may also be included.
- *PAPIER COLLE* is the French term that refers to Georges Braque's invention in 1912 involving pasted paper combined with drawing.
- FOUND OBJECT is a natural or manufactured object not originally intended as art but considered to have aesthetic value. FOUND MATERIALS (without the sense of object-hood) are those ordinarily meant for other purposes but incorporated into the making of artworks. Both found objects and found materials are the core ingredients in making assemblages.
- ASSEMBLAGE is the three-dimensional counterpart to collage. It is a variation on the additive method of sculpture in which an object is made by joining together various parts (compared to the historic tradition of subtracting material from a single mass or block). Found objects and found materials are its main ingredients, but assemblage can also include traditional art materials.
- RELIEF is an artwork that has a pictorial orientation, that is, it hangs on a wall but has three-dimensional objects or materials attached to its surface that project into space. Low relief (or bas relief) has slight projections while high relief has greater projections.
- READYMADE is the term invented by the artist Marcel Duchamp to identify a manufactured object that the artist declared a work of art. These objects' identities are undisguised but are often modified by the artist.
- TO APPROPRIATE in the art lexicon means to take possession of an object, artwork, or some item with an existing identity and to manipulate it so that it becomes a different artwork in a new context. The resulting art or action taken may be called an APPROPRIATION.
- JUXTAPOSITION is the adjacent relationship between two unrelated or contrasting materials, forms, or images. In collage and assemblage, placing items close together or side-by-side is a strategy used to emphasize their interaction and dialogue.
- MIXED MEDIA is simply any artwork that combines or mixes two or more different materials. This umbrella term describes most of the definitions above.

COLLAGE AS A MODEL FOR MIXED MEDIA

Collage is probably the most common mixed media genre as well as the one with the most specific methods and strategies. In most of what follows, I will describe the collage process since its concepts, materials, and techniques parallel those of the other mixed media genres including photomontage, assemblage, and relief.

Though collage is a relatively recent innovation in artistic practice, another factor that may cloud its understanding is its association with early education when each of us first learned the important motor skills of cutting with scissors and applying paste to locate pieces in a picture. At the grade-school level, only the most rudimentary approaches to collage expression would have been possible. Many who take a college course in mixed media may not have done a collage since those early school days!

My experience in teaching mixed media is that many students assume collage making to be a more logical and simple procedure than it actually is. In fact, I think collage is one of the most difficult genres to master because its broad appeal with diverse materials and images makes it immediately seductive and distracting. Thus, it has a tendency to self-indulgence and gratuitous effects. One can easily get lost in its wide-ranging imagery, sensuous materials, and limitless possibilities for combining and mixing. Its visual freedoms can become either an exercise void of expressive purpose or paralyzing in its openness and tendency to excesses. Without sufficient structures and frames of reference, collage can become a glut of surpluses rather than a statement of dramatic focus. I want to outline ways of thinking about and doing collage that get beyond the pitfalls of simplistic solutions and clichés on the one hand, and overwhelming abundance and confusion on the other.

CHANGING CONTEXTS

What makes collage so challenging is that you attempt to intervene with materials and objects that have a prior life. Their baggage of meaning and content threaten to carry more weight than the art itself. Photographs, printed matter, and materials manufactured for specific purposes are not the "anonymous" art supplies you purchase at an art store. Collage materials generally have a meaning and function designed for a purpose different from art. Their context in life must undergo a modification to a new context, to that in art. The hazard is this: If that previous context is left too intact—if we continue to recognize its function primarily as a product of commerce—its visual transformation into art is lost. This is the greatest single pitfall I have witnessed in beginners' collages.

Sometimes the dialogue between what the materials of collage meant in life and then becomes in art can be its expressive content. It may take the form of satire, social or political commentary, or simply the absurdity or humor of the contrast. The light cast in this dual way must be fresh and new, or the effect can devolve into cliché and mediocrity. The best examples of bridging these contexts may be the photomontages of the Dadaists, such as John Heartfield, Hannah Hoch, Raoul Hausmann, and Alexander Rodchenko. A clear example of bridging art and life contexts is Marcel Duchamp's appropriated urinal titled "Fountain" and made in 1917. He signed the iconic ceramic vessel with the pseudonym R. Mutt, placed it on a museum pedestal for exhibition, and declared it a work of art. This object is now an icon of art history and continues to conflate our impressions of the object's standard utility and its proclamation as artistic statement. We cannot see one without its relation to the other.

"Fountain" may be an extreme case of art holding an uneasy equivalence with life. Usually the tensions of context are not so demanding. The artist can choose whether to disguise his found materials or feature its prior references to make expressive contrasts. In either case there must be a balance between prior meaning and the new context of art. That means that the art must be more assertive than any of the found images or materials that comprise it.

The opportunity to creatively alter parts and pieces derived from the world-at-large in order to make art can be a heady and exciting prospect. But it is a challenge that takes artistic courage and demands firm and resolute actions. No cows are sacred, and nothing is too humble or lowly.

ALTERING COLLAGE MATERIALS

Although much in collage and mixed media involves starting with materials and objects as they are found, you do not have to accept them at face value. You can alter them physically (even before their *placement* in a composition alters them) by cutting, tearing, breaking apart, reattaching, sanding, scraping, sawing, drilling, painting, or drawing. In addition, you can make your own collage material. Take sheets of paper and cover them in paint, colors, textures, and patterns of your own making. Cut them into desirable shapes and pieces for collage or mixed media works. You can apply tooling methods to nearly all materials, including found objects.

I suggest that you keep drawings and paintings with which you are unsatisfied as collage material. "Cannibalizing" your less successful art this way can be both creative and cathartic. The feeling that you are retrieving something useful from your mistakes can be motivating and reassuring. It is another way to stretch your artistic muscles.

THE NATURE OF COLLAGE

In order to capitalize on its best qualities and unique features, it is useful to consider the formal characteristics of the collage medium:
- Cut or torn edges (think lines "drawn" with a razor knife or by tearing, instead of charcoal) are visual elements to exploit. Edges can be made to seem soft and subtle or hard edged and sharply defined. Much depends on how the surfaces affect the edges.
- What happens at those cut or torn edges is of great consequence. The sensation of suddenly stopping and abruptly starting something else, which the edges facilitate, is called juxtaposition. It is the drama behind any collage.
- When two unlikely or unrelated forms or objects are laid side by side, their contrast becomes a phenomenon of interest for contemplation. Often, their combination is striking because their differences arouse immediate questions, challenge our ability to reason their coexistence, and convey the sensation of something invented or not seen before. In this way, collage causes us to wonder about reality.
- The laws of physics (What's micro, what's macro? How far is far?), gravity (What's up, what's down?), and linear perspective do not apply to collage. Place and space become dream and fantasy. Collage is the science fiction of the visual arts.

- Time collapses into spontaneous contrasts. Collage has the ability to encapsulate in the same unified image elements of the past and present. An antique object or an early photograph can be accommodated into the content of a collage and still seem connected and contemporaneous with all the other materials and images of its making.
- By definition, collage is compatible with all media and materials. There is a solution to making extreme contrasts and contradictions effective and unified if you have the imagination.
- The *entire world* is available to you for both your subject matter and art supplies. You are limited only by your ability and good fortune to find them. With access to so much in the environment, you need only go on a scavenger hunt. Most of it, other people overlook or discard. And so much of it is free!
- Despite the fact that collage is a kind of visual anarchy dependent on fragmentation, contrast, collision, and contradiction for its content, coherence and unity are essential for its effectiveness as art. Composition is just as critical in collage as in traditional media.
- Collages become their own realities. They imply a universe different from the objective representations and plausible illusions found in earlier traditions of drawing and painting, and they cannot be likened to nonobjective abstractions since collages freely incorporate fragments and images of everyday life. Think of collages as hybrids of other realities.
- Collage has its own set of myriad techniques that may include cutting, tearing, scraping, sanding, and altering the surfaces of various materials. Its assembly is roughly akin to putting together an elaborate jigsaw puzzle with neither directions nor predetermined fittings to aid the process.
- Like mirages, the surfaces of a collage often transmute by the power of visual suggestion, that is, seem to become illusions of materials other than what they actually are. Often these transmutations recall the technical effects of drawing and painting media. For example, a printed texture from a photograph might imply the sensation of charcoal rubbed over a rough surface, or a roof tile may appear to be paint mixed with gravel. These equivalents help us see collage as not limited to its found characteristics. Collage expands the way we experience surfaces, materials, and images.

TOOLS AND SUPPLIES

- RAZOR KNIVES are known in the art world as mat knives and in the general world as utility knives. A *mat knife* consists of a single-edge razor blade held in a metal or heavy plastic handle. The handle unscrews into halves to change and store blades. *Box cutter knives* are inexpensive and one of the most versatile tools for cutting paper and cardboard. They are available in a lighter or a heavier plastic handle from which the blade extends in a continuous band. To renew the blade when dull, the end is snapped off at the next serrated mark with a pair of pliers. A third kind is the *craft knife* (X-acto is the major brand) with a pencil-like metal shaft. These have limited use for delicate or detailed cutting in relatively thin paper.
- SCISSORS come in a great variety of shapes and sizes. Choose those that suit your hand and the material to be cut. I keep about ten different kinds for various tasks, but a couple of good ones are adequate.
- CUTTING MATS are crucial to good cutting practice. They are about as thick as mat board and are made of a seemingly magical NASA-like composite material in which knife cuts promptly close up and "heal." They come in the standard sizes of 9 × 12, 12 × 18, and 18 × 24 inches with convenient one-inch grids printed on the surfaces. You can cut on cardboard sheets (not corrugated), but they soon acquire so many gouges that you cannot make clean cuts on them for long.

- METAL STRAIGHT EDGES of 24 to 36 inches long are indispensable for measuring, planning the format shape and size of collages, and especially when you want straight, cleanly cut lines.
- DRAFTING TRIANGLES come in various sizes and two distinct angles (45s or 30/60 degrees). At least one medium size triangle is essential for establishing accurate 90-degree angles.
- A SET OF FRENCH CURVES is optional but most useful when you need a specific curve or precise contour. If careful not to cut into the plastic form, you can trim along the contour of a French curve with a knife and use its shape as a template. Also you can design an entirely new shape by using several French curves for its various contours.
- GLUES and ADHESIVES abound, but only a few are suitable. First, here are the ones to avoid. Rubber cement is an abomination. It has too many chemicals, its hold is temporary, and it discolors to dark brown anything it touches within a short time. Glue stick is really a temporary adhesive and is only practical for "spot" gluing. Glue guns are also temporary fixes and meant only for heavy-handed solutions with mostly three-dimensional materials.
- The standard WHITE GLUES are acceptable, such as Elmer's Glue-All or PVA glues. They tend to dry fast and are quick to hold and set material. You have little time to maneuver a piece of paper with white glue. If you need to move it after contact, it may be impossible if the paper or material is fragile. Thinning with water (no more than a third of water to glue) can help speed application with a brush and give more time to setting pieces in place.
- ACRYLIC GEL (preferably matt finish) is the best glue for collage in my experience. Gel comes in tubes or jars and has the consistency of wet plaster. It must be thinned in another container with about one part water to two parts gel and mixed thoroughly. Make it soupy but not stiff. Keep in an airtight, waterproof container. Gel is essentially acrylic paint without pigment. Though it appears translucent white when wet, it dries clear and virtually invisible.
- ACRYLIC MEDIUM is excellent and similar to gel except it is already thinned in manufacture. The gloss versions are undesirable because they leave shiny stains on surfaces. Gels and acrylic mediums are flexible when dry so they can take a certain amount of rolling up or bending around a tube without cracking. White glues are inflexible and brittle. They have the disadvantage of cracking or losing adhesion if bent too far or applied too thickly. Gels, mediums, and white glue serve materials that are porous only. These include paper, cardboard, fabric, canvas, wood, ropes, and yarns.
- EPOXY GLUES, SUPER GLUES, and others if they designate so on the product are meant for nonporous materials such as glass, ceramics, plastic, and metal. Always follow directions on the label since some must be applied with ventilation and in a particular manner.
- EASEL BRUSHES (long-handled compared to watercolor brushes) of natural bristle or nylon are used to spread glue before attaching pieces. The chisel-shaped brushes called flats are the most useful since they can spread glue more evenly. You will need several, and the numbered sizes 2 through 10 are desirable.
- TWEEZERS are effective for those small, pesky pieces that do not want to be picked up in any other way.
- BRAYERS and ROLLING PINS eliminate air pockets and ensure that pieces are glued flat to the mount. They are optional since you can use the heel of your hand or a small wood block to apply pressure. I use wallpaper seam rollers (just over an inch long) for small pieces, ink brayers for medium sizes, and wooden rolling pins (the kitchen type) for large sheets.
- WAXED PAPER of the supermarket variety is ideal to cover pieces with freshly applied glue so that the pressure applied by hand or rolling pin does not touch wet glue or tear the collage. You can use plastic wrap but it is difficult to handle or to use more than once. Waxed paper can be used indefinitely and cleaned with a cloth rag.

- COTTON RAGS are a good way to wipe away excess glue. Wiping with paper towels is likely to cause damage since they tend to stick to the glue and tear the collage.
- HEAVY MOUNTS of sufficient ply and thickness are necessary to resist the tendency of glues to warp paper. Bristol paper and card stock are fine if heavy enough. Illustration and mat board are even thicker and resist warping altogether. Collages may be mounted on Masonite, plywood, or stretched canvas as well.
- Of course a COLLECTION OF MATERIAL is the basis for making collages and mixed media works.

THE STAGES IN MAKING A COLLAGE

Gathering Material

The hunt for materials and clippings can be one of the most engaging parts of the collage process. Look where other people discard. Trashcans, dumpsters, and recycling bins have abundant materials if you are willing to risk appearing desperate. I have no pride in this respect so I look everywhere for diamonds in the rough. After years of raiding curbside deposits, I am amazed at what people throw away. It is best not to have a preconceived idea about what to collect. Be open to what you find while looking for items that arouse your visual interest and imagination.

If you want slightly better pickings or specific items, flea markets, thrift shops, and garage sales are wonderful sources. Wherever you gather your collection of materials, accumulate all that you can find and reasonably store. You need the inventory to have sufficient artistic choices.

Be wary of collecting in a narrow range of material in order to develop a theme. Themes in collage and mixed media tend to work against the desirable attributes of contrast and variety. Too often, they drive verbal meaning rather than visual content, —and risk meanings that are simplistic and clichéd. Collage depends on surprises and contrasts, insurrection and contradiction, and, most of all, mystery and multiple interpretations. Avoid assembling materials that are too homogeneous and carefully aligned for similarities. They risk becoming predictable and dull. Boredom is a pitfall to avoid in art generally, but especially in mixed media. So mix it up.

Retooling Context

Once you have a load of materials and clippings, you can start to cut and shape them into aesthetic forms. For example, I often tear whole pages from magazines but later cut out only select portions that interest me. Usually the figure or object represented in a photograph or design will help determine how I cut it. The objective is to begin to edit out the existing context so that what is retained becomes fresh and new and assumes a mystery about where it originated. Physically changing the original clippings is a key step in beginning the creative process and later in making the collage image your own.

Starting a Collage

Starting may be the trickiest part of making a collage. There are a few different approaches, but not as many as you may assume. Choosing a theme first can be limiting because if you do not have sufficiently related material your theme can suffer artistic anemia. If the theme is too obvious and literal, the image will become simplistic and clichéd. Many beginners feel the need to stay connected to the logic of the everyday world and so choose themes with verbal messages or social commentaries. Unfortunately, the quickest way to bore viewers is to preach lessons or appeal to sentimentality. As you can imagine, I do not recommend this approach unless your theme is broad enough and predominantly visual so that it is open to multiple interpretations. Bear in mind: Collage making is not about logic and reason. In fact, it depends on contradiction and contrast—the kind of leap of the imagination that keeps asking the question, "What if?"

Planning and drawing a compositional structure first can be just as limiting since the pieces you want to use may not fit into the shapes or compartments you have predetermined. Working with rigid plans also tends to dampen the excitement of discovery. What is an artist to do? Play—in a cunning way. Lay out a lot of pieces all around your work area. Be surrounded by the abundance of what you have collected. Then take just a few pieces that especially strike your fancy—at this point, do not worry about why. Let your intuition guide your choices. Try to find other pieces that will interact with those first ones in ways that enhance a gradually expanding area of space. The first pieces you choose function as focal points that you can place anywhere in your composition and move around at will as you add pieces near them to try to start some visual sparks. Watch for interesting interactions as you test various placements and try to encourage visual relationships among all the parts.

Another good strategy is first to lay down in your composition large pieces that cover much of the area to form a spatial background. Here is a useful metaphor: Think of a collage as a two-dimensional theatrical play. The background is the set design with spaces and environment defined by architecture, landscape, or abstract forms. Next, into this stage scenery actors and props take their positions. Superimposed over this space, begin placing smaller figures, objects, and other pieces depending on your subjects. Do not be concerned yet whether the various pieces relate by similarity or contrast or even whether they seem appropriate together. They only need to give off energy at this stage. Do not judge too fast. You may miss something. Revel, contemplate, and brood as you play. As the collage develops, it will begin to tell you (if you are listening!) what it wants. Collage making is a process of exploration, of finding what you did not know before starting. Do not have a preconception about how your composition should look—except in a broad and open-ended way.

Some artists glue as they go. You can create a background and decide to glue it down before "inhabiting" it with players and props. If you need to change parts of the background later, you can still do so by pasting new pieces over the ones that no longer work.

Resolving the Composition

Do not be distracted by the complexity and variety of collage material. Its given state with images and forms found, not made by the artist, does not exempt him from the practice of sound composition. The principles of formalism apply to all the disciplines of art making. Remember that art is about *how* you use your materials, not *what* they represent.

The great feature about making a collage is that you can change the composition quickly—more quickly than in drawing or painting. Keep adding and removing pieces to test your judgment about what works and what is ineffective. When I work on a collage, I will experiment with the composition to such an extent that I will see twenty to thirty different pictures before I settle on the best one. The thoroughness of this searching process assures me that I have found the best expression for my image. No one needs to see my mistakes and, at the same time, I get to see a lot of art in a given studio session. Sooner or later, the image will seem to fall into place—as if the artist is a channel taking cues from the work itself—and fewer additions and changes become necessary.

Before you get to that point, it is essential to see your collage from a distance at many stages of development. If you are working at a table, carefully place the mounting with your unglued collage directly on the floor. Look down at it while standing for a better perspective to judge its composition. For more distance and better viewing, stand on a bench or stepladder to see the effect as if from across the room. If possible, spot glue your collage temporarily with a glue stick. (You can break the spots of glue with a palette knife without damage to the pieces.) Pin it directly to the wall where it is meant to be viewed. Look critically and make revisions as necessary.

Finally, try to arrive at the feeling that everything in the collage is inevitable, that it is arranged in the way it must be. Another way to gauge a collage is to anticipate that anything added or subtracted would compromise its optimum state of expression.

Framing the Image

There are two ways to frame a collage: Carry the image all the way to the edges of the mount or stop short to form a margin around it. About an inch or so of exposed paper at all four sides is a reasonable margin to set the image effectively against the sheet. Measure accurately with a straight edge so the composition is centered on the sheet. It is optional to make the bottom margin slightly wider than the other three sides. Draw the rectangle or outer shape of the composition lightly with a hard pencil.

The Gluing Process

Once you are sure of your composition, you can glue the collage to a mount. If your collage is complicated— many pieces with considerable overlapping—taking it apart to start gluing without any reference may be risky. It is difficult to remember where all those parts and layers need to be located. Furthermore, where overlapping is complex, you must be sure to get the pieces glued in the right order or else discrepancies will change your composition.

There are several ways of making a record of your composition. A rough free-hand sketch of your collage on separate paper will help you recall. Add notes and measurements as needed. A tracing is more accurate and faster to make. Take a sheet of tracing paper and carefully lay it directly over the collage. Trace with pen or pencil all the relevant pieces and cut edges. It helps that this traced drawing is also exactly the same size as your collage. Another alternative is to take a digital photograph of your composition and refer to your screen as needed or make a print. Any of these methods serves as a reliable tool by which to recreate your intentions so that you can glue the pieces from the ground up with confidence. Of course, if you think your memory is up to the task, you can forego doing any reference images and glue up.

There are three gluing methods. Apply the glue to the mount, to the back of the piece to be attached, or to both. Applying glue to the mount is recommended:
- Make a light tracing with pencil around the piece to be glued on the mount so you know where to put the glue.

- Apply the glue liberally with an easel brush going a fraction beyond the borders of your tracing.
- Immediately position and gently press the piece into the wet glue.
- Carefully wipe with a soft cloth any excess glue at the edges.
- Place a sheet of waxed paper over the piece and apply pressure with the heel of your hand or a rolling pin.
- Slowly lift the waxed paper and wipe away any excess glue again.
- Repeat pressure as necessary until you are sure of uniform adhesion.
- If any edges around a piece are not sticking to the mount, lift carefully with the edge of a razor blade or a palette knife and apply more glue.
- With any very small piece, place it on the glue by holding it with tweezers.

Be sure to cover all surfaces that make contact with the mount thoroughly with glue before attaching to avoid air pockets and distracting wrinkles. Remember that spot gluing is the Amateur Hour because it shows air pockets, uneven shrinkage, and warping so badly that the art will be greatly compromised.

Sealing the Surface

Once a collage is completed, you may want to apply a very thin coat of matt gel to the entire surface for protection. This seal will slightly deepen the colors (adds a little spatial depth as well) and limit to some degree any printed inks from fading. Apply the gel thinly. Brush vigorously and quickly so that brush marks are not visible when dry. A second coat may be applied but only after the first coat has dried completely. Practice on some scrap pieces to see if you like the effect. Be aware that some inks, especially those of copier printing, may run when brushed with water-based mediums. If any doubt, test a sample first.

Living with Art

After you have completed your collage, it may not yet be finished. Hang it on a wall and look at it frequently. Live with it for a while. Time is the test of art. Repeated and critical viewing will reinforce what is effective and reveal what is not. Flaws and areas that are unsatisfying will become apparent if the work has your attention. Do not hesitate to go back into the work to solve a problem or make a revision. Whether or not you are successful in finding a solution is less important than your need to find out.

ADVICE ON ADVICE

Take my advice with a grain of salt—or a pot of glue. You may find ways of working that suit your needs better. What I have said is mostly what I have discovered through trial and error. It is important—and unavoidable—that you go through your own process of experimentation and discover methods that are uniquely yours. Because collage and mixed media involve such varied processes and techniques, a word of caution is appropriate. Focusing too much on technique, rather than the interaction of line, shape, color, form, and imagery, can result in an exercise of considerable physical activity but with limited meaningful expression. Technique is a means to artistic vision, not an end in itself.

CHAPTER 10

COLLAGE AND THE CONTEMPORARY WORLD

It amazes me to observe that so much in contemporary life is a product of collage. One can see it in the way that the computer screen organizes and compartmentalizes images and text, and with a single click can skip instantly to the next, and the next. This collage concept of seeing in quick fragments and organizing the world in grids and boxes has existed throughout the Industrial Revolution with its divisions between rural and urban life, its countless inventions and innovations, and its tendency for science and technology to expand awareness through comparison and contrast. Printed media, high-speed transport, television, film, photography, computers, cell phones, and countless other devices and discoveries have all created various layers of new realities. The digital age has certainly compounded that effect. Art today reflects the speed and fragmentation of how we live as never before. Where for centuries, and as recently as fifty years ago, one medium dominated the art world, we have countless styles and genres and a great expansion of new media to express ourselves. The artist's task is to make sense and order out of civilization's galloping montage.

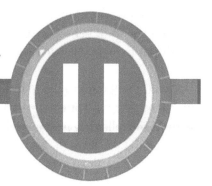

chapter **II**

KEEPING A JOURNAL SKETCHBOOK

Values, beliefs, and opinions—from the internal domain that shapes an adult life—change and develop rapidly during the postsecondary years. Nearly every day, new ways of thinking emerge and old ones are updated or discarded. An art education multiplies that effect because the nature of creativity is a seemingly boundless and complex undertaking. Add to that the information glut of our technological age. Psychologists confirm this early adult phenomenon of rapid change and great upheaval on both emotional and intellectual levels.

The complexity of developing mature viewpoints and an artistic vision is daunting, a tall order at any age. What to do? First, take it all in with an open mind and unquenchable curiosity. This is your Age of Discovery—one of life's great passages to be savored and embraced. Nurture it, heed its promptings, and document it.

Keep a journal sketchbook. This personal volume of the creative process is a combination of written entries and rough drawings. Consider first the journal portion. You groan? Don't like writing, you say? This is not a writing assignment, not the requirements of a topic you have not chosen. This journal is about *you*—what you think and feel, what you make of your art and life, how you make your life in art. No one needs to read it but you. Entries can be as personal (or outside of yourself too) as you wish. If your sketchbook is submitted for evaluation, you can remove or cover those passages that you want to keep private.

Since art comes from life, from the experiences and reactions to people, the world, and the environment, writing about your responses is crucial to understanding your development. Art is neither made in a vacuum nor void of outside influence. Making art and living in civilization are messy and entangled. As Robert Rauschenberg, the premier mixed media artist of the late twentieth century, said, "I want to bridge the gap between art and life."

Many valuable ideas and good impressions vanish when not documented. Nail them down by writing them. Daily contemporary life is such an information overload that it is wise to separate the useful from the indiscriminate, the wheat from the chaff. Art classes are creative crucibles, veritable hotbeds of ideas, viewpoints, and possibilities. Time spent in social dialogues reveal new ways of thinking and feeling. Solitude to reflect on these events is important in order to process and understand them. Write down as much as you can. Recording your thoughts will help you sort, sift, and filter through to what really matters—and take advantage of the opportunities that clear thinking promotes.

Hereafter, I will refer to the journal sketchbook as simply the sketchbook. The verbal and visual parts are entered together and often overlap—appropriate to the messiness of art and life. For now, consider the verbal portion. The following is a partial list of suggestions and questions for writing:

- What did you learn in class today? What advice or practical tips will be useful? What surprised you? Did you disagree about anything? Why? What comments in the critique do you want to remember?
- Have you written down all the directions you need to know about a project or an assignment? Write down any questions and ask during class.
- What do you feel when planning a project? Excitement? Anxiety? Impatience? Anticipation? Too many ideas? Creative block?
- What is going through your mind as you work? Are you focused? Distracted? Do your thoughts race among possibilities? Do you feel productive? Are there rituals that help you work?
- When you are finished with a working session, what do you think about your effort? Are you self-critical? Satisfied? Do you know what the next step will be when you work again? Do you waver between conflicting emotions? Or are you more even-tempered and rational?
- Are you interested in looking at art in galleries and museums? Which styles, periods, and artists move you the most? The least? Why? Do you seem to understand when you look? Are there qualities in other art that you would like to explore in your work?
- What responses do you have to reading stories, poetry, and articles about current events? What films and photographs seem compelling? Do you listen to music? What specific qualities do other art forms have that hold your interest?
- What are your visual and sensory impressions of your environment at home, work, and school, in the landscape, in new places, when traveling?
- Do the impressions noted above inform your art? How so? Describe how you might take more advantage of the world at large as a creative resource.
- Have you recently experienced strong emotions? What incidents or impressions ignited them? Are they positive or negative? Is that strength of feeling something that can be harnessed into art? What parallels are there between your feelings in life and those in your art?
- Do you have dreams or nightmares? Are they recurring? Vivid? The Surrealists used their dreams as sources of subject matter in their paintings. Is it possible to connect any of your dreams to art making?
- Do you have unusual experiences such as déjà vu, remarkable coincidences, memories spurred by a smell or a taste, or other sensory or even psychic phenomena? Do these impressions affect your approach to art making in any way?
- Do you have inspired moments when ideas and thoughts seem to flow effortlessly? Or do you feel you must work to get them most of the time? What conditions seem to influence a creative state of mind— that is, a readiness to receive ideas and produce work?
- Do problems arise that you cannot resolve or complications that make decisions difficult? Try writing about a dilemma to explain it to yourself. Does that help clarify what needs to be done?
- What other circumstances or relevant issues would writing help illuminate?
- Feel free to improvise, to be spontaneous in your writing. Making lists, recording single words or phrases in or out of context, and even thoughts that pop up out of the blue are valid entries. Try practicing free association or automatic writing, recording any thoughts that come to mind. Sometimes *nonsense* can

sound poetic and lead to more substantial ideas. There is no need to censor anything about how you think or feel. It is all grist for the creative mill. You can sort out later the gems of wisdom from the crumbs of gobbledygook.

The drawing and pictorial parts of your sketchbook can be just as diverse and multipurpose as the journal portions. I suggest you mix them freely and not worry about separating one from the other. You can move instantly between words and images. What is important is to be able to respond immediately to a stimulus. Be spontaneous. Take up pen or pencil wherever that next blank page is. Because art is your main subject, you may naturally have more visual entries than verbal ones in your sketchbook. It is essential to have both, but the ratio is whatever works best for you.

The following are suggestions (you may think of others) for drawing in your sketchbook:
- Make preliminary sketches that explore ideas for planning either required or independent projects. It can be fun to make plans for something that will never be made. Architects and fashion designers are examples of artists who often make pie-in-the-sky fantasies.
- Illustrate or diagram what you need to understand about project requirements or other ideas presented in class.
- Draw to stay in practice or as a warm-up before starting a project. Just as athletes do aerobics to limber up before an event, artists can test their readiness by rapid sketching as a preparatory step.
- Draw from life to sharpen your skills of observation. It might be just a five- or ten-minute effort in between other tasks, or even left unfinished.
- Draw from imagination in response to a dream, fantasy, or vivid impression.
- Doodle. Draw *mindlessly and aimlessly* just to satisfy the impulse to use a tool to make shapes and forms. This is the visual counterpoint to free association or automatic writing. It is another tool of the Surrealists who found compelling images in the seeming nonsense of the unconscious. You can make discoveries this way too when inhibitions about *what* to draw are dropped.
- Draw images or diagrams when visually complex forms or images serve the purpose better than verbal descriptions. Such drawings can highlight technical problems or construction methods.
- Draw to record a moment in time. When you do not have a camera, a sketch can be a worthy substitute.
- Draw in response to anything else not covered by the above suggestions.
- Make clippings from magazines, newspapers, catalogs, and other printed matter (but not from books!— make photocopies from those) that have interesting images, forms, and patterns. Paste them on blank pages. Draw on them if you wish or alongside in response to their content.
- Before you throw away a failed drawing or painting, cut up the better passages and mount them in your sketchbook—as a souvenir, a learning experience, or because this or that part might be the stimulus for something new. "Cannibalizing" your work conceptually or physically is a valid artistic practice.
- Experiment with new tools and materials. Mixed media should have a welcome place in your sketchbook. When you are unsure what to do technically, try it out on a page. Make a mess? So be it. No blank page is precious.

Though invaluable as an internal record of progress, the sketchbook may be one of the most undervalued and underestimated tools in the art making process. The reasons for resistance may be: (1) seeing a sketchbook as an obligation; (2) lack of interest in the thinking and pondering aspects of art making; (3) concluding that drawing in a book is not *serious* art, and (4) complacency or indolence about forming new habits. If you think you may be resisting for these or other reasons, I ask you to get over it! The sketchbook is a barometer of your interest, energy, intellectual capacity, and visual curiosity. It is your artistic mind extended to the immediacy of pages and pencils. It is not coincidental that the most capable students keep the most thorough and engrossing sketchbooks.

Make it easy for yourself to carry a sketchbook wherever you go, whether to classes, work, or travel. Therefore, keep it small like any other book you might carry and that would easily slip into a bag or backpack. The sizes I recommend are simple: the standard 8½ × 11 inches or 9 × 12 inches—but no larger. The pages must be line and graph free, just blank white paper. There are two main styles available, hardcover or wire bound. Hardcover sketchbooks are more deluxe, will stand up better to wear, and add a little more protection to the pages. They are also a bit more compact because of their binding. Wire bounds have the advantage of opening flat to one page. The choice is yours.

I recommend that you enhance your sketchbook by attaching pockets to the front and back covers to hold clippings, articles, class handout sheets, and those inevitable hasty sketches made on the backs of envelopes and odd pieces. Since I clip from printed media and draw on scraps, pockets and folders are indispensable to my practice. Make pockets by attaching half sheets of heavy paper to the bottom of each inside cover. A good alternative is to keep a large 9 × 12 inch mailing envelope or manila folder at the back of your sketchbook for storage of these items. Fasten to the cover with clips.

Get in the habit of bringing your sketchbook to every art class, whether required by your professor or not. Keep it open during class and make quick, simple entries (that might be expanded later) about projects, assignment requirements, worthy ideas, and useful advice. Write questions you want to ask in class and material you want to know more about or do not understand.

Once you have made a conscious effort to initiate this process, sketchbook entries will become second nature. Afterward, the few times you forget you will feel that something is missing—as if you left the house without your keys.

To give you an idea of the richness and variety of how artists past and present have made sketchbooks, do a little research on the internet or at the library. There are many excellent sketchbooks and artist journals that have been published for public viewing. One of the most famous is Vincent van Gogh's letters and sketches to his brother Theo and other artists. Paul Gauguin's illustrated journals of his South Seas travels give us an intimate view of a lesser known culture. Leonardo da Vinci's career as both an artist and a scientist is mainly known through his voluminous notebooks filled with exquisite drawings and detailed explanations. Picasso's sketchbooks reveal much about his creative process and his ability to see the artistic in everyday experiences.

I think of a sketchbook as a garden and its pages as seeds to be fertilized into art. Throw a lot of seeds onto those pages. You reap what you sow. The best part is you do not have to buy expensive seed packs, just paper. You never know what splendors, what kernels of thought, might blossom into art. Sketch and scribble away.

SECTION III

2D AND 3D NECESSITIES:
SPACING OUT WITH TRUE COLORS

chapter 12

PERSPECTIVE

Anyone who draws or paints, especially if he represents by observation the three-dimensional reality of nature on a flat surface, uses perspective. Since virtually all two-dimensional art involves the illusion of objects in space and distance, understanding the concepts of formal perspective is integral to an art education.

The most common brand of perspective—linear perspective—is a spatial system for projecting three-dimensional objects on a pictorial surface, called the picture plane, from a single fixed vantage point positioned at eye level, called the horizon. Within this pictorial space, certain kinds of objects have perpendicular structures and parallel lines (buildings, boxes, and cubes) that recede in space and appear to converge (if those lines are fully extended) at their vanishing points on the horizon. One of the most obvious examples is to stand on railroad tracks and to look from your feet toward the most distant point as the tracks seem to disappear.

As applied to mechanical drawing, perspective is a technically complex practice of accurate steps and procedures. Fortunately, for most purposes of artistic expression, perspective is a series of straightforward, reasonably simple concepts that can be applied readily. Though you may not always handle the urban subjects of streets, buildings, and interior architecture for which linear perspective techniques were designed, you will still need a basic understanding of its ideas to effectively represent a broad range of subjects.

RENAISSANCE PERSPECTIVE

Linear perspective, an accurate system of representing illusionistic space based on mathematical precepts, was invented during the Renaissance as a consequence of artists striving to construct a convincing representation of their visual observations. Perspective in this scientific and aesthetically dramatic format dominated composition in two-dimensional art for over 500 years until the invention of photography in the mid-nineteenth century. Though photography has largely relieved the artist of the obligation to apply perspective in the strict Renaissance tradition, its concepts are still the basis for constructing all kinds of pictures, including abstract and nonobjective art. We instinctively and correctly "read" space into pictures as a result of historical consensus, a cultural acceptance of the basic tenets of western perspective that viewers take for granted.

Painting was conceived in the Renaissance as a window into the visible world more or less literally. The window is the picture plane or the flat canvas as bounded by a rectangular frame. In modernism, the picture has changed from a window to "being there"—that is, the feeling of being *in* the picture or *moving around* in it—and assuming the role of participant rather than voyeur or onlooker. This "in your face" composition has been achieved by thrusting the subject matter closer to the picture plane, emphasizing the foreground rather than background space, and cropping subjects so that they seem life-size or compositionally dominant. Despite these spatial changes that modernism has added to pictorial structures, linear perspective is still a basic complement to seeing and understanding two-dimensional illusion.

CONE OF VISION

When you look through a window inside a building, or through the viewfinder, or at an LCD screen of a camera, you are seeing the basis of perspective. From a fixed position as you view the subject, your vision of the pictorial field spreads from the point of your eye to the size of the window (which when transferred to the art becomes the picture plane). This framing as you look directly at three-dimensional reality is called the cone of vision—with the apex your eye and the base the picture. See the illustration at the end of this chapter. The same principle is in use when you look at your still life through a viewfinder in order to align your composition as described in the Chapter. However, the cone should really be called the *pyramid* of vision since most pictures are rectilinear. In any case, the subject matter that is seen through the window and thus projected onto the picture plane will appear in perspective with receding planes converging to the horizon, diminishing sizes in the distance, and overlapping of objects in space. Whether depicted in the vision of a Renaissance master or through the lens of a digital camera, perspective in some comprehensive form is inescapable in all kinds of pictures.

ONE-, TWO-, AND THREE-POINT PERSPECTIVES

The specific functions of receding planes, vanishing points, and horizons in relation to eye level can be fairly quickly understood by studying diagrams and illustrations of perspective that are widely available in drawing textbooks and at websites online. If you search the words *perspective drawing* online, you will get many accessible sources of basic instructions. Libraries are an excellent source for books on the subject. See the illustrations of one-, two-, and three-point perspectives at the end of this chapter.

However, it is useful to summarize briefly the three major linear perspective systems so that when you study them you will know what to look for and what they illustrate. One-point perspective is the simplest and describes an object—imagine a box or cube—seen from its optimum frontal view with the receding planes of its interior space converging to a single point on the horizon. Imagine looking at the cube as if transparent in which the back wall is smaller than the front. The interior planes at the left and right will converge to the same point directly behind the object. The bottom (floor) and top (ceiling) planes will be visible and converge to the same point as well. In two other views, you may see a second plane of the cube (but slight in width) recede to the vanishing point at the left or at the right, but the main frontal plane will still appear as a wide perpendicular shape.

Two-point perspective occurs when the viewer sees two sides of a receding object at the same time. Look at a cube positioned so that one of its four corners is visible with its receding planes at the right and the left. For example, rotate the previous frontal cube in one-point perspective to about 45 degrees so that you see the vertical edge between the left and right sides. Each side's upper and lower edges rush to the left and right vanishing points, respectively. Imagine standing on a street corner as you view a block of buildings so that the roads and the buildings' walls on both sides converge to those vanishing points.

So far, you have been viewing your subjects from an eye level that does not permit seeing either the bottom or top of the (cube) object. Three-point perspective is perceived when viewing that object from above as in an aerial view or bird's eye view, or at (or below) ground level as in a worm's eye view. In an aerial view, the receding planes continue running to vanishing points left and right, but the same planes will also rush vertically to a vanishing point below ground level. In addition, you will see the top plane of the object as it recedes in both right and left directions. In a worm's eye or ground-level view, the opposite will take place: the third vanishing point will converge in the sky and the bottom of the object may be visible if it does not reside directly on the ground. See illustrations at the end of this chapter.

Isometric perspective essentially ignores three-point perspective regardless of viewpoint, and all vertical edges remain parallel to each other. In this practice, two-point perspective applies to all spatial conditions. Isometric perspective is the system used in industrial design and mechanical illustration, in which depth of field is not relevant.

Learning perspective may seem like a dry and mechanical process, but the concepts are essential in developing your ability to construct illusion on a flat surface. In fact, the process need not be dry. You do not necessarily need to use a straight edge and the drafting techniques of mechanical drawing to create the effects of linear perspective. However, I recommend that you copy by drawing freehand the basic illustrations you find about perspective to strengthen your understanding. An indispensable exercise is to set up a few simple cardboard boxes on the floor or on a tabletop as in a still life, observe them carefully from various heights and angles, then draw them in perspective in various positions.

In fact, once you understand the basics you will apply perspective consistently in drawing, not by the mechanical means of drafting tools and measurements, but conceptually, with your informed intuition. Most mechanically drawn perspectives are for the special purposes of architecture and industrial design. An experienced art student who understands the concepts from study and practice can draw objects (e.g., buildings) in a freehand manner without diagramming the horizon or vanishing points. Practice makes perspective second nature.

SIGHT PERSPECTIVE

Applying perspective intuitively is called sight perspective. A simple application of this technique is to note carefully the *direction* of a receding edge of an object as you observe it before you. Hold a pencil or brush handle at arm's length exactly adjacent to the receding edge in question. By <u>underlining</u> it this way, you can more easily comprehend the direction your line should have in your drawing. Then draw the line immediately according to how you estimate the direction from your tool's measurement. You will not always need to perform this task literally with all the diagonal edges you see, but only with those that seem visually problematic. With experience, you can learn to apply the concept in your mind's eye to most subjects.

FORESHORTENING

Foreshortening is a special problem in perspective for drawing the human figure and for objects with physically greater length than width. A foreshortened object is one that *appears* shorter than its actual length. The object's length is pointed straight toward the viewer's eye level. For example, in a given pose the model may hold out an arm so that the hand is pointed toward the viewer in a way that its length may appear to be little more than its width. This is a good example of how truth can be stranger than fiction. If you draw the arm with the length that you *know*, it will not be in a foreshortened position. Although the arm in reality may look odd in its compressed dimensions, draw as close to how you *see* it as you can. Only when you are drawing with attention to observation will the arm become convincing. Also, note that in a foreshortened object the part closest to the viewer—in the above pose the hand is closest—will appear much larger in size than its normal proportions.

A helpful technique to understand foreshortening is to take photographs of models or objects in these positions. Since the photo prints do not allow you to peak around the corner to see the foreshortened part's normal length, you can see more truthfully what shape and form it has in that position. In addition, the fact that the print is as two-dimensional as your drawing should help to understand what you are seeing.

LATERAL SPACE AND PERSPECTIVE

The difficulty in perceiving western pictorial structure is the need to integrate the lateral space of the picture plane (its flatness) with the illusion of receding space in perspective. The former is literal, while the latter is figurative and abstract.

The two systems work together despite the seeming contradiction. In lateral space, the lower third of a picture, the foreground, is closest to the viewer while the upper third of a picture, the background, is the farthest. The central third is the middle ground and will usually contain subjects at the viewer's approximate eye level. The horizon in this scheme may be located at any level in any of these three divisions. If the horizon is high in the picture, the observer will be above ground at an aerial view. If the horizon is low, the observer is closer to ground level.

What all this implies is fairly straightforward: Objects lower in the picture, at the foreground level, will be larger because they are closer to the viewer, while objects higher in the picture, in the background, will be smaller because of the illusion of distance.

ADDITIONAL STRATEGIES TO ENHANCE SPACE

The following methods of depicting space complement perspective by exploiting the properties of lateral space:

- Diminish sizes of objects as they recede in space.
- Locate objects strategically according to their locations in foreground, middle ground, and background.
- Exaggerate size. Make an object a little larger or a little smaller than it appears.
- Intensify contrast of sizes. Place a large object adjacent to a small one.
- Overlap objects so that the one in front crops the one behind.
- Describe objects, depending on whether they are near of far in space, with greater or lesser definition, focus, and detail.
- Intensify light and dark contrast in adjacent areas.
- Assign light, warm colors to advancing forms and dark, cool colors to receding forms. Highlights advance, shadows recede. Brilliant colors tend to move forward, while neutral colors tend to fall back.

BREAKING THE RULES

Of course, there are limits to what perspective can do for creative expression. Once you master an understanding of perspective, you may want to explore opportunities to "play" with illusionistic space in ways that break the rules and exceed expectations. For example, Cubism is the first movement in modernism that deliberately undermined traditional perspective. If you do so knowingly, it is a valid creative challenge to use multiple perspectives in the same picture. A collage incorporating various photographic fragments from many image sources (photomontage) into striking juxtapositions of contradictory scale and space is a good example. Some artists today have taken cues from Salvador Dali and M. C. Escher to create perspectives that are clearly ambiguous or contradictory to the eye in order to surprise. Practitioners of Op Art and hard-edged abstract painters often intentionally deny space and perspective by emphasizing the flatness of decorative forms and colors. Whether you decide to apply, contradict, or deny traditional perspective, you need to know the concepts so you fully understand your artistic options.

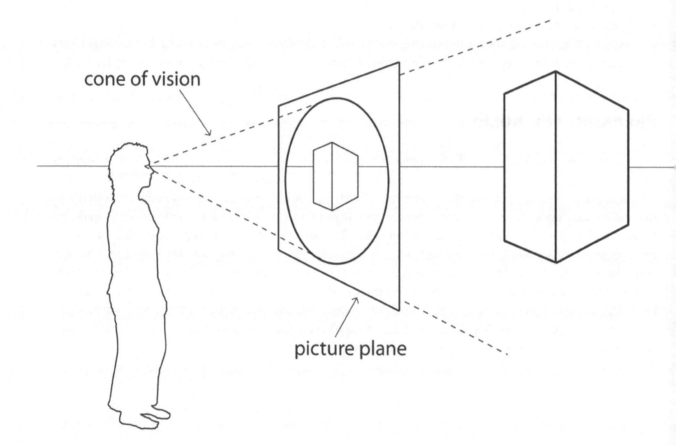

cone of vision

picture plane

CONE OF VISION

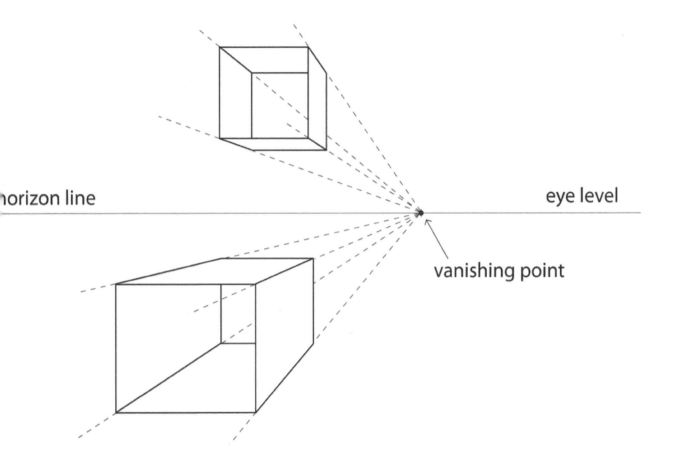

horizon line

eye level

vanishing point

ONE POINT
PERSPECTIVE

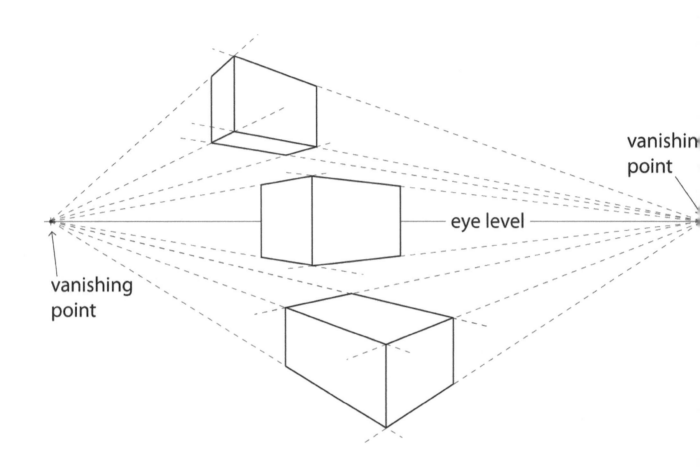

vanishing
point

eye level

vanishing
point

TWO POINT
PERSPECTIVE

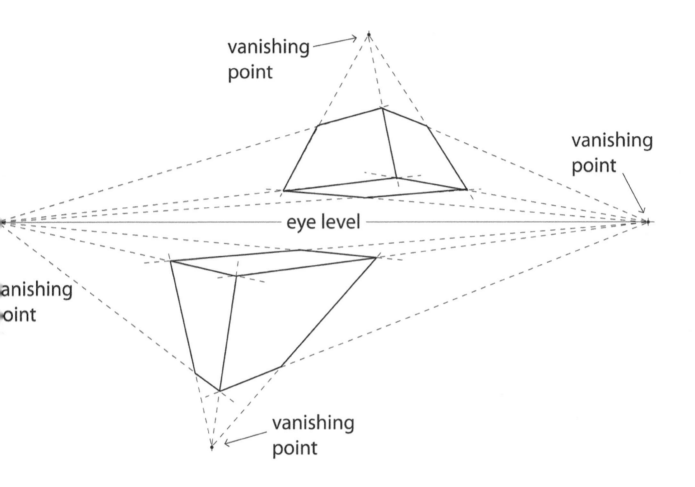

vanishing point

vanishing point

eye level

vanishing point

vanishing point

THREE POINT
PERSPECTIVE

Illustration contributed by Jerry Zinser. Copyright © Kendall Hunt Publishing Company

chapter

THE COLOR OF ART

Of all the formal elements, color may be one of the most challenging to practice. When is color effective or ineffective in art? How do you learn to make color expressive? Why are some color schemes more satisfying than others? While it's possible to reasonably explain a shape, line, object, or figure, why is it an exercise in futility to describe a color in words? It's impossible to know red, green, blue, and yellow without seeing them. If painting from observation, how does one interpret the colors of nature with the manufactured pigments of oils or acrylics? The answers to these and many questions about color are … imperfect … but necessary to pursue.

The rub is that all styles and genres from fine arts to commercial graphics depend to a greater or lesser degree on the quality of color for expressive impact. I believe that one of the main functions of color is to reinforce the emotional undercurrents that characterize all artworks. Furthermore, works in black, white, and gray are still evocative of some aspects of the color spectrum since monochromatic values are never purely devoid of color. If color is one of the most expressive elements in the visual arts, then it surely behooves the student and the artist to understand color and its interactions.

There is a great deal of literature about color theory from both scientific and artistic viewpoints. Much of it is lengthy and dry in language. While interesting to a general readership, the content may be too inclusive, scattered, and less than on-target for the art student. It is my intention to give concise guidance about color to allow you to apply the information expediently to the practice of art making. I readily admit that what follows may be the "Cliff's Notes of Color." As your interest and requirements dictate, you should seek additional information from your professors, textbooks, and other sources to give a more complete picture of this enormous and complex subject.

THE NATURE OF COLOR

The ability to see color depends completely on its exposure to light. No light, no color. At the same time, color is modified by lights and darks—that is, highlights and shadows—as observed in reflected light. A major principle of color is that its hue (the *color* in color, or its intensity or saturation) is relative to the type of light in which it is seen. For example, the differing effects of color outdoors are obvious on a day of alternating sunlight and cloud cover. The greens in foliage will seem more intense in sunlight and duller, possibly grayer, under cloudy conditions. A good example of this phenomenon in modern art is the series of haystacks, cathedrals, and other subjects painted in different seasons and times of day by the Impressionist Claude Monet.

Indoor lighting is critical to our experience of color. The position, type, and amount of light dramatically affect our perceptions. Fluorescent lighting is blue compared to the warmer yellow of incandescent light. Overhead lighting will make color more flat and uniform than single-source lighting. All these variables have notable effects on color perceptions. When you draw or paint from life, it is essential that you take lighting conditions into consideration. Lighting is even more dramatic for the photographer whose equipment may respond differently from the eye. Thus, before the artist or photographer can effectively interpret the colors observed in nature, he must understand from careful observation the dynamic effects that light and dark have on them. Looking carefully and comparing adjoining surfaces are the best strategies for understanding the physical properties of color.

THE PSYCHOLOGY OF COLOR

In the larger world, color has many associations as symbols and reflections of mood and feeling. Color may stimulate, soothe, agitate, or inspire a variety of emotional responses. Sometimes these effects of color on the psyche may seem grounded in reason. For example, blue implies calmness or serenity since its association to water, sky, and the horizon feels reassuring. On the other hand, red may be excitable, with its cultural suggestions of violence, sex, melodrama, and action.

In many other instances, color mixtures and their effects, whether in life or in art, may not be easily explained or rationalized—despite the fact that their expressive impact may be strongly felt. In those cases, we may be well to trust our spontaneity and intuition. Mystery is part of the art experience too. In fact, the mystery that often pervades art—whether color is responsible or not—may be the most important experience to both the artist and the viewer from an emotional standpoint. Nonetheless, you should use language to try to understand what you are doing with color, but remember that nothing else is its equivalent.

LOCAL AND EXPRESSIVE COLOR

Until the arrival of the Impressionists in the 1870s, color in art reflected the artist's observation of nature. Interpreting local color—the rich greens of grass and foliage, the luminous blues of afternoon skies, and the earthen tones of stones and soil—was the given tradition of depiction. Local color is the color seen in reflected light. All of that changed with the innovations of Claude Monet and his Impressionist colleagues. They greatly exaggerated the colors in nature to explore the imagination and to express feelings—to place the inner reality of the mind on a par with the outer reality of visibility. The shift to the *mind's* eye was a new artistic gate that, once opened, changed forever the way we think of color in art.

At the start of the twentieth century, the Fauvists and then the German Expressionists exploited the Impressionists' ideas by painting with greater emphasis on feeling than on sight. They dared to paint grass in bright pinks or magentas, the sky lurid yellow greens, and buildings in brilliant reds and blues. Once the Dadaists and Surrealists joined the party, color became a tool of fantasy and dreams. Since then, the possibilities of color for the contemporary artist have expanded to include more than local color—though that is still a choice for artists who have purposes for which local color is most suitable. What the mind can imagine is what color can be. Now we take bold splashes of highly saturated hues or "outrageous" color schemes in the fine arts and in the commercial world for granted. Even the Fauvists, Expressionists, and Surrealists look tame to us so many decades later. We can rejoice in our age's chromatic declaration of independence but appreciate at the same time that it was not always so.

THE COLOR WHEEL

The structural basis for understanding color is the color wheel, invented by the great mathematician Sir Isaac Newton after first experimenting with reflecting light and color through prisms. He diagrammed his findings on a color disc (now called a wheel) in a book published in 1704. This deceptively simple device has been the standard tool for understanding the spectrum of existing colors visible to the eye, for developing color mixtures, and for organizing color into charts and scales for the manufacture of paints, dyes, and even cosmetic products.

Most of us understand from grade school that the color wheel begins with the primaries of red, yellow, and blue, which are placed equidistant on the wheel. See illustration at the end of this chapter. Mixing the primaries (as with paint pigments) results in the secondary colors of orange, violet, and green. Mixing these adjacent colors makes six tertiary (third-level) colors. Continue the process, and soon there are hundreds of adjacent colors that become extremely close in hue to one another. If you go to a commercial paint store, you can see charts of hundreds of distinct colors. The mixtures the eye can distinguish are remarkably far ranging.

Color mixture does not stop with color itself. The monochromes of tints and shades add great differences and possibilities to color for the artist and designer. A tint is any amount of white added to a color, while a shade is black added to a color. Adding either white or black to a color diminishes its hue depending on the quantity combined. Black tends to dull a color because its value (thus its strength) is greater than any single color. White added to a color will maintain its hue quality longer since all colors have values darker than white. Adding both black and white (that is, a given mixture of gray) to a color will alter both its value and hue. These gray mixtures will "soften" colors and are often called pastels.

(*Note*: The subtractive mixing of colors in reflected light that I have described on the color wheel along with tints and shades should not be confused with additive mixing, that is, mixing colors of light through a prism or, in the case of theater practice, through transparent colored gels and spotlights. Mixing light seems counterintuitive. For example, the sum of the wavelengths of the primary colors results in white, while mixing two colors such as red light and green light make yellow light.)

Colors that are directly opposite one another on the wheel are called complementary colors. Complements are remarkable for their contrast in color "temperature." One will appear cool, while the other seems warm.

Examples of complementary colors are red and green, blue and orange, and yellow and violet. If complements are placed adjacent they will seem to intensify each other. Each color will appear more strongly saturated by comparison. Ironically, when complements are mixed in equal measure, the resulting color will be a brownish-gray (or grayish brown) neutral hue in which both colors will seem to have disappeared.

Analogous colors are any two that are adjacent on the color wheel, such as red and orange or blue and green. Their mixture will result in a hybrid of the two colors and will retain their mutual hue strength unlike the mixing of complements. Analogous colors are appealing because their transitions are soft to the eye and, if mixed closely in values, can give the illusion of gradation. Triadic colors are any three colors equally spaced on the color wheel. The primaries are the most obvious example. Artists and designers often use complements, analogous, and triadic colors to create color schemes and to organize their ideas and expressive intentions.

COLOR INTERACTION

To understand how colors react to one another, open a box of Color-Aid papers (brand-name product consisting of 240 or more sheets that have been painted with the spectrum colors including tints and shades) and place them so that they overlap or juxtapose. If you do not have a Color-Aid pack, you can paint your own sheets of paper with acrylics or tempera colors—you do not have to paint 240 sheets, two dozen or so may do! You will notice that a color will appear to change its hue or value when placed against one color versus another. This sensation is called simultaneous contrast. If you place two equally sized sheets of contrasting colors adjacent and "float" two smaller shapes of the same color (as long as they are not the same as either of the adjacent colors), one in the middle of each color field, you will likely notice that the two floating colors now look like different colors. Depending on your choices, the effect can be mildly different or remarkably dramatic in contrast. A reverse experiment is to choose two colors close to each other in value and hue (but still visibly contrasting) and then attempt to find color fields that will make them appear to be the same color. These are fun and fruitful explorations since you will see quickly how colors really do change each other.

Try placing a color on a field of black. Then, follow with white, gray, its complement, an analogous color, and finally, colors chosen at random. Notice that the color will seem especially saturated against black or its complement. Other color placements may be surprising and unpredictable. A simple but valuable lesson is that if you want to intensify a color, place it against black or its complement.

Have you ever wondered why the edges between some adjacent colors seem to vibrate while some do not? Highly saturated complementary colors with similar values appear to flicker or move where their edges meet. This phenomenon can be put to useful effect if you want an object or a form to carry a strong visual impact. The opposite effect, melting or soft edges, occurs with adjacent colors that also have similar values but which are much closer in hue, as in analogous colors. Color subtlety of this type can be a strategy to suggest that an object or a form is receding in space. In addition, it is good to keep in mind that in two-dimensional art cool colors or those mixed with gray tend to recede in the distance, while warm or saturated colors tend to advance toward the eye.

For further study about color behavior, consult the bible on the subject in a little paperback book entitled *Interaction of Color* by Josef Albers, first published by Yale University Press in 1963 and still in print.

TRANSPARENCY

Transparent color can be readily made with watercolor washes or with acrylics or oils greatly diluted with mediums. Transparency depends on the visibility of the white ground beneath the color—the more white seen through the color, the lighter the value and the more transparent. When two or more transparent layers are place on top of each other, the optical mixing of the colors is much different from the literal mixing of opaque colors on a palette.

With opaque colors, transparency will be illusionistic. Try this experiment: Select two opaque colors and imagine the color that would result if they were mixed. You can actually mix that third color or simply choose one that seems reasonable even if not exact. Arrange the colors in a configuration so the mixed color area seems to be an overlapping shape created by the first two passing over each other. You will see the illusion of transparency. Whether applying the optical transparency of watercolor or the illusion of it with oils or acrylics, this is another useful tool for manipulating space, form, and color.

COLOR AS WEIGHT AND EMPHASIS

Color seems to have visual "weight." The greater the hue saturation or the darker the value, the heavier the color will seem. For example, primary red has a greater weight or feeling of mass than primary yellow. This illusion works in both two- and three-dimensional art. How you control the viewer's eye will be due in large part to the way you assign colors to various areas of your work. To that extent, color plays an enormous role in matters of composition. The "right" colors will reinforce the clarity and effectiveness of forms and their relationships.

Sometimes, extraordinary color schemes can compensate for otherwise weak compositional structures. Likewise, bad color can weaken good composition.

THE ARTIST AS COLORIST

So how do you know when you have "good" color in a work of art? Is the cliché, "Those colors just do not go together," ever true? What makes an artist a good colorist? How much does color matter to effective art making? As with so many questions about art, these are difficult but not impossible to answer. There are two factors that must be satisfied. First, color should articulate clearly but forcefully the space and forms of composition. Color must reveal its subjects efficiently and effectively—that is, play the role of enlightening the image—so that no color seems arbitrary or merely decorative. Gratuitous colors call attention to themselves rather than to the subject matter of the art.

Second—and most problematic because it is so difficult to measure rationally—color must be expressive of the whole. Color is the skin that we see first in the art and it must support the mood or tone that everything else is about. Because color is so *there* when we look, maybe the first visual quality we notice, it will tend to contribute immediately to our emotional reactions to the art. It is with color that one's artistic emotions may be greater than one's intellect. The experienced artist knows when color works or not—he does not have to explain it to himself in verbal terms. But it takes a great deal of curiosity and practice to understand color dynamics to that degree. Be patient.

Whether you work with a wide range of colors or with a tightly limited or even monochromatic palette, you are a colorist whenever you make art. Art is always understood to be "in color." However, you can always limit the importance of color by emphasizing any number of other visual preoccupations. After practice and experience, if you still feel that color is the least of your concerns, you can build on those other areas that do arouse your interest.

There are a number of artists who seem to be gifted colorists and whose work "sings" with chromatic drama. They tend to be the artists who put color at the top of their lists. Their work seems to be unthinkable without the dimension of color. Whatever role color eventually plays in your art, now is the time to experiment and find out what is possible. Color your world!

TRADITIONAL COLOR WHEEL

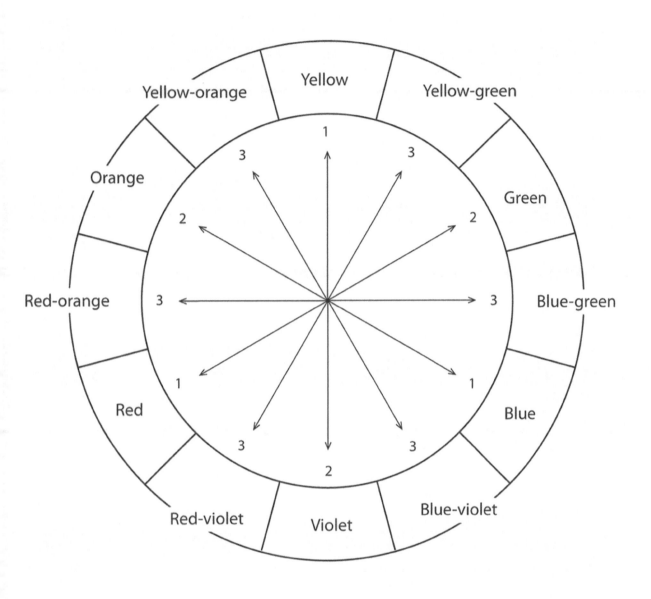

1= Primary colors
2= Secondary colors
3= Tertiary colors

Adjacent colors are analgous

Opposite colors are complementary

EXPANDING DIMENSIONS: THINKING AND MAKING 3D FORMS

Though we live in a three-dimensional world, we are connected to multifaceted systems that yield much of our information via two-dimensional surfaces. Think of computer screens, mobile devices, films, videos, books, magazines, signs, and even car dashboards. A historical consequence of civilization's preoccupation with two dimensions is that for centuries in art history (the mid-1300s through modernism) pictures have dominated sculpture. Sometimes, I think we use our perception of space primarily to avoid bumping into other objects! Thus, many of us may have a deeper understanding and appreciation for two dimensions rather than three dimensions.

This cultural bias would seem counterintuitive since we are, after all, three-dimensional entities who move around in the spacious environment of planet Earth. Nonetheless, my experience as a teacher is that students generally are less sophisticated about thinking in the third dimension. It is as if catching up is necessary as we begin to make objects in real space since we are especially attuned to the everyday exposure of verbal messages and pictorial images. The good news is that with practice and experience most of us can readjust our sensory gauges to make inroads into acquiring skills to operate effectively in the complexities of three-dimensional form and space.

THE CHALLENGE OF ADDING DEPTH

Of course, adding depth to length and width makes a surface into an object. While the picture is dependent on the wall or other devices such as an easel for viewing, the object is "free" to occupy the environment with greater variety to its placement. When we view pictures, there is an ideal frontal viewpoint, one that is essentially fixed, as in looking through a keyhole or window. But in three-dimensional form, we must become mobile and view the object from countless different positions in space. Walking around, literally, as in a circle, is the way to fully understand and appreciate a three-dimensional form. To that extent, the artist must view his own work in the same spatially sensitive way, that is, from many viewpoints. From the beginning of the art making process, the sculptor must fashion an object so it is engaging in form and content from all the possible angles in which it may be seen.

Compared to picture making, you can easily understand how varying vantage points complicate the artist's task. It is not enough to have just a frontal view since the object now occupies the space we move around. Ultimately, it is this bodily connection that makes art objects so compelling. We can easily imagine holding them if they are small or occupying them, as in entering a chamber, if they are larger. As artists, we must appeal to this natural sensation and manipulate the object's potential to resonate with the observer's body and the fact that both she and the art now exist in the same space.

ART AND CRAFT

Though a picture can be said to have some degree of object-hood, as in a painting on a stretcher or installed in a frame (even a work on paper has some depth in the thickness of the paper), once the paper or canvas surface begins to be developed by the artist, any craftsmanship is concentrated in the paint or drawing material being manipulated. The craft of the "object" is already complete in the cut paper or stretched canvas. But in sculpture, craftsmanship is an ongoing concern with both the object and the materials with which it is made. In fact, part of the content of an art object is *the way it is made*, the manner of how its structures have been connected and realized into a cohesive whole, a composition of satisfyingly firm and sturdy forms. Even if delicacy and fragility are part of the content, those elements must be fastened so as to stand up to reasonable handling, storage, and transport.

Practice is necessary to acquire these building skills. Every form made and connected is a problem-solving process. No manual exists to tell you how to do each step of constructing your forms. General advice about good craft—how to fasten, glue, cut, saw, drive nails, drill for screws, carve, sand finishes, and a range of other techniques need to be mastered. All those techniques can be learned, but using the right procedure for any given step along the way is a process of trial and error. You try something, then, if it does not work, you try something else. It has always seemed to me that what distinguishes the artist is his ability to commit to following through until he finds the right method. Amateurs usually give up too quickly out of impatience. You can be taught various, essential methods of construction, but how to use them effectively in any given project is through experimentation. You must embrace the practicality that, when you are alone in the studio manipulating materials, you teach yourself how to make art.

THE HYBRID BETWEEN THE PICTORIAL AND THE SPATIAL

There is one format in three-dimensional art making that shares much with picture making—the art relief. A relief hangs on the wall like a painting, but it has projections and/or recessions that penetrate the picture plane, often in such a way that any flatness as a continuous surface is no longer visible or apparent. Reliefs that have limited depth are called low relief and those with more pronounced forms are called high relief.

Relief as an artistic practice has been historically abundant since ancient times. Think of ancient Egyptian incised walls, Gothic carving, and Renaissance architecture. In modern art, relief has taken on a special status, emerging out of Cubist practice and occupying a special place as an art form that may combine painting and sculpture, while mixing a variety of both art and nontraditional materials. Its practice has led to the present-day genres of mixed media in objects, pictures, and installation art. See Chapter 9, Collage and Mixed Media.

MODERN SCULPTURE

Though Cubism, as invented by Picasso and Georges Braque around 1908, led to a revolution in the pictorial arts, it also fundamentally changed sculpture just as dramatically. In the old tradition of making sculpture, roughly from ancient times through the nineteenth century, sculpture making was a subtractive method. To make a figure or a representation, the artist carved, chiseled, or otherwise removed material from a large bulk, whether wood, marble, or ceramic. Metal sculptures were usually made by fashioning a positive form in the additive method, making a cast of it in plaster or wax, then filling the void with molten metal.

When Picasso and Braque began making collages around 1911, it was not long before they realized that they could also incorporate three-dimensional objects into their paintings. Hence, they made reliefs that contained bits of everyday materials, such as rope, wood scraps, metal fragments, wire, corrugated cardboard, printed fabrics, and a wide variety of what we now call found objects. Picasso extended this practice into freestanding sculpture, attaching objects and fragments of materials to each other with glue, nails, twine, and other fasteners. Born was the new additive method of making sculpture. It has radically changed and greatly expanded the possibilities for how we make art objects today. New too was the invention of the assemblage, the construction of sculptural forms that included manufactured objects as well as nontraditional materials of art making. The seemingly unrelated connections among different found objects bound together into one composition held special appeal to the Surrealists who exploited its fantasy-like qualities and imaginative juxtapositions.

Later, the German artist Kurt Schwitters, the Russian Constructivists, and American artists such as Robert Rauschenberg and Jasper Johns expanded Picasso's experiments by intensifying the quality and quantity of found materials and scaling up the art into sometimes mural-sized reliefs and larger sculptures that went beyond the normal scope of Cubism's domestic sizes.

TO BASE OR NOT TO BASE

In traditional subtractive sculpture, an inconspicuous base usually held the art object to the floor, or if small, was set on a pedestal. The base or pedestal acts like a frame is to a picture, setting if off from the real world so that it can be seen without interference. In the mid-twentieth century, bases began to disappear with some kinds of art to acknowledge that sculpture does occupy the real world and should be unencumbered when possible by the third parties of bases and pedestals. Perhaps too, the inclusion of found materials and new subjects suggested alternative possibilities for presentation. It is not uncommon today to see sculpture placed directly on the floor of a gallery, set on shelves instead of pedestals, or even hanging directly from the ceiling on wires. In the case of installation art, the sculpture may even span the spaces of floor, wall, and ceiling within one work of art.

THE CASE FOR ELEVATION

When making sculpture, I have noticed that some beginning students tend to fashion their art objects close to the floor or pedestal, that is, they have adequate size or scale but lack an engaging rise into space, called elevation. It is as if they are still thinking pictorially, that the base, floor, or tabletop is a kind of wall on which to conceive the art. I encourage students to make a bigger deal about making sculptural forms that have greater physical presence and drama by getting away from the ground and raising a fuss in the space of the air above! It does not mean that lower formed objects cannot be good art, but just that the tendency to resist height can be misguided until you understand more about working in three dimensions. Remember too that we subconsciously compare what we look at in sculpture with our own bodies, and we are, indeed, fairly vertical entities.

SURFACE AND FORM

It should not be forgotten that 3D art has surface just as pictures do. While priority should be first given to composing an object's form in real space, those surfaces that inevitably result can also make or break how we look at the art. Color, texture, pattern, or imagery applied to a sculpture can change the feeling of weight, degree of simplicity or complexity, areas of focus or interest, and how the three-dimensional form is clarified or camouflaged. At its extremes, the surface can be left free of finish in its natural state or embellished heavily with paint and other materials to change its character. Various possibilities in between those ranges are also practiced. Whatever you do to the surface, it should enhance and clarify the three-dimensional forms you have already invested with the effort of design and construction.

SUPPORT EQUALS ART?

A case can be made for allowing some of the necessary fastening, such as nails, screws, twine, and braces, to be visible in the art. Have you ever noticed how houses under construction with their exposed studs, beams, and rafters look terrific in their overlapping, highly spatial complexity? The very elements that are covered up may actually be more attractive than the plastic windows, doors, and vinyl siding that finally finish the house! There can be a refreshing expression of integrity or honesty of materials when you do not try to cover up everything that went into the construction of an object. In any case, it is certainly one more possibility to add to the content of what a sculpture can contribute to our visual experience.

PLANNING VERSUS IMPROVISATION

Art making generally is a balance between planning and spontaneity. For those who thrive on the abilities of reasoning, planning the design of artworks may take precedence over improvising. I do think that planning is more critical to three-dimensional art making than picture making, if only because it is so much more difficult to change a 3D form than to erase charcoal marks on paper or paint over previous layers on a canvas. The construction process is so labor intensive that you want to be reasonably sure that minor changes may be in store, but that major shifts in form can be minimized since those can mean starting over from scratch, or taking too much time disassembling rather than fabricating.

As with so much in art, you will understand this through practice and experience. Know thyself. Are you an intuitive person, trusting in your instincts, or do you need considerable planning to counteract unknowns and surprises? I think you need healthy doses of both reasoning and intuition, but the individual needs to find out what amounts of each are best for her brand of art making. I rely heavily on intuition, but at the same time, I must always have a planned starting point before launching into uncharted waters.

THE WORKING PROCESS

Related to reason and intuition is acquiring the habit of paying attention to what is happening in the working process. First, do not preconceive the end product in your mind to such an extent that the art becomes impossible to realize in concrete form. You set yourself up for disappointment. Fantasy is so often better than reality. You must be open and flexible to change, accidents, and mistakes. These are opportunities for discovery and invention—and may even pull you in a direction you did not plan or intend. In fact, sometimes these discoveries can lead to better results than what you started in the first place. I think this is what makes art exciting to make. I do not want to know in advance where I will be at the end. If that were the case, then I do not need to make the art after all!

Art is a search that takes you to new places you have not been before. It is a kind of travel in the mind's eye. If there is anything muscular in art making it is this: Revel in the search for the unknown treasure and let your imagination stretch and flex in the process.

Whether 3D or 2D, it's important to stop and look critically at your art during the studio process. Think, reflect, and look again and again at the work in progress. If you are listening, it will tell you what it needs in the next step. But, every step you take will change the art, so you must do this frequently. Changes demand changes, so be sensitive to the fact that even a small addition or subtraction from your art object will alter the composition in such a way that you may not have anticipated.

In addition, it is always better to work in many sessions over several days before completing a project. Overly long sessions can rob you of fresh approaches and insight while the feeling of wanting to finish may take precedence over the considerations of quality in your decisions. When you break it up into smaller and more numerous sessions, you also remove much of the pressure of worrying about the result. You are smarter each time you start work from the previous time. Your subconscious mind processes a lot of your problem solving, so that you will see your project anew each time you start again. I think an awareness of these described practices is especially important for three-dimensional art making since working in space is visually, conceptually, and technically complicated.

chapter

ABSTRACTION, REPRESENTATION, AND REALITY

Abstraction, developed in the early 1900s by a number of enterprising artists, has exponentially expanded the possibilities for art making. Soon after the basic implications of Cubism's hide and seek disguise of academic subjects were understood, abstract experiments began to dispense with recognizable subject matter altogether. The means of representing nature now became the ends, that is, form and color became the subject matter. How lines, shapes, color, and other formal ingredients were expressed became the art's meaning and content. It must have been a heady time at the start of these new practices to realize how pure form, especially in all types of picture making, could become **the** subject matter without dependence on representing the illusion of figure, still life, or landscape. In short, the art became the object itself in equal relationship to nature's reality. No longer was the artist obliged to fit his vision into the window world of artifice and illusion.

Literally, the definition of art has become vastly more inclusive.

If music, throughout its history, has always had the advantage of pure sound as its formal basis, the visual arts have only achieved that in the last 100 years. That these two important art forms should be so far apart in their respective realities is something of a cultural mystery. That artists were thinking about this conundrum at the beginning of abstraction is evident in the work of the Russian master of abstract painting, Vasily Kandinsky. In 1910, Kandinsky wrote the first treatise that laid the groundwork for the practice of abstract art and its relationship to music, *Concerning the Spiritual in Art.* His writing established the insights by which we consider color and form to be the main ingredients for creating abstract art. That alone is not the meaning. Kandinsky maintained that abstraction could express the magisterial and sublime content that had flourished in classical music for several centuries. He claimed that this special content came from the artist's "inner necessity." In short, form could be transposed into the feeling and mood derived from experience.

While abstraction was slow to become accepted by the viewing public—as all new innovations tend to be in the arts—artists from all over Europe in the early 1900s eagerly experimented with its possibilities. Imaginative forms could now be investigated by artists without reliance on specific representations in nature. Initially, the emphasis on inward experience rather than outward appearances put abstraction into a special class of its own. However, this radical departure from the Old Tradition of eyeball appearances eventually changed the way we consider all art. The contrast of inner and outer expression between the nineteenth and the twentieth centuries could not be starker.

A consequence is that visual terms assumed the greater part of meaning. The cues so characteristic with representational art are no longer as compelling. Abstract art has to be understood through its deployment of visual form. Verbal description might provide clues for the viewer, but nothing more. As the contemporary American artist Frank Stella once said, "What you see is what you see." Hidden messages or special keys to meaning do not exist for understanding. You must have the frontiersman's attitude of seeing art as if for the first time and confronting it on its own visual merits.

More specific than Frank Stella's quote is what the Pop artist James Rosenquist said, that he is not interested in subject matter, but rather in visual invention. That can be interpreted to mean that all subject matter is OK, grist for the artistic mill. However, those subjects are not interesting as they are not ends in themselves. Rosenquist was a master of imbuing ordinary objects and figures with the aura of newness and fantasy. His work is a wonderful meld of pure form and illusion, a marriage of the abstract and the representational, void of any negative conflicts between those differing worlds.

Because the public often confuses subject matter with content—or insists that only representation has content—abstraction to this day continues to be met with scratching heads or even outright dismissal. You have no doubt heard comments by viewers such as, "What is it?" or "Why is it art" or "My child could do that." A number of questions shed light on why there can be a sharp disconnect with some viewers between representational art and abstraction. Consider the following list:

- If the viewer must exercise more imagination when viewing abstract art and hasn't been educated to do that, how will he respond?
- Is abstraction less accessible to viewers because it is still too recent a development in the history of art?
- Has the increasing proliferation of photography, especially in the digital media of today, oversaturated our culture and shortchanged the experience of abstract art, of pure visual form and color?
- Is there a hierarchy in how images are judged? Is abstract art more acceptable in advertising and graphic design, rather than residing on a pedestal or hanging on a wall in a gallery or a museum?
- As humans, are we programmed through our DNA to favor subjects in nature because they may affect our well-being, as in friend or foe?
- Do some viewers require the familiarity and security of subject matter that they can name and identify?
- Is there a misconception that abstraction is elitist and meant only for the highly educated or affluent?
- Do some viewers mistakenly expect that a hidden secret, some little known knowledge, or special key to meaning is necessary to understand abstract art? Can that response discourage engagement altogether?
- To what extent is public education responsible for nurturing visual literacy? Has it failed to provide students with quality aesthetic and artistic experiences?
- Do viewers assume that looking at art is a passive process rather than an active one? Do they not trust their intellect to call up their own experiences, to explore their emotional responses and connections to art?
- Is there the misguided assumption that understanding abstraction should be equivalent to a verbal explanation?
- What biases may be interfering with how we view art? Do humans tend to reject the unfamiliar and the new?

CHAPTER 15

Wherever these questions lead you, know that abstraction and representation are not in opposing camps. One is not greater than the other. No style or art movement is superior to another, nor does its placement in history have anything to do with art quality.

The concept of combining or thinking simultaneously in both abstraction and representation is true in a literal sense. Before an object or figure is identified, it is first a form and a color. For example, a tree is a cluster of organic shapes, a building is a jumble of planes and edges. All artists throughout history understand that designing their subjects with form and color is a first consideration. Knowing the subject is both real and abstract is a double vision that all artists cultivate. The dual capacity to see reality in this multifaceted way is the powertrain by which art becomes expressive and compelling.

As an art maker, you can create works that are either representational or abstract, and not worry whether you are more advanced or more avant-garde than anyone else. There was a brief time in the mid-twentieth century when artists were expected to choose either representation or abstraction and to produce work consistently in that way. The great freedom today is that you can combine abstraction and representation in the same artworks, or work back and forth between them. Adherence to a single style or consistent content is no longer required. Take advantage of that freedom to experiment, to try out as many different approaches to art making as may appeal to you. The consequence of your open mindedness to experiment will eventually reward you with the direction and content you seek in your art.

Ultimately, art asks us to consider reality. Is it what we see or what we think or feel? Is it fantasy, dream, nightmare, or what ordinary appearances provide? Is it past, present, or future? Is it concrete and tangible, or symbolic and metaphoric? Is it knowable or mysterious? Or, is it all of the above? Can reality be agreed upon or does each of us understand individually different frames of reference? Art is about making visible these realities, any of which are really abstractions of our own states of mind. As it does so, art prompts us with questions. We provide the best answers when we understand that the questions may actually be more important.

NONOBJECTIVE ART

Nonobjective (no objects) is the ironclad term for art that does not depict nature. However, in general discourse abstraction or abstract art generally means nonobjective. When communicating, you can use either term and assume you will be understood. Abstract art or abstraction is somewhat of a misnomer. All art, including various styles of realism, are abstractions of nature. Art is an artifice of what we express in response to nature. The only "realism" is reality.

AUTHOR'S OBSERVATION

When I was a freshman at Miami University in Oxford, Ohio, my first-year drawing professor asked the class in a show of hands whether we preferred representational art or abstract art. Nearly everyone opted for the former. The professor said that was predictable, but that by the time we graduated we would prefer abstraction. At the time, I was amazed and disbelieving.

But, it came to pass. I must confess to a bias. Abstract art is the highest form of visual expression. I have a rationale, so the bias is not entirely subjective. Too much figurative art is discouraging since it is ubiquitous (it is everywhere!) and unrelenting. It is collective narcissism. Yes, that is an overstatement to make a point. Put another way, our reflections are everywhere in art and the wider culture. That makes me want to step out of the mirror, get out of myself.

As species, we need to consider the planet and not just ourselves. Abstract form, though humanly made, deliberately expresses needs and desires outside our bodies and possessions. Each artist's version of abstraction is a new galaxy. I want to see the whole universe. That, above all, is the Big Picture.

I am aware that abstract art is both the easiest and most difficult art to make. It's easier to make a triangle than a pine tree or a cube rather than a building. It is unique to itself, a language untranslatable. The best abstraction expresses a magisterial state, exalted, often strange, almost always enchanting, and open to multiple ways of interpreting and appreciating. I like its challenge as something to ponder again and again.

chapter

HOW TO EVALUATE THE QUALITY OF ABSTRACT ART

What tools does the viewer need to evaluate abstract art and access its aesthetic rewards? Below is a list of characteristics the viewer should bring to the process. Note that many of these attributes apply to viewing all artworks and all styles.

- A predisposition to visual experience is a must. A healthy appetite for looking at art and a curiosity to explore its vast ranges of form and content are prerequisites. We all get our best rewards from what visually interests us.

- Open mindedness is essential. Too much of human judgment is based on prior conditioning and preconceptions—we are brainwashed by propaganda. Accustomed to the debased in popular culture, we may not realize how that eclipses our appreciation of the unique and unfamiliar.

- Understanding how the principles of formalism and composition affect the success or the failure of art is paramount. These same concepts apply to all art, representational and abstract.

- Basic history about modern art is essential. Art has connections with the rest of civilization. When you understand how art styles evolve alongside developments in the social, political, and industrial climate, you have a reference to know how a style (or an artist) relates to its predecessors. These cross-influences inform the viewer of what art is about and what commonalities various artists and styles share. Bernard Berenson, a great historian of Renaissance art, is quoted as saying: "You see as much as you know."

- Embrace the mysterious, the strange, and the new. Do not demand too specific a meaning from a work of art. Abstraction is not about pat answers, singular themes or messages. Viewers too often look for definitive answers, but art asks more questions. In the scientific method, a given discovery seems initially illuminating, but that same discovery prompts ten or more questions. Art tantalizes us to seek more than we already know.

- Know that the more you look, the more you understand. You see more patterns and relationships when you consider the similarities and differences among various styles of abstract form. Picasso said that everyone wants modern art explained, but that the best way to understand is to look—and keep looking.

- Allow room for differing viewpoints. There is both reasonable consensus and thoughtful disagreement about the quality of abstract art. Critics and artists often argue about the merits of certain artists or styles. A good argument will bring reasoning and evidence to the discussion. Know that your best opinions are those in which intellect and emotion attain a balance. Art is both objective and subjective.

- Abstraction will transport you to another world. Be motivated to go there. You may find it strange, beguiling, infuriating, welcoming, or scary in countless ways. Regardless of your assessment of what you contemplate, the abstract experience will always enlarge your perceptions and the scope of your world.

chapter **17**

HOW TO MAKE ABSTRACT ART

The title of this chapter may seem like an oxymoron or a contradiction, as if there is a correct or a particular way to make abstract art. In fact, there are multitudes of ways, and each way is related both to realism and to the creative approach of the individual artist. In all cases, the result is a product of imagination. Your imagination is exponential, limitless if you exercise it forcefully, freely, and frequently.

Abstract art is often beset by doubt or disbelief with entering art students. This is a misguidance perpetuated by cultural conditioning. The general population prefers realistic or recognizable subjects, objects, or figures that can be named or labeled. What's worse is that people may not understand that their views are being shaped by uninformed outside influence. Abstract art is more than hundred years old, so it seems surprising to me how many people still dismiss or ignore so much of our artistic heritage.

You should never assume that representation (including realism) and abstraction are in opposing camps or that one or the other is more advanced. Art is bigger and more equitable than that. In fact, reality and abstract form are made of the same substance. Picasso said that in order to start a work of art, you must begin with something in your surroundings, although it may eventually become more abstract. But that approach might be applied in reverse. If you start without reference to reality, you may create forms that eventually become symbols, references, metaphors, or otherwise suggestions of realistic features or objects—without any of them becoming explicitly recognizable.

Furthermore, abstraction can include recognizable forms. A valid practice is to mix abstract forms with representational ones. Many abstract painters deliberately place "impurities" from the real world into their canvases. You don't have to be a purist. Think of art as the ultimate democracy. In today's art world, anything and everything can be mixed together.

The following is a list of the multitude of approaches to make abstract art. The list is inclusive but not exclusive. There are surely many additional approaches to the ones here. You might invent a different abstract process more suited to your brand of imagination.

The suggestions here can be combined or mixed, that is, you can apply ideas from several methods to make your art. Since you have to start somewhere, think of these points as a launching pad into the universe of your abstract fantasies.

- Begin a doodle anywhere on your picture's surface. This is spontaneity on steroids. Then expand it, "mushroom" it into increasingly larger areas until the pictorial space is full and satisfying as a composition.
- Plan first as a variation on the doodle. In your sketchbook or on small paper, make spontaneous drawings of proposals for how your picture might work as a composition. Drawing informally in an "automatic" approach can unlock the possibilities lurking in your subconscious. By making lots of small drawings quickly none are too precious. That can make your attitude more open to an expanded range of forms.
- As Picasso suggested, start with something in reality, an object, figure, photograph, or memory. Change, add, subtract, or otherwise enhance that reality until it becomes more experiential, and less recognizable. Expand with more additional forms that seem appropriate to where your picture is going.
- Shoot photographs of a variety of subjects. Experiment with close-ups, severe cropping, contrasting lights and darks, and any other way that might reveal the subject in a new and unexpected context. Sketch plans for how the photographs would become more abstract while still drawing on the uniqueness of the subject matter.
- Make a collage with or without photo-realistic details. Collage naturally emphasizes the abstract form. Use it as a model to make your picture, but feel free to depart from the collage if it suits a better purpose.
- Explore the possibilities by chance. Drop found objects onto a panel or a sheet of large paper. Notice the positions of how they land, overlap, and interact in that space. Use this arrangement as a starting point or foundation for designing your abstraction.
- Wing it. Willem de Kooning often started a painting by writing with a brush a simple word on his canvas. The forms of the letters may be enough to stimulate the imagination with additional lines, shapes, and colors. As the painting develops the words will likely disappear.
- Speaking of words: think of nouns, verbs, or adjectives as possible routes to stimulating abstract qualities. How can you express the feelings or sensations of those words in the formal language of abstraction? Thinking in opposites is a fruitful way to consider the expansiveness of expression: exuberance versus quietude, complexity versus simplicity, purity versus contamination, stability versus chaos, or tension versus relaxation. Perusing a dictionary or thesaurus can stimulate new ideas.
- Vary your technique. Although a brush is the major tool for painting, there are so many other ways of spreading paint. Squeegee, rag, stick, pouring from a can, and spattering are just a few ways to describe your forms. Read again Chapter 9, Notes on Painting, for the full list of techniques. Much of the same is true for drawing. Pastels, inks, and watercolors can all be applied with imaginative techniques rather than the conventional methods.
- This last cue may mistakenly seem an art cliché, but worth consideration as a prompt to thinking in the abstract language. Many of you may recall in public school classes listening to music while attempting to interpret it into picture making. You need not be that literal in approaching music with art. Nonetheless, listen to music, good music that suggests images, storytelling, or moods. Music (without lyrics) is inherently abstract. Its sounds, at whatever octave or with a given variety of instruments, are not representations of visible reality. Rather, its expression is through moods, feelings, and subtlety of suggestion just as is pure form and color is in abstract art.

I listen primarily to classical music. Its orchestral nature with many varied instruments in dialogue as they engage and change passages is an exalted panorama of contrasting sounds and audial forms. Classical music is the Big Picture of Sound. Its counterpoint in nature is the dazzling variety of song heard in a countless number of bird species, often heard singing to or answering each other, similar to "conversation" in orchestral music.

A popular misconception is that classical music is mainly historical, its presence past, composed of the old masters like Mozart and Beethoven. Not true. Contemporary composers abound and continue to compose music that adds depth and richness to the canon. At the same time, the old masters of music and art continue to provoke inspiration and innovation for contemporary composers and artists.

A good supplement is to listen to music while you make art. Music may suggest visual possibilities, consciously or subconsciously as you work. Vasily Kandinsky, the great pioneer of abstract art, believed fervently in the kinship between music and art. His important treatise describing the foundations of abstraction, *Concerning the Spiritual in Art* published in 1911 and still in print (and required reading at many art schools), is the first major document to address the relationship between these two great art forms.

If any of these approaches help you get started, that is the point. Once started, often in the process of making art, the road changes and you suddenly see a better method or approach. Take the leap, trust your intuition, and draw or paint until you have arrived at a desirable destination. Your picture is traveling in your head.

SECTION IV

TAKING THE DIVE: ACTIONS SPEAK LOUDER THAN WORDS

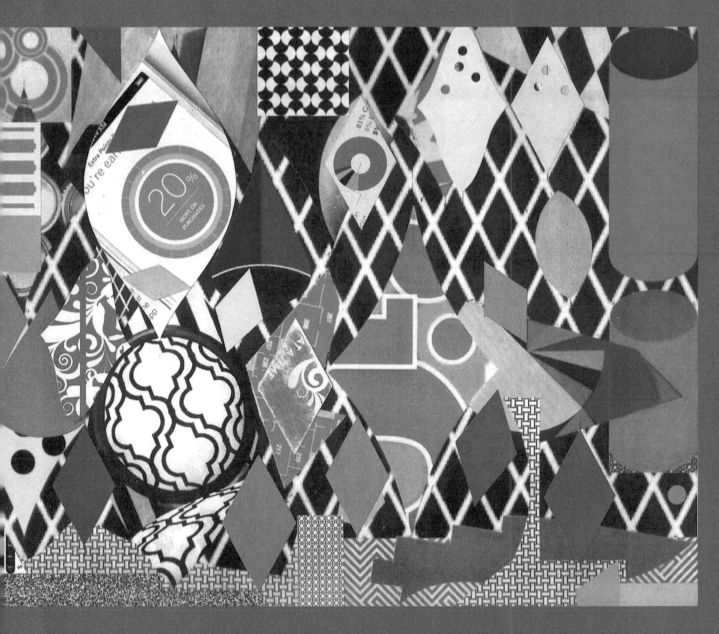

chapter 18

AN ARTIST'S CREDO

The *will to work* is indispensable to art making. Making art is labor intensive. You must be prepared to wrestle physically and intellectually with materials to transform them into images, objects, and ideas. Without a work ethic, your ability or talent will remain undeveloped at best or squandered at worst. However, if work becomes habit, making art will not seem like obligation or "work."

Good working habits may not come easily. Negative thinking often prevents starting projects. Are you a procrastinator? Do you delude yourself that you work better under pressure? Procrastination is really a foil to cover doubts and fears about your abilities. Lurking somewhere between consciousness and unconsciousness, a little negative voice says, "I won't fail if I don't try." Procrastination may also reflect a lack of motivation or a perceived lack of imagination. Be assured you do not need to dive through hoops, jump hurdles, or change your personality to make art on a regular basis. But you do need to *start*—and if you get stuck, you need to start *again*.

Once the prospect of work becomes anticipation instead of anxiety, you're on your way to *enjoying* art making as a consistent feature in your life. Enjoying art is key. We all want to do what gives us pleasure. That scary feeling in the pit of your stomach, that fear of failure, should be replaced with an adventurous spirit of discovery.

The following ten guidelines, not listed in any order of importance, are a proven way to get going in art making and to free you when you get stuck. If you have already put into practice any of these critical strategies, so much the better. Familiarity with these practices is essential to their mastery.

1. Cultivate Curiosity. Cultivate curiosity about art, life, the world, and the universe. An inquiring mind is the most important precursor to creativity. Without this attribute, you are dead in the water. To be curious is natural, but our culture does much to distract us and stultify our childlike (but not childish) sense of wonder. Stop listening to all those programmed messages and commercial demands. Find a place to be quiet and listen to your own voice. What do *you* think? What do *you* want to do that is not derived from a prompt you have absorbed from the outside world? Re-experience that sensation you had as a child that everything is new and worth exploring—because it *is*. Try to get past the fact that you have been "civilized" and socially brainwashed to focus only on the popular and the commercial.

One secret about art making is that great ideas are not generated by the exotic or by divine intervention. Good ideas derive naturally from the experiences of the everyday, from the mundane world that others discard or overlook. Be curious about what is immediately around you and what is already part of your world. As a simple exercise, pick up something familiar in your environment, such as a tool, a fruit or a vegetable, or a toy. Look carefully at all its details as you turn it around in your hands. Study it for a prolonged time. Dare to be naïve—imagine that you are an alien and have no idea what this thing is. Then you should be able to see it in a way few others know. This is curiosity—rethinking the familiar as new and strange. It is easy to be jaded.

Just as important, your curiosity must extend to the unfamiliar, to all subjects that you do not know about and have yet to explore. It is no contradiction to say that the content of art comes from everything else *except* art. Subject matter comes from thinking, feeling, and living in the real world. Become well rounded. Be a generalist.

2. Make Anxiety Your Friend. Get used to it. Anxiety is a natural part of artistic practice. Fears and doubts either can cripple your creativity or can intensify your concentration by keeping you in a heightened state of alert. Use that tension as the edge of your seat, as the toehold for the next step. Oscar Wilde said, "The anxiety is unbearable. I only hope it lasts forever." The good news is that anxiety usually dissipates quickly once you have broken the ice by taking some initial action. It is a little like the stage fright of actors. Once the curtain opens the butterflies vanish.

With a little experience and practice, you will inevitably make something that pleases you. Bank on that to give you confidence in the next challenge: I have done this effectively in the past, therefore I can do it again.

3. Plan, Then Be Spontaneous. Concentrate, then improvise. Plan enough to get started. You need only a rough blueprint: a subject, a material, a particular series of shapes and patterns, and an approximation of how to organize them. A rough sketch in your mind or on paper may be enough. Then, at some early point in the working process, step back and look. Listen to the work. What does it want? Now allow your intuition to work the problems.

At the start of a project, it is not possible to preconceive the art object to completion, intact, in your head. It is a misconception that anyone can do that. When you work with art materials, all kinds of incidents, including accidents, occur that you could not anticipate. Manipulation with tools and materials brings unpredictability. Do not let your intellect prevent the spontaneous. *Welcome the unexpected*, even the accident, as an opportunity.

Don't try to predetermine a project before it has had its day in the studio. I think the reason that students sometimes want to have their compositions completed in their minds first is to avoid the unknown. Understand that *the unknown* is part of the creative process.

Remember, anxiety is a tool to find your way. When anxiety threatens to overwhelm you, stop and do something else. Your subconscious will take over the task. You will not realize this is happening. But in the shower, eating, driving, or doing some other mundane task, you may discover new possibilities and solutions that did not occur to you in the initial process of construction. That eureka moment did not pop out of the blue. The problem festered in the back of your mind and the solution came to consciousness because you were thinking about it all along—which brings me to the next step.

4. Work in Increments. Space your art making over a number of sessions and days. If you try to finish a project in one session, you set yourself up for frustration. The enormity of completing a project from start to finish at one time can be overwhelming. Also, you are not likely to do your best work. (The exception is when limited time is intended, as in a gesture drawing or a rough sketch.)

Pace yourself. Become sensitive to the rhythms in your working process. Some tasks must be done carefully and methodically if they are to be successful. Others may be done with fluency and ease—as if *you* are the instrument of the art's making. Changing the momentum of your work as the circumstances allow is also a way to keep your involvement from becoming predictable and monotonous.

Each time you start and stop working, you are alternating between the best of two worlds—deliberate planning and intuitive insight. Those breaks give your mind a chance to sift the possibilities and to explore the variables that may be too numerous and unmanageable in a single studio session. You are a different person each time you work. Each working session informs the next. You know a little more with each passing hour, with each new day. Take advantage of how time allows the creative process to build on its own past. Your work will be richer as a result.

5. Pick Up Something and Play. Pick up something and play especially when you have trouble getting started. But I find that this technique works anytime. Decide that what you are about to do is No Big Deal. Do not harbor grandiose intentions. They intimidate. Willem de Kooning, the great American Abstract Expressionist, sometimes would start a picture by writing a word in paint directly on his canvas. As a collage artist, I often start by cutting shapes from patterns and images that catch my eye. Perhaps getting started can be as simple as sharpening your pencils. Then suddenly you get the desire to use them. Before you know it, you are caught up in the process and on your way. Sneaking up on the artistic act is a useful trick. Try it.

6. Entertain Opposites. Connect ideas, themes, and materials that seem unrelated. The beauty of opposites is that they often enhance each other. Black looks richer and darker next to white. White looks stark and pristine next to black. With complementary colors, each enhances the brilliance of the other. Large looks larger next to small and vice versa. You get the picture.

Sometime, opposites can just duke it out and the energy that flies can be dynamic, surprising, and effective. For example, the contrast of observing something in nature and then adapting it to art can be a fresh and creative challenge. A form or pattern found in nature can give you an idea for a painting or sculpture. The elaborate striping of colors found in a seashell might be the structure needed to unify a series of forms in a drawing or a painting. Opposites are often closer to each other than we assume.

7. Sow More Seed Than You Need. Consider a lot of possibilities. Sometimes, a student will ask me immediately after I have assigned a project what I think of his suddenly inspired idea. I am suspicious when someone is in such a hurry to settle the matter. Is he merely relieving his anxiety by grasping at the first straw? Jumping to a conclusion this way short-circuits what is both the most fun and the most effective way of generating ideas—entertaining in your mind the great variety of possible directions your work might take. I say *entertain* because this process can be a movie in your head. With no special skill or tools, you can efficiently travel great distances and explore new worlds in your imagination.

Consider the absurd alongside the sensible. Do not censor anything at this embryonic stage. When you have saturated your curiosity, you can start the process of elimination. In this way, quality is linked to quantity. Think about this: You would not buy a camera or other expensive equipment without researching and comparing a number of different models for performance, price, and suitability. The quality of your finished art will depend on critically examining many possibilities and choosing the one to put into form that offers the greatest potential.

8. Dare to Sail into Uncharted Waters. Art is exciting because it ventures into new experience. Do something that feels *unfamiliar*. Getting out of your comfort zone is a must. Surprise is a keystone in art. Relying on familiar and safe solutions is a dead end in the studio. The result is dull and hackneyed content. You want to arouse your sense of excitement by discovering something you have not encountered before.

How can you do this? Free association is a good exercise to start this process. The Surrealists were experts at envisioning new and compellingly odd combinations of subjects and themes. Consider the classic surrealist fantasy, "Beautiful as the chance encounter of a sewing machine and an umbrella on an operating table." Try this! Open a dictionary and randomly choose groups of nouns, verbs, and adjectives. Mix and assemble them as improbable sentences or phrases. Then imagine how you might depict these sentences as images or objects.

Automatic writing is another way to discover something new. Write as quickly as possible without censoring the thoughts that come off the top of your head—nonsense and all. Another method can be done visually. Close your eyes and imagine images passing through your mind's eye. Use a stimulus by listening to music or looking at artworks as a catalyst. Write down or sketch quickly whatever appears in your mind. Trust the powers of your creative instincts.

9. Make a Big Deal Out of a Little. Sometimes, less is more. When you feel overwhelmed by too many choices, narrow your sights. Impose limitations. The rigor you must exercise when using only a few variables will stretch your ability to imagine within that range. Limitations will force you to understand the visual elements in ways you had not considered when distracted by clutter. Some of us have an inherent inclination to put everything into an artwork, including the ubiquitous kitchen sink. If you indiscriminately and repeatedly overload your work, you risk exhausting yourself. The art may become a literal display of your own confusion and unfocused excess. Set priorities. What is necessary to make this work clear and effective? Leave everything else out.

10. Turn Off the Inner Dialogue. That is right, ignore the above suggestions except this one when you start working. Once you take action, your intuition is the guiding force and puts you in the most direct contact with the artistic process. Remind yourself that art is a *visual* medium. Verbalizing while doing art will make you self-conscious and distracted with worry. Raphael, the great Renaissance master, said, "When one is painting, one does not think." Turn off your mind and let your body do the work.

chapter

STUDIO STRATEGIES FOR ART MAKING

Working in the studio will invariably have stops and starts. Progress has an uneven pace. Thorny problems and unexpected hurdles arise at unwelcome moments. When that happens, check this list to see if there is a prompt or a solution to ease your way. If these statements sound like commands, remember that everything in this book is meant as a suggestion. You can experiment through trial and error to discover what works best in the way you approach art making. These twelve strategies are essentially an abbreviation of the advice given in previous chapters about the art studio process. Use as a quick reference.

1. **Start any place.** There is no rule about what must come first. Breaking the ice with action, even a small action, can get your creative juices flowing.

2. **Plan ahead.** Planning promotes a narrowing of choices so you can focus on essential ideas. The limitations required by organization make you become more creative. But do not prepare so much that you completely eliminate surprises and uncertainties. These are opportunities for discovery. Trust that your intuition can solve problems when planning no longer serves the purpose.

3. **Do not be in a hurry.** If you are working under a deadline because you did not get started early enough, you will be forced to accept compromises that diminish your best efforts. Procrastination is the enemy.

4. **Avoid "safe" choices.** Playing to the middle of the road in art is a fast ticket to mediocrity. Worse, relying on easy solutions derived from pop culture is a faster ticket to triviality. Avoid clichés. Art is about sabotage and extremes. Take a risk. Go off on that tangent. Art should express *new* responses to experience, not what you and the viewer already know.

5. **Pay close attention to formalism and composition.** These may seem to be fundamentals that masquerade as academic exercise, but they are not. They are the costume art must wear to convey its deepest content. Formalism and composition make expression visible.

6. **See your work as the viewer does.** Step back during the process and look. Then look again. Often. Working distance is different from viewing distance. The latter is how art is seen, so you must see it at a distance from the start.

7. **Look, then listen.** Your work will tell you what it needs. Clues and evidence abound in a work in progress if you are paying attention. Ask the art, "What do you want?"

8. **Do not be too easily satisfied.** Did that last brushstroke or constructed form seem false or too facile? Ingratiating effects may be momentarily welcome, but if it happened too easily, you may be in shallow waters. Art is hard won—there are no shortcuts. You must be convinced that that mark or form is inevitable, that *it* must be there.

9. **Be tough.** Eliminate for the greater good. Understand that "tiny bits" of the wrong stuff can diminish or destroy art. For example, the wrong patch of color or one too many repeated shapes can weaken a composition. All parts must enhance the whole. No one thing can serve itself only.

10. **Make art in the spirit of work and play.** Work alone soon becomes tedium, while unrelenting play can quickly descend into boredom. But a balanced combination keeps you challenged and amused at the same time. If art making seems too much like work, you are doing something wrong. Viewers do not want to see the monotony of labor in art even if some of that was required. Keep it fresh, surprising, and as spontaneous as possible.

11. **Make it as if you mean it.** Intensity and urgency of expression are far greater attributes than technical abilities. Whatever you do, your attitude about making art is the real subject matter. The viewer will sense your feeling about what you create.

12. **Ask: Is it really finished?** When you complete an artwork, live with it and look at it wonderingly and critically—and frequently. Does it need tweaking here, finessing there?

Does the art hold the feeling and intention you had when you made it? Are the forms unified? Is the subject coherent? Have you included sufficient description and detail to sustain attention? Does the work add up to more than the sum of its materials, that is, is it expressive? Time is the test of art.

chapter

ONE APPROACH TO ART MAKING

Jasper Johns, a pioneer of the Pop Art movement, once said in the course of an interview, "I don't know much about art"—this from the man whom many critics consider to be one of the preeminent artists working today. Shocking? It is a tongue-in-cheek remark. Johns was trying to describe how he works. What Johns does is *think*. He imagines a problem or a plan, but it's open to the working process, subject to change. He doesn't want to preconceive the end product of his efforts. That would be too predictable and not much fun to know the result and how it will look in advance. So, like many artists, Johns embraces risk and uncertainty to arouse his curiosity and to enjoy the element of surprise as he makes discoveries.

The artist does not worry whether what he is doing is art. Questions and curiosity drive the art making process. Is this image worth investigating? Will I find something new? Is this problem interesting? Am I satisfying my urge to uncover my feeling about this subject, this object, this material? Or it can be as simple as: What if I did this or that? The answers to these and countless other questions that tap into the imagination manifest themselves in images, in objects, in materials, in techniques, and become the work of art.

Johns also said,
> "Take something.
> Do something to it.
> Do something else to it.
> Do something else to it."

These four deceptively simple sentences are nearly a manifesto for the artist. Let us examine this little credo a moment. What is "something"? It is whatever strikes your visual fancy—not necessarily exotic, but something that arouses your sense of inquiry. In fact, it is not the *what* so much, it is the *how*—which is the second sentence. Ask the question as you do something to it: What if I change it or change its context. Do whatever it takes to alter its reality. That can mean
> Dismantling it,
> Reassembling it in a new way

With all or only some of its parts,
Altering all or some of the parts physically,
Combining it with similar—or dissimilar—materials, Objects, or surroundings,
Or, mixing any of the above.

Your first attempts may be tentative and only scratch the surface. Johns softly admonishes, do not be too easily satisfied. You have only just begun, "Do something else to it." That is still not enough. He repeats, "Do something else to it."

When you have done more "somethings," investigated a number of possibilities, you have a basis for comparison and determining effectiveness. This works, this does not, maybe this will be better, maybe this is best. You need to feel that you are getting the biggest bang for your artistic buck.

Making art is always a matter of follow through, exploring an image or an idea in a set or a series of works, rather than in a dead-end, one-shot-is-all syndrome. If the concept or approach is worth its salt as art, there is always much more to mine below the surface. That is another message in Johns' refrain. If something is worth doing, it is worth doing more than once to find out what it is about or what it can become. Call it variations on a theme. This is why a solo exhibition of an artist's recent output invariably seems consistent in style, content, and expression. You never need to worry that you are repeating yourself as long as you feel the excitement of revealing something new or the satisfaction of significantly improving the quality. Sometimes, a small variation, just tweaking a color or a single form, can have a monumental effect. It can be the difference between flawed and effective—or so different that it sets off new ideas.

In short, seek choices
But not just in your head.
Carry them out,
Take action.

chapter

PSYCHOLOGY, PROCRASTINATION, AND HABIT

Because art making is a challenging undertaking it is easily postponed. One of the most common art ailments is procrastination. Nothing attempted, nothing failed. When I ask a student why she forestalls, often the response is "I'm a perfectionist so I avoid what can't be done in exacting terms." This is passing the buck. Fear of failure is really a ploy to avoid effort. The delusion that you can avoid the task until later is a pretense, a brand of self-dishonesty. It is more positive to be realistic. When you are developing a skill, you are not going to immediately make masterpieces. In fact, you will surely make many mistakes. But mistakes are the most valuable lessons when learning how to make art—if you dig deeper to understand them. Understanding mistakes is a way to avoid them and to navigate toward better solutions.

Some students claim they work better under pressure. Not so. Pressure may assist you momentarily via the force of a deadline, but the stress of delaying and the prospect of not finishing in time will surely be a distraction away from clear thinking and creative problem-solving. The art process requires that you be on high alert for all that is happening from moment to moment because every mark or material you add to the work is the result of countless critical decisions made and applied.

Another excuse to avoid action is distraction. Some people are too easily diverted by outside influence and indifferent activities. It is human nature to avoid the act of thinking, especially thinking that requires physical effort. However, there are ways of approaching art that can change all these negative stoppers.

The secret (there are not many, but this is one) is that the process of creating art is greater than the end product. To put it another way, trusting in the making of art and doing it often, as a habit and with enthusiasm will eventually yield good results. In other words, the art will take care of itself if you invest fully in the process. So how do you make art a habit, a regular routine that is motivating and gives you confidence that you are improving and developing your work? In short, habit and positive skills are closely related and interdependent. One leads to the other. You cannot have one without the other. When you perceive that you are developing positively, the resulting self-confidence will be the motivation to work habitually.

You must learn to appreciate the unknown. Drifting into brand new territory is a way to see what others do not. That is the start of originality. Discovery is the heart and soul of art making. Intense curiosity to find new forms and experiences is the motive for making it. Emphasis on the quality of the end product implies a rigid frame of mind that cares only about results. Self-consciousness combined with an overly precious attitude about your art will rob you of the essential pleasure of making art in the first place. Get your ego out of the picture.

I strongly urge you to read Chapter 18, An Artist's Credo and Chapter 19, Studio Strategies for Art Making. These chapters are pointed lists of practical actions to take to enhance your art experiences, to get out of trouble when feeling stuck, to throw out doubts and anxieties, and to help you get motivated to make art on a regular basis.

A great method I have found is to just start with something, anything in the studio. I think of starting to work as play, not labor. Many artists have rituals to get going: Sharpening pencils, looking through art books, scrawling in a sketchbook, mixing paint, or just putting a stroke of color on a blank canvas. Once you are underway, then the process becomes more serious, but you do not realize when that happens. Why? Because as you manipulate materials it is fun and that pleasure is enough to keep you going.

To reinforce play as an essential attitude, here is a quote by the eminent twentieth-century psychologist Carl Jung: "The creation of something new is not accomplished by the intellect but by the play of instinct acting from inner necessity. The creative mind plays with the object it loves."

I have often thought that you need a high visual appetite to make art. Wanting to see new form and color is a curiosity all artists have and more people should have. The more you work the more you will cultivate this desire. A good way to consider curiosity is to ask questions. What if I do this? What happens if I apply paint without a brush? How will these colors interact when placed adjacent? How can I interpret my subject so that it becomes more symbolic and less imitative? Can I make something that does not look like art at first, but is art after all? Do you get the picture? Once you hone in on satisfying the "what ifs," the rest of the art process takes care of itself. You must trust that your instincts and intuition will get you to your destination.

Ultimately, we all do what we think is important in our lives. If you keep avoiding art for prolonged periods, then it is not essential for you. No one needs the guilt and stress of hanging in limbo. Find what you can and will do that is sustaining and get on with it.

In my experience, art offers so much in its multifaceted complexity, intellectual, emotional, physical, and spiritual, that I must have access to it on a daily basis. The completeness of how art engages all our best human faculties is a monumental draw to its flame. If I can have a hand in helping students realize that art can positively and profoundly transform their lives, then my rewards are doubled as both artist and teacher.

SECTION V

KNOWING YOUR PLACE: UNDERSTANDING THE BIG PICTURE

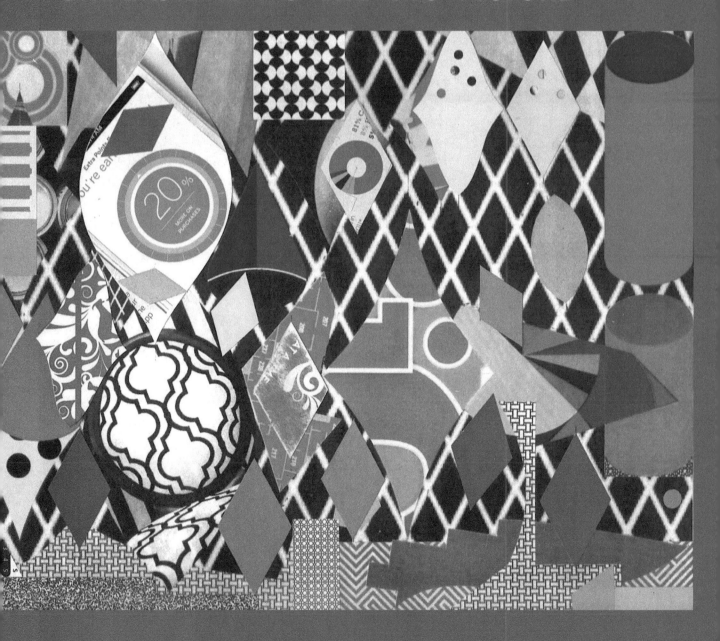

chapter

A SHORT LESSON IN THE LONG HISTORY OF ART

If you pursue a career in art you need to understand your place in the Big Picture of your predecessors and artists working today. I will attempt to describe in a nutshell, in admittedly stark and incomplete terms, what art history means to me as an artist. My response to the past is skewed to my interests, as it is with all artists. However, the achievements of great artists who have made significant contributions should be understood and appreciated whether or not that work seems to have resonance with your own endeavors. Their influence will have had effects on the styles that *do* interest you. Art is a giant tapestry in which all the threads are connected and where both opposites and similarities speak to one another. Substance is substance. Art that is a different species than your own inclinations always deserves respect and attention. Past art is a beacon that lights the way in the present.

Art history is not progressive or linear—not like a river rushing to a single destination. The early twentieth century notion that "industry is progress" has been discredited in recent decades. That revelation is reflected in how we reassess all disciplines, including art. The idea that later art improves on earlier art is a myth. It is better to think of art history as a gigantic wheel where each of the countless spokes is a branch to a unique time and place. The outer circle of the wheel reassures us that differences have connections after all.

Each generation of artists responds to the art of the previous, often in the spirit of rebellion and overthrow. Making art is really cultural mutiny. Emerging artists tend to be convinced that their work has greater relevance compared to the current masters who are their established counterparts. Sometimes this attitude seems arrogant and self-possessed, but at other times it is the acknowledgement of artistic debts, a tribute or homage to the influence of the great masters.

The best artists understand the abundance in art history and mine it unapologetically to extract ideas from all periods and styles for their own work. This process of mining or recycling the past can be seen throughout history. Examples abound. It strikes me that the stiff, frontal and semi-geometric figures of ancient Egyptian art are similar to the flat, stately, and stylized figures of Gothic painting and sculpture from more than a thousand years later. We can see the naturalism and idealizations of the ancient Greeks and Romans reemerging in all the arts and architecture of the Renaissance. The art of many twentieth century and contemporary masters can be traced to their origins in history too. Andy Warhol revisited the adaptation of popular culture first opened by the Cubists. Roy Lichtenstein painted his versions of the modern masters by transforming key works of Cubism, Expressionism, and Surrealism into his trademark comic strip style. Robert Rauschenberg has expanded collage and assemblage to a monumental scale inspired by Cubist collage and the assemblage art of Kurt Schwitters fashioned out of street detritus in post-World War I Germany. Jasper Johns "steals" subjects from other great modern masters including Edvard Munch, Picasso, Marcel Duchamp, and the Renaissance painter Hans Holbein.

Of course, no self-respecting artist is content with imitating previous masters. The intent is to overturn or expand on previous approaches. Borrowings become transformed into the artist's own interpretation. Art has always been about expanding horizons and definitions. These rich sources in the distant and immediate past can never be exhausted.

You ignore art history at great risk to your development. One of my former students who transferred to the Tyler School of Art said that if you do not have a working knowledge of art history "you are not part of the current conversation." Those art history courses are the sails on your ship into the studio. Do not be put off by the memorization of names, dates, and styles. They will eventually take hold in your mind as you assemble the Big Puzzle of Art and come to appreciate the dialogue the masters have with your own endeavors.

Because no scientific method exists by which to accurately measure quality in art, you must scrutinize carefully and develop your knowledge and critical skills to derive meaningful experiences that you can apply to your work. It is essential to your art that your analysis of history is based on sound reasoning and insight rather than reactionary emotions and prejudices.

While critical assessments in art change to some degree through the generations, there is always a basic informed consensus among professionals. Art as a discipline of study is not a free-for-all in which all opinions expressed are equal. The social anarchy in some parts of our culture that condones an I-like-it or I-don't-like-it attitude as the end of discussion about art is simply willful ignorance. If we want to raise the quality of discourse and engage in meaningful interaction, we cannot practice our democratic privileges of free speech at their lowest common denominator. This is a point at which art meets issues in both ethics and politics. If we are willing to raise our expectations, we can bring more meaning to our lives at many levels.

To some extent, art history is pliable and elastic. What we value in the present as we look across the ages in art is different than what was valued in 1950 or 1900 or 1850. We are shaped to a considerable degree by the values and traditions of the culture we inhabit. To that extent, our tastes may be corrupted by the trends and fashions we acquire while living in the present at a particular point on the globe. But we need not be the victims of our own near-sightedness if we acknowledge our biases.

One of the most satisfying, if difficult, ways of appreciating history is to put yourself in the time and place of study. It takes reasonable background in the history of a period—how people thought and lived—before you can stand in their shoes. If you develop an acquaintance with historical trends, the process of studying art becomes more satisfying because you are no longer a prisoner of your own limited cultural cocoon.

The lesson to remember is that art today is in constant dialogue with the art of the past. What has happened in previous movements often influences contemporary art and affects how we understand ourselves. For example, you may revisit Baroque art when your efforts reflect a passion for the drama of light and shadow. In the climate of political consciousness of the 1990s, many artists looked more closely at the social relevance of American Regionalism of the 1930s and Soviet Realism of the Cold War era. As more artists adopt the mixed media genres of installation art and performance art, and new sculptural forms and materials, the more we are reassessing early twentieth century collage, assemblage, Constructivism, and Dada. These are all desirable and valid pursuits since they are based on fresh awareness and creative need.

Whatever your interests are, there are precedents for them in art history. It is your duty to find them so that you do not reinvent the wheel. Your acknowledgment of those discoveries in your work will lend credibility to your art. By knowing your sources, you can be more confident of leading rather than following.

Art history is user friendly. You can take heart that you are walking the same paths as the great masters, that you share the angst and exultation of all artists, and though you may be alone in your studio, you have ample company in the creative pursuit of beauty, truth, and excellence. You can take comfort in the fact that any subject or style, no matter how ancient, obscure, or seemingly retrograde, might serve you in a contemporary purpose.

Regardless of history and its effects on culture, an artist is fortunate if his subject matter speaks directly to his times. You must pursue your interests no matter how unfashionable they might seem to others. Every artist depends on his authentic core to make meaningful work. You make art for yourself first (including what you make as a student). Always. Insincerity is the only unforgivable sin in art.

The daunting range of creative freedom you have today was not possible in the art of other periods. With the rise of democracies, their accompanying radical social changes, and the rapidly developing scientific discoveries and technological innovations of the post–Industrial Revolution era, artists' choices have expanded exponentially. You can be thankful for your predecessors who have blazed this trail. We artists walk in their well-worn path as their compatriots even as each of us must also find his own trail to champion. At the risk of seeming maudlin and egotistical, every artist yearns to contribute something of value to the posterity of art through the ages.

chapter 23

ONE ARTIST AND MODERNISM

An attempt here to describe art history from its beginnings in prehistory to the present is not necessary. You will get this and more in your art history courses. Since the advent of modern art with the Industrial Revolution of the early 1800s has an especially direct bearing on contemporary art, I will assess modernism as an arbitrary but relevant starting point for the art student. I should note that most artists are trained with Western viewpoints and concepts, and, that until recently, most art history departments covered only developments in Western art. Since the 1990s, Asian and other Eastern arts courses have been offered as welcome supplements to the traditional curriculum.

Because I am a pictorial artist trained before the diversity of the current climate, I have studied the history of Western painting more than anything else. Painting has always been about the illusion of space on the flat surface of the picture plane. There are three major concepts of handling space that can be identified in art history: (1) schematic and stylized flatness with emphasis on symbol, narrative, or iconic figure; (2) naturalistic illusion accompanied by perspective and light and dark modeling; and (3) a blending or melding of flatness and illusion. In most premodern periods, only one of these concepts was practiced and permissible. Today, the artist can choose.

Although naturalistic illusion reached the height of sophistication in the Renaissance with the invention of mathematical perspective and the perfection of light and dark modeling, we can see reasonable illusionism with partially effective attempts at perspective in ancient Roman painting. Flat space has migrated throughout art history from medieval illuminated manuscripts to modern abstraction. Remember, formal changes in art are not progressive. Themes and ideas can punctuate history in surprising ways.

What is compelling is that Renaissance illusionism reigned supreme in art for about 500 years. In the late nineteenth century, that concept of a window into the distance was challenged. The most significant contribution of the Impressionists and Post-Impressionists may not be the vivid color and light of observed landscape but the suggestion that the painting's surface must be as visible as the illusion. Many artists began to apply paint directly from the tube without thinning it with oil and turpentine first. This impasto application ran counter to the centuries-old technique of building paint layers in accumulated applications of transparent glazes. The two immediate effects of this technical departure were (1) an emphasis on the painting's picture plane with the implication that a picture is also *an object*, and (2) the increasingly visible *emotional state* of the artist as he applied his paint with highly visible brushstrokes and spontaneous gestures. The tracks the artist's hand left behind in the new technique of direct painting are not only a record in time of his activity (so-and-so was here) but also a telling reflection of his state of mind. These seeming by-products of style (compared to Impressionism's major tenets about color and light) would become the basis for a new art in the twentieth century.

When the Impressionists first started their quest, they went to the source of their interests and painted on-site before the open landscape. That act itself was a new idea since paintings for centuries had always been done in the studio. Ironically, what began as an intense study of the external world as experienced by the eye in real time and natural light would become the foundation for exploring the interior world of the artist's mind. Paul Cezanne was the artist who most realized the profundity of these new possibilities. He attempted to reconcile the seeming contradiction between intense observation and responsive experience. Cezanne felt that objective, universal values needed to be found in nature while simultaneously insisting that he satisfy the subjectivity of his reflection of nature. It is the conflict of the ages, and no wonder that Cezanne suffered doubts when he said he had great difficulty "realizing my sensations." His conundrum would become the bridge between the nineteenth century's ties to the visible, objective world and the twentieth century's need to express subjective experience and creative vision.

The beginning of the twentieth century was arguably more revolutionary in scientific, technological, social/political, and industrial developments than our own computer and digital revolution today. The nearly simultaneous advent of the automobile, the airplane, the cinema, and the production-line factory all conspired to reorganize populations from rural farm settings into tightly clustered urban centers of commerce and labor pools. To cope with this emerging stressful environment, Sigmund Freud proposed the new field of psychoanalysis in which the unconscious mind and dreams played seminal roles. Our interior world of emotions was changed forever. Albert Einstein's theories about the interchangeability of energy and matter combined with the speed of light altered our understanding of time and the universe. Our viewpoint of the exterior world would never be the same.

Does historical background matter to art? Absolutely! Art does not develop in a vacuum or drop out of the blue by divine intervention. Art is always a direct reflection of the times and places of its making. The events in art from 1900 to the 1920s parallel the radical changes just described. What's more, *all the styles* in art since the 1920s—including *those in our own time*—have their roots in one or more of these three seminal movements: Cubism, German Expressionism, and Surrealism.

When Pablo Picasso and Georges Braque began their collaborative experiments around 1908, they both said in retrospect they did not set out to invent Cubism. Instead they were looking for a new way to *see*. Picasso clarified seeing by saying that he wanted a way to make paintings that were closer to the way we experience our world. We don't stand fixed in one position and see life through a keyhole or a window. We walk through and move around in it. Our viewpoints shift as we do so. Cubist space was a way out of the dilemma of 500 years of linear perspective in a new and rapidly changing age that demanded another way to understand reality. The viewer could have, for the first time, the experience of moving around inside the picture instead of standing outside it as a voyeur. The shift from sight to experience, or sight *combined* with experience, would soon change everything in art.

Picasso and Braque reduced pictorial space to a compressed, shallow box or grid of seemingly tangible forms. Everything in deep space is pushed to the front of the canvas as if the viewer is in intimate contact with the subject. If the subject matter is a sprawling tabletop (think of still life or landscape), it is as if the table is turning nearly 90 degrees toward the picture plane. Everything seems to tumble down and out of the picture rather than fall back into the distance. Suddenly the contents of the picture feel like they share space with the spectator. You need only reach to pick up something.

To achieve this tangibility, the painters dismantled objects as if with a hatchet or hacksaw. The parts got put back together again to re-form the object, but in such a way that the object could be *felt* to exist in a number of viewing angles simultaneously—that is, all or most of its sides seen at once. To emphasize the exposure and accessibility of objects, they were drawn or painted fully despite the opaque overlapping that would have occurred in traditional illusionism. A peculiar sensation in looking at Cubist paintings is the feeling that objects are seen in X-ray vision—where they do overlap or they appear transparent. Furthermore, objects seem to open up—their contours stop short or are interrupted—and share their contents with other objects or the surrounding space. This quality of objects and background "leaking" into each other is called passage. Passage is another device developed by Picasso and Braque to bring background and foreground closer together in space.

Early Cubist paintings often look like sculptural reliefs with light and dark shadows exaggerated to create the illusion of a more palpable reality. Early Cubism from 1908 to about 1912, called Analytical, was usually monochromatic to emphasize three-dimensional form and spatial structure. The conclusion logically can be drawn that Cubism started with little color because Picasso and Braque needed to understand their experiments with forms and space first.

Around 1910, Picasso and Braque found another way to nail down their new concrete reality. They cut and pasted bits of newspaper, wallpaper, fabric, oil cloth, rope, and other nonart materials into their drawings and paintings. The seemingly simple act of gluing real newspaper to canvas not only challenged the traditional technique of painting the illusion of a newspaper, but led almost immediately to the invention of collage, assemblage, and mixed media. These new materials and their expansive implications would have powerful effects on the many art movements that followed: Dada, Russian Constructivism, Surrealism, Pop Art, and the mixed media genres of today.

Collage further flattened pictorial space, and soon the Cubists abandoned traditional modeling and imitated the flat planes of collage with generous applications of textured paint and patterns. These paintings—with lavish sweeps of color and generally lighter in feeling—came to be known as Synthetic (late) Cubism. By now, the Cubists were at the brink of abstraction.

When you look initially at Cubist paintings, you may be struck by how abstract they appear since the subject matter is often camouflaged in the breakup of forms. How to represent an object or figure structurally was more important to Picasso and Braque than its cognitive role as subject matter. Before the outbreak of World War I, several artists saw clearly the implications of Cubism. Piet Mondrian said "the logical consequence of Cubism is abstraction." The Russian painter Vassily Kandinsky was struck one day by unexpectedly seeing a painting of his leaning against a wall upside down in his studio. It was no longer recognizable and the freshness of seeing the forms and colors first rather than the subject matter excited his imagination. His creative leap after that was a revolution of monumental consequences. In 1911, after conceptualizing and rationalizing his plans by writing a treatise, Kandinsky painted the first abstraction without reference to nature or observed subject matter. Nonobjective art was born. Kandinsky's landmark treatise on abstraction, "Concerning the Spiritual in Art," remains an accessible and poignant classic of modern theory for those who wish to understand the original motivations for the twentieth century's greatest single contribution to the history of art.

At the same time that others were developing abstraction, Picasso extended the idea of collage into sculpture. Prior to the twentieth century, sculpture was carved, modeled, or cast from a single material. Starting with a block of marble or wood, the artist removed material by *subtraction* to reveal his form. Picasso saw that he could make sculpture by fastening one piece to another and that different materials could be attached to each other as well. This *additive* technique greatly expanded both the technical and expressive possibilities for sculpture. The practice of sculpture today can be both subtractive and additive, but the latter so dominates now that we take it for granted.

The sculptural counterpart to collage that Picasso invented is called assemblage because it involved the bonding of separate objects to each other in the same composition. Many of these objects were altered but retained much of their original identity. Their relationships to other objects and materials triggered new connections and surprising effects. The Surrealists were especially fond of the abrupt and irrational juxtapositions that assemblage so dynamically conveyed. Since its methods were never dependent on an "ism" or style, assemblage is still a vital practice in art today because the technique is so readily adaptable to an individual artist's vision.

As Cubism yielded to other styles after World War I, Cubist tenets were often incorporated into those styles. Once Cubism had infiltrated the European art world, it ceased to be a style and became an institution. Any artist wishing to stay on the cutting edge of his field had to reckon with its concepts and wider implications for art making. Cubism not only radically changed the arts of painting, sculpture, architecture, graphic design, and fashion, but it also fostered a staggering array of new styles, genres, techniques, and materials. Consider the metaphor of a large boulder tossed into the middle of a lake. The initial impact that Cubism made in the art world was stunning. The outlying ripples that impact made continue to inform art making today. It is no exaggeration to say that Cubism may be the most shattering and far-reaching revolution in art history.

Consider some of the ripples. Dada, the multidisciplinary movement of revolt against the inhumanity of World War I, depended on the stylistic elements of chance and irrationality that first appeared in Cubist collage. With Dada as its forerunner in the 1920s, Surrealism inherited Cubism's disjointed and contradictory combinations of subjects and themes. Although Surrealism introduced dreams and fantasies as its subjects, it carried on the collage tradition of abrupt contrast as a mainstay device.

When New York City became capital of the art world after World War II, Abstract Expressionism—the first international art movement originating in America—borrowed heavily from the fractured forms and the shallow, all-over space of Cubism. You can see those broken Cubist forms in the early paintings of Willem de Kooning and that all-over space in the drip paintings of Jackson Pollock.

In the 1950s, a new generation of artists demanded more concrete subject matter to replace the brushstrokes of private angst that suffused the canvases of the Abstract Expressionists. Robert Rauschenberg and Jasper

Johns fashioned collages and assemblages on a grand scale from street discards and incorporated into their art commonplace motifs such as targets, numbers, words (a direct borrowing of the stenciled letters of Braque's paintings), maps, and flags as tangible connections to the real world.

With roots in Cubist materials and subjects, Pop Art mined the world of everyday culture like never before. By the late 1960s, Pop Artists' unabashed celebration of popular culture was complete. Andy Warhol, Roy Lichtenstein, James Rosenquist, and Claes Oldenburg all derived subjects from the commercial world and synthesized them into the gallery and museum world. Picasso and Braque's idea of experience in the reality of the everyday was never so complete.

By the 1970s, Pop Art's heyday was eclipsed by an unprecedented pluralism that included such diverse movements as Minimalism, Conceptual Art, performance, film and video, and installation art. Painting saw a revival in styles called color field painting, pattern and decoration, and hard-edged abstraction. But painting as the dominant expression for centuries has fizzled ingloriously with Neo-Expressionism in the 1980s—commonly regarded as a pastiche of the original German Expressionism of the early twentieth century. While its leadership has apparently waned, painting will continue for those who know its rich possibilities can never be exhausted.

Since the 1990s, art has been like a ship at sea with neither rudder nor compass. Pluralism and creative freedom abound as never before, but none of it seems to offer the kind of breathtaking direction, range of possibilities, or profound insight that we have seen in the earlier twentieth century movements. Modernism has relentlessly pursued the cult of the new to the extent that we may have run ahead of ourselves. Have we exhausted the creative possibilities that seem now to have been thoroughly explored? Perhaps our culture is so frayed by an overabundance of subcultures and media distractions that art can no longer hold the attention of the public as it once did. Or maybe our artistic malaise has become so entrenched that few can see a horizon from the bottom of the ditch. Is modernism really finished as a succession of rebellious movements turning the artistic house upside down? Surely, the creative potential of artistic practice does not dry up for long. If the past is any indication, the time is ripe for a group of gifted artists to take culture by the collar and declare a postmodernist insurrection on a monumental scale.

See the modern art history and American Art diagrams at the end of this chapter. They are a quick glance at the complexity and expansive variety that has characterized art since the Industrial Revolution. To the novice, modern art can seem formless and indeterminate. The diagrams are meant to show that art develops with structure and chronology. These three "Big Pictures" should encourage you to investigate the artists and movements of the modern and contemporary eras.

THE FAMILY TREE OF MODERN ART 1800-1940

Select pioneering *artists* are listed only.

PHOTOGRAPHY Invented 1830s
Daguerre, Atget, Muybridge, Evans, Cartier-Bresson, Lange

Literal realism of photography freed painting to reinvent itself with qualities that expressed the gestures of the hand, the tactile properties of art materials, and emotional content.

REALISM early 1800s-1870
Delacroix, Courbet, Manet

Myth and religion were replaced by everyday, secular subjects, often rendered on site. Real had more to do more with subject than with style.

POST-IMPRESSIONISM 1880s-1910
Van Gogh, Gauguin, Cezanne, Seurat

Interpretation was greater than appearance. Patches of paint, distinct planes, and expressive color became more important than traditional light and dark illusion.

IMPRESSIONISM 1870s-1890s
Monet, Degas, Renoir, Sisley

Direct painting of color and light focused on the duality of illusion and surface. Tactile paint became as important as subject.

CUBISM 1908-1920
Picasso, Braque, Gris, Leger, Delaunay

Radical formal innovations dismantled Renaissance perspective by reducing subjects to planes and facets rendered in a shallow box-like space. Multiple viewpoints imply we move around in the world instead of from a fixed point seen through a window.

FUTURISM 1909 - 1920
Boccioni, Balla, Carra, Severini

The Italian version of Cubism promoted speed, industry, and violent politics in the quest to move Italy beyond it's tradition bound past.

ABSTRACTION 1907- present
Kandinsky, af Klint, Malevich, Mondrian

Subject matter became the magisterial expression of form and color. Illusion was reimagined by the physicality of materials and the art work as object.

SURREALISM 1920s-1940s
de Chirico, Miro, Dali, Ernst, Magritte

Dreams, nightmares, and fantasies became the new realities of art. Artists freely juxtaposed unlikely subjects that provoked fascination with the strange and mysterious rather than the familiar.

DADA 1918-1920s
Tzara, Ball, Hans Arp, Hausmann, Duchamp

Chance, experiment, and absurdity made ad hoc statements in all art forms as an anti-art protest after World War I. The means of expression were greater than the end products.

COLLAGE 1912- present
Schwitters, Hausmann, Heartfield, Hoch

Picasso and Braque were the first to paste cutouts of paper, fabric, and found materials into drawings and paintings.

EXPRESSIONISM 1915-1920s
Kirchner, Beckmann, Nolde, Grosz

Dramatic outpouring of protest and critique of social/political mores led to charged expressions in raw, gestural paint.

FAUVISM 1905-08
Matisse, Derain, Vlaminck

Spontaneous execution of imaginative color replaced local color. Matisse became the Anti-Cubist of flat color and textural brushwork.

SCULPTURE AND ASSEMBLAGE 1915-present
Picasso, Schwitters, the Constructivists

The additive process of connecting pieces to each other replaced the subtractive method of removing material from a block. Found objects were incorporated into 3-D art works.

Illustration contributed by Jerry Zinser. Copyright © Kendall Hunt Publishing Company

AMERICAN ART SINCE 1890

Various artists from other countries participated in the isms starting with Abstract Expresionism. Many more artists than space allows can be added to these lists. Some styles relate as reactions to others, while there are similarities between some. These are indicated by arrows.

ASH CAN SCHOOL 1890s-1910s
Bellows, Henri, Sloan, Glackens

The grit of urban scenes in New York City was a more earthy brand of European realism, expressed in thick, gestural brushwork.

EARLY MODERN 1910s-1930s
O'Keeffe, Dove, Hartley, Demuth, Davis, Sheeler, Bruce, Marin

A post-Cubist response combined both representational American subjects and innovative abstract forms.

REGIONALISM 1930-1940
Wood, Benton, Curry, Wyeth, Hogue

This realist rejection of modern art trends featured subjects of Midwest to Southern rural and small town America.

ABSTRACT ESPRESSIONISM 1945-1960s
Pollock,Krasner, de Kooning, Motherwell, Mitchell,Hoffmann, Kline, Gorky

The first American ism that became an international style of a highly personal, existential abstraction filled with spontaneous, roughly applied skeins of paint. After the devastation of Europe after WW II, New York replaced Paris as the world's art capital.

POP ART 1960-1970s
Warhol, Lichtenstein, Rosenquist, Oldenberg, Wesselmann

Johns and Rauschenberg opened the door to using found materials and subjects from popular culture. Pop artists freely explored the banality of everyday objects and commercial products, causing us to see our consumer excesses in a new and critical light.

OPTICAL ART (OP ART) 1960s-1970s
Riley, Anuszkiewicz, Stanczak, Vasarely

Strong optical effects of pulsating, vibrating, and warping forms were made via intense, hard-edged geometry, often disorienting to the viewer.

MINIMAL ART 1965-1975
Judd, Andre, Serra, Ryman, Kelly, Martin, Herrera

The industrial look of clean, simple design was a response to the crass subjects and messy brushwork of the above isms. Less is more, simple can be Wow!

COLOR FIELD PAINTING 1950s-1970s
Noland, Louis, Poons, Olitski, Held, Stella, Hodgkin, Gilliam, Halley, Zox

Differed from Abstract Expressionism in its lack of angst and existential content. Great spills and pours of color celebrated the upbeat traits of unorthodox paint handling. This raw approach was also countered with pristine geometry by means of tape separating colors.

NEO-EXPRESSIONISM 1980s
Schnabel, Salle, Basquiat, Kiefer, Clemente, Auerbach

Narrative, social subjects were handled with rough, emotion-laden paint as a reaction to the coolness of Conceptual and Minimal art.

PATTERN & DECORATION 1970s-1980s
Kushner, Kozloff, MacConnell, Zakanitch, Jaudon

Blurring the line between art and design, these artists celebrated the rollicking patterns of wallpaper, printed fabric, and quilts.

ONE ARTIST AND MODERNISM

Illustration contributed by Jerry Zinser. Copyright © Kendall Hunt Publishing Company

AMERICAN ART SINCE 1890 Part II

The following movements are largely independent of each other. However, content may overlap and some artists can be included in more than one movement. The art here is often interdisciplinary and involves multi-media or mixed media. These lists are not inclusive and more artists can be added.

SCULPTURE 1950s-present

Nevelson, Noguchi, Bourgeois, Pfaff, Brancusi, Hesse, Westermann, Murray, Calder, Smith, Chamberlain, Cornell, Bontecou, Duchamp, di Suvero

While painting dominated art for centuries, finally sculpture took its rightful place in mid-century. The range of subject matter, materials, and content is as staggering as the variety in New Genres.

ART OF CALIFORNIA 1950s-present

Wiley, Hudson, Diebenkorn, Parks, Bischoff, Frey, Saul, Arneson, Shaw, Jess, Price, Nagle

Art of the West Coast is often distinct in form and content compared to the rest of the USA. Humor, playfulness, exaggeration, unlikely materials, an adventurous spirit, and even climate play roles in the exuberant expressions of these artists.

FLUXUS 1960s-present

Maciunas, Cage, Ono, Watts, Hendricks

This interdisciplinary group is nearly impossible to identify in specific terms. These art experiments manipulate a wide range of materials and may even involve performance. Fluxus artists are committed to broadening what can be considered art.

PERFORMANCE 1960s-present

Schneemann, Kaprow, Beuys, Burden, Nitsch

Happenings of the Pop Art era introduced performance as art that seemed an extension of theater but not necessarily with the usual literary narrative. These acts by artists may be scripted or spontaneous or some combination in which content is made compelling but mysterious.

NEW GENRES 1970s-present

Viola, Acconci, Huebler, Smithson, Irwin, Flavin, Holzer, Goldsworthy

New attitudes, materials and technologies have expanded the field, including film, video, animation, performance, conceptual art, installation art, earthworks, art furniture, & environmental art with more on the way.

CONCEPTUAL ART 1970s-present

Duchamp, Acconci, Huebler, LeWitt, Weiner, Burden, Cage

Idea or concept is greater than the art object. Visual form is predetermined by a careful planning process. Art expressions vary widely from photo documentation to a variety of materials.

INSTALLATION ART 1980s-present

Pfaff, Sze, Christo & Jeanne-Claude, Weiwei, Solcedo, Broodthaers, Walker, Kusama

Art beyond the single object may fill a room, gallery, or outdoor site with a variety of techniques and materials meant to transform space into a theater-like envelopment.

NEW PHOTOGRAPHY 1990s-present

Sherman, Crewdson, Casabere, Baldessari, Mann, Wall, Gursky

Since the advent of digital tech, photography has attracted many new practitioners. A vast range of subjects and technical approaches has insured a major role for this medium.

chapter

24

ART HISTORY TIMELINE

An art history timeline is a linear representation of important periods, styles, and artists arranged in chronological order. Timelines can be found on the Internet and in many art history survey textbooks. They vary considerably in quality, inclusiveness, and legibility. Timelines are useful as reference guides for understanding context and providing a basis for further exploration of an artist or an era. When you wish to know more about an artist or style, you will need to research texts that describe ideas and contributions. Timelines are locators rather than explainers.

The following is a condensed timeline that will give you a convenient overview—the bare-bones minimum—of the great expanse of art through the ages. If this simplified version seems overwhelming, be assured that knowing art history is a gradually accumulating process. You will add names, styles, and concepts continuously to your cerebral data bank without realizing you are doing so. All you need is a healthy visual appetite. Art history will grow on you like English ivy on a brick wall.

Artists' names are not identified prior to the Renaissance since most art before 1300 was done anonymously. Artists then were considered artisans, skilled workers on a par with other tradesmen such as blacksmiths, masons, and carpenters. Starting with the Renaissance, many artists acquired superstar status in their own lifetimes as society began to value human achievements and secular pursuits over adherence to theological doctrine.

Bear in mind about art after 1500: The High Renaissance was a time of great tension and social upheaval between the patronage of the powerfully entrenched Roman Catholic Church and the rising wealth of the aristocratic and emerging merchant classes. Since secular patronage had different demands, subject matter expanded into portraiture, landscape, and still life. These worldly and less theological subjects reflected the tastes of a new, acquisitive clientele. Patrons had something to say about the art that got made. These tendencies continue today.

Dates specifying the time spans of styles and periods are always somewhat arbitrary and relative. Since artistic influences tend to be overlapping and diffused, estimating the precise years of an art movement's inception and demise are not possible. Reasonable approximations will suffice.

Vital dates of birth and death are useful as comparisons among peer artists. How an artist fits into the time scheme of a movement (for example, as a leader or a follower) and how much (mortal) time he had to make his contributions are additional considerations that may be gleaned from his dates.

Some artists supersede their niches as listed under periods or styles. Their importance and influence have been far greater than particular "isms" or movements. Besides the obvious examples of Picasso and Braque, William Turner, Edouard Manet, Henri Matisse, Vasily Kandinsky, Marcel Duchamp, Jackson Pollock, David Smith, Robert Rauschenberg, and Jasper Johns have each had an enormous impact on subsequent developments in the visual arts.

Viewing just one or two examples of an artist's work can be misleading. Understanding the essential components of his legacy and the role his work has had in the larger scheme of history is far more complicated than a couple of examples can ever suggest. Those two art works may only represent a few days in the lifetime production of that artist, which in some cases may exceed 50, 60, or even 70 years. Make an effort to examine a body of work by an artist before you claim an understanding of his contribution or an appreciation of his aesthetic qualities.

In the category of Abstraction, I have listed only the founders of nonobjective art that developed in the early 1900s. These artists spawned a virtual flood of abstract styles that have thrived in all subsequent periods and into the present day. With the onset of Abstract Expressionism, artists in nearly every category afterward have practiced or now practice some form of abstract or nonobjective art. Abstraction has become an institution, a language of its own form and content, and will always have practitioners.

One of the most important and practical points to take from art history, which these timelines illustrate, is how the burgeoning accumulation of styles (especially since Modernism) continuously expands the definition and the boundaries of art. Since styles do not go out of fashion (or if they do, their ideas do not), the benefits to artists are incalculable. The most courageous and creative artists have and will always resurrect new possibilities out of the ashes of seemingly spent art movements. It is just one of various reasons you need to know art history.

The modern and contemporary timelines have more emphasis and detail because the artists and movements since the Industrial Revolution have a more direct impact on your development. I have included brief summaries of most styles starting with the "isms" of modernism. These may serve as quick reference, but they are only that. What you discover in your art history courses or through your own research will be more comprehensive. Think of these descriptions as signposts to point you in a chosen direction.

ANCIENT	NEAR EASTERN	9,000-500 B.C.
ANCIENT	EGYPTIAN	3,000-500 B.C.
ANCIENT	GREEK	800-100 B.C.
ANCIENT	ROMAN	500 B.C.-395 A.D.
EARLY CHRISTIAN		200-500 A.D.
BYZANTINE		500-1450
MEDIEVAL		600-1100
ROMANESQUE		1000-1100
GOTHIC		1150-1450

EARLY RENAISSANCE 1400-1450

Giotto (1266-1337)   Donatello (1386-1466)
Masaccio (1401-1428)   Jan van Eyck (ca.1396-1441)
Filippo Brunelleschi (1337-1446)   Leon Battista Alberti (1406-1472)
Andrea Mantegna (1430-1506)   Piero della Francesca (1412-1492)

HIGH RENAISSANCE 1490-1600

Botticelli (1445-1510)   Leonardo da Vinci (1452-1519)
Raphael (1483-1520)   Tintoretto (1518-1594)
Michelangelo (1475-1564)   Titian (1488-1576)
Pieter Brueghel (active 1551-1569)
El Greco (1541-1614)   Giorgione (1478-1510)
Albrecht Durer (1471-1528)   Giovanni Bellini (1430-1516)

MANNERISM (OFFSHOOT OF THE HIGH RENAISSANCE) 1520-1600

Agnolo Bronzino (1503-1572)   Parmigianino (1503-1540)
Jacopo da Pontormo (1494-1556)

BAROQUE 1600-1750

Peter Paul Rubens (1577-1640)   Frans Hals (1580-1666)
Caravaggio (1573-1610)   Jan Vermeer (1632-1675)
Diego Velazquez (1599-1660)   Rembrandt (1606--1669)
Nicolas Poussin (1594-1665)   Jean-Baptiste-Simeon Chardin (1699-1779)

ROCOCO 1700-1800

Jean-Antoine Watteau (1684-1721)   Jean-Honore Fragonard (1732-1806)

MODERN ART 1750-1970

ROMANTICISM 1750-1850

Romanticism was not an organized movement with a consistent style, but more a diffusion of individual styles that rejected the old order of the aristocracy and the excesses of the Rococo. These artists also rejected ancient classical forms including mythological narratives and symbols of imperial ambition.

The Romantics favored subjects drawn from the imagination that provided escape from the dry rationalism of the Enlightenment and the increasingly gritty realities of Europe's burgeoning cities. Romanticism may be thought of as a kind of wish fulfillment in a time of rapid industrial change and social upheaval.

Driven by the anxiety of an age of great uncertainties, these artists sought consolation through spirituality, individual expression, and personal sentiment. They are especially modern in the sense that felt experience became the creative force for making art rather than external appearance.

William Blake (1757-1827)   Pierre Puvis de Chavannes (1824-1898)
William Turner (1775-1851)   Francisco Goya (1746-1828)
Eugene Delacroix (1798-1863)

NEO-CLASSICISM 1770-1840

Time ran out for the sensual follies of the Rococo when national politics began to overturn monarchies in favor of more democratic civilities. The French needed a new expression to reflect the revolutionary experiments they passionately and courageously undertook. Classical art, especially that of ancient Greek (remember, the cradle of democracy), untainted by religiosity or authoritarian power, provided suitable heroic subjects for the periods' emerging democratic ideals.

There may be a contradiction in the period's embrace of ancient art to express the revolutionary spirit of radical regime change. New art might seem more in order to reflect great upheaval. Perhaps symbolism at such a time is more important than art. In any event, Neo-Classicism's tendency toward moralizing optimism and political propaganda was balanced at the same time by the brooding and extravagant melodramas of Romanticism.

Jean Auguste Dominique Ingres (1781-1867)   Jacques Louis David (1748-1825)

REALISM 1840-1875

Gustave Courbet was nearly a one-man art movement in casting out the urbane niceties of official academic art and introducing a new genre of subject matter that reflected the growing power of an emerging bourgeois (middle class) society. The man in the street, the worker in the field, and the woman doing laundry replaced the old aristocratic and religious subjects.

Realism in this sense refers more to the radical reconsideration of what makes suitable subject matter in art than to the technical or formal manner of how to represent those subjects. At the same time, direct observation from nature rather than the traditional practice of painting in the studio from memory was a critical new precept. Painting on site, that is, working directly before the subject, became a nineteenth century innovation culminating in the work of the Impressionists.

The switch to scenes of everyday life was an inevitable consequence of the political struggles that beleaguered France from the inception of her revolution in the 1790s until its resolution well into the mid-1800s. To our modern consciousness, it seems unthinkable to imagine a time when the subject matter of ordinary people and ordinary surroundings would have been unacceptable. All of art since Courbet is based on the subjects of its own time and place. What seemed so unnatural then, we take for granted now.

Gustave Courbet (1819-1877)   Camille Corot (1796-1875)
Honore Daumier (1808-1879)   Edouard Manet (1832-1883)
Jean Francois Millet (1814-1875)

IMPRESSIONISM 1870-1886

In one sense, the Impressionists took Courbet's Realism to its zenith. They painted the ordinary moment in time and its transitory effects of light and color as if their lives depended on it. They were the painters par excellence of working on site. Because these artists worked quickly to capture the necessary effects before the light changed by spreading their paint spontaneously and expressively, Impressionist paintings retain the immediacy of their making and subject, and as a result still look fresh and vibrant to our contemporary gaze.

While they continued to focus on their everyday surroundings, the Impressionists turned up the volume on color as they saw it in the brilliance of sunlight. Instead of mixing colors on a palette, they placed innumerable small dabs or short strokes of pigment as adjacent primary colors so that the eye would optically mix them from a distance. Impressionist paintings have the uncanny attribute of looking crusty and unfocused at close range but perfectly seamless and comprehensible from afar.

Because of the immediacy of response demanded by the Impressionist idea, paint was applied in thicker, rougher patches than ever before in the history of art. Though Courbet really pioneered this impasto technique, the Impressionists made it a trademark. The nature of paint as a visual force, that is, colored pigment as a material form and texture with its own artistic interest, was an innovation of this style that has been retained in painting into the present day.

Claude Monet (1840-1926)   Camille Pissarro (1830-1903)
Auguste Renoir (1841-1919)   Edgar Degas (1834-1917)

POST-IMPRESSIONISM 1886-1900

Post-Impressionism was not a unified style but a period of individual reactions to Impressionism. These artists felt that Impressionism had become too diffused and formless, too dependent on superficial atmosphere and insubstantial effects. They made important contributions that would become the vocabulary for radical innovations in the early twentieth century.

Georges Seurat nailed down darks and lights as if they were palpable forms by means of a carefully crafted dot technique called Pointillism. His rational and deliberate methods were in sharp contrast to Impressionist spontaneity. In fact, the mechanical texture of his points of paint look disarmingly like the later Ben-day dots of twentieth century newspaper photographs. In contrast, Paul Gauguin took his cues from the flat color shapes and incisive contour lines of Japanese prints to make his images more defined, simplified, and dramatic. At the same time, Van Gogh took the immediacy of emotion and passion and painted the French landscape as psychic melodrama that became a model for the Fauves and German Expressionists. With his south of France landscape and still life motifs, Paul Cezanne—easily the most influential artist of the nineteenth century and the one with the greatest impact on the twentieth century—remade the transitory effects of Impressionism into a new framework of solidity, mass, and volume, but all within the concrete reality of the picture plane. Later, Picasso took these formal lessons and pushed them to their limits in the Cubist revolution that followed in 1908.

Georges Seurat (1859-1891)   Paul Cezanne (1839-1906)
Paul Gauguin (1843-1903)   Vincent van Gogh (1853-1890)
Odilon Redon (1840-1916)   James Ensor (1860-1949)
Edvard Munch (1863-1944)   Pierre Bonnard (1867-1947)

FAUVISM 1905-1910

In the 1890s, one could hardly imagine canvases more liberated in color than those of Impressionism. Henri Matisse led a movement quickly tagged Fauvism (Fauve = wild beast) and did just that—wielded brilliant and raggedly applied color that was as fully charged and saturated as paint allowed. Colors were chosen for their highly expressive purposes and not for the local colors seen in nature. This is a movement that put a premium on subjective impulses and intuitive responses. Fauvism is the first movement in the twentieth century to stress the importance of inward expression. Feeling is greater than the eye.

Henri Matisse (1869-1954)   Andre Derain (1880-1954)
Maurice de Vlaminck (1876-1958)

CUBISM 1908-1920

I have said much about Cubism in the art history chapter, so this is a nutshell. Cubist invention depended on the influences of Cezanne and African sculpture—seemingly random and different choices but united in their emphasis on strongly defined structure and simplified forms. For Picasso and Braque, these models became tools to develop a new way of looking (quite literally) in response to a world radically and rapidly transformed by scientific advances and industrial development.

In one fell swoop (not quite, it took some years to be understood), Cubism destroyed the 500-year-old Renaissance window of single, fixed-point perspective and replaced it with simultaneously shifting viewpoints that reflected the physical experience of looking (we walk around in our world) and not just the optical. Cubism's multifaceted precepts have reached into every corner of the arts, culture, and society to forever change the way we see and understand it.

Pablo Picasso (1881-1973)   Georges Braque (1882-1963)
Fernand Leger (1881-1955)   Juan Gris (1887-1927)
Robert Delaunay (1885-1941)

FUTURISM 1910-1918

Futurism is essentially the Italian version of French Cubism. These artists wrote their own high-handed manifesto and insisted that they would embrace everything new, industrial, and aggressive in spirit. They were especially preoccupied with time, speed, and the possibility that war (close at hand with World War I in 1914) would clear the decks of the old, outmoded order and replace it with the exciting optimism of a new technologically driven world. Whether the Futurists' enthusiasm was naïve, tongue-in-cheek, or deliberately nose thumping matters less than their conscious effort to renew art making and finally supersede the all-too-evident Renaissance heritage that seemed to restrain their beloved Italy.

Giacomo Balla (1871-1958)   Umberto Boccioni (1882-1916)
Gino Severini (1883-1966)   Carlo Carra (1881-1966)

GERMAN EXPRESSIONISM 1912-1920

Disenchanted with the direction of European civilization—with its moral restraints, corrupt politics, consumer excesses, urban congestion, and industrial intrusion on the landscape (sound familiar?)—several groups of German painters in major cities responded with an outpouring of emotional turbulence. They were the first social protest painters of the twentieth century. Their impulsive and urgently painted canvases described the period's yearning for simpler, freer, and more humane lifestyles. The movement's messages and aspirations anticipated the arrival of World War I. If this sounds a bit like the ideals of the American counterculture of the 1960s, there may be similar lessons and parallels indeed.

Ernst Kirchner (1880-1938)   Emil Nolde (1867-1956)
Max Beckmann (1884-1950)   Franz Marc (1880-1916)
Georges Grosz (1893-1959)   Oskar Kokoschka (1886-1980)
Kathe Kollwitz (1867-1945)   Kurt Schwitters (1887-1948)
(Founders of)

ABSTRACTION 1913-PRESENT

Mondrian said that Picasso could not accept the logical consequences of Cubism—abstraction. However, it was Kandinsky who first proposed the idea of a subject matter-free art. One day when entering his studio, he was struck by the immediate beauty and impact of one of his own paintings leaning upside down against the wall—and at a glimpse looking unrecognizable in both subject and style. After two more years of careful study, studio experimentation and voluminous writing, Kandinsky finally made one of the first abstract pictures, a watercolor in 1913. He laid the foundation for developing abstract art as a new language of color and form that could be at once epic, thrilling, complex, and complete as a visual experience without the props of representational subjects.

Recently rediscovered, the art of Hilma af Klint has challenged the traditional belief that Kandinsky painted the first abstract picture. Her abstractions were painted as early as 1905. Whoever was first is less important than the expansion for the future of art that abstraction provoked. After these pioneers carved out a vast mine of new possibilities for art, painting and sculpture would never be the same.

Vasily Kandinsky (1866-1944)   Piet Mondrian (1872-1944)
Kasimir Malevich (1878-1935)   Hilma af Klint (1862-1944)

DADA AND SURREALISM 1918-1930S

Dada was, in a word, antiart, a social protest that immediately followed the horrors of World War I. Its practice began in the nightclubs and cafes of neutral Switzerland and took the form of mixed media, including poems, verses, songs, and performances (in addition to the traditional painting and sculpture). Daring, risk, chance, and experiment were its calling cards.

But Dada was a warm-up exercise for the main event. Surrealism followed in more organized fashion in Paris in the 1920s with poet leader Andre Breton and his written manifesto. Freud's theories about dreams and the unconscious and the idiosyncratic paintings of Giorgio de Chirico are the great influences of this movement devoted to the visibility of dreams, nightmares, and fantasies. An argument can be made that the invention of collage a decade before, with its unlikely juxtapositions of materials and images, is an important forerunner to the Surrealist impulse—put two or more items together that do not belong and let the sparks fly. Since its beginning, Surrealism's footprints have trod everywhere in the arts and popular culture.

Giorgio de Chirico (1888-1978) forerunner   Salvador Dali (1904-1989)
Max Ernst (1891-1976) Joan Miro (1893-1983) Rene Magritte (1898-1967)

MODERN UNCLASSIFIABLE EARLY TO MID-TWENTIETH CENTURY

Paul Klee (1879-1940)   Egon Schiele (1890-1918)
Gustav Klimt (1862-1918)   Julio Gonzalez (1876-1942)
Francis Picabia (1879-1953)   Constantin Brancusi (1876-1957)

Marcel Duchamp (1887-1968)   Henry Moore (1898-1986)
Amedeo Modigliani (1884-1920)   Alberto Giacometti (1901-1966)

EARLY-TWENTIETH-CENTURY AMERICAN

These artists applied the lessons of European modernism but forged an art especially unique to American experience. Often, they reinvented Cubism, Fauvism, Expressionism, Surrealism, and abstraction to suit their circumstances.

John Marin (1870-1953)   Edward Hopper (1882-1967)
Milton Avery (1893-1965)   Charles Sheeler (1883-1967)
Alexander Calder (1898-1976)   Marsden Hartley (1877-1948)
Stuart Davis (1894-1964)   Arthur Dove (1880-1946)
Georgia O'Keeffe (1887-1986)   Charles Demuth (1883-1935)
Joseph Albers (1888-1976)   Charles Burchfield (1893-1967)

ABSTRACT EXPRESSIONISM AND NEW YORK SCHOOL 1945-1960

Abstract Expressionism (or AE as it is sometimes abbreviated) is the first style of the New American Century that coincided with the emigration to the US of many European refugee artists as a consequence of World War II. Take the pioneers of abstraction, meld with the German Expressionists, add a dash of early Kandinsky, and put all into a pot of subjective feeling expressed in spontaneous and urgent outpourings of paint on big canvases and you have American Abstract Expressionism.

Jackson Pollock took the canvas off the easel, put it on the floor, and made the act of painting the virtual subject of art. The influence his work had on scale (how big can art be?), installation and performance art, mixed media, and all the painting that has followed is incalculable.

Jackson Pollock (1912-1956)   Willem de Kooning (1904-1997)
Hans Hoffman (1880-1966)   Philip Guston (1913-1980)
Arshile Gorky (1904-1948)   Barnett Newman (1905-1970)
Ad Reinhardt (1913-1967)   Mark Rothko (1903-1970)
Joan Mitchell (1926-1992)   Romare Bearden (1914-1988)
Robert Motherwell (1915-1991)

PRE-POP ART

Johns and Rauschenberg are artists who bridged AE and Pop since they reintroduced representational subject matter and mixed media into art. Ironically, both continued the brushy gestures of AE but tied them more specifically to imagery that reflected a more gregarious culture. They dared to dip their art into the real world and so inspired the Pop artists who quickly followed.

Jasper Johns b.1930   Robert Rauschenberg (1925-2008)

POP ART 1960-1970

Fed up with the private meanderings and insular navel gazing of the AEs, the Pop artists wanted to rub shoulders with the growing clamor and vibrancy of popular culture and commercial advertising. This is art that gets real with the tangibility of consumer objects, pop icons, and artifacts of a society in love with brand names and celebrities. Warhol's riffs on coke bottles and soup cans and Lichtenstein's reinvention of the comic strip as a major pictorial style are now legendary. Whether their subtle social critiques of American culture register with meaning depends on the sophistication of art viewers.

Andy Warhol (1928-1987)   Roy Lichtenstein (1923-1997)
George Segal (1924-2000)   Claes Oldenburg b.1929
James Rosenquist b.1933   Tom Wesselmann (1931-2004)

MINIMALISM 1970s

These artists wanted no more crass commercialism or messy angst. This is art as industrial object. Leave the hand out, make it clean and clinical. Their philosophy is "less is more." Simple can be "Wow"!
Don Judd (1928-1994)   Carl Andre b.1935
Ellsworth Kelly (1923-2015)   Dan Flavin (1933-1996)

COLOR FIELD AND HARD EDGE ABSTRACTION 1960-1970s

These artists extended AE but with more charm, unabashed color, and optimism. Painting can be a bag of tricks, treats, and sleights of hand. Many of these practitioners turned painting inside out and showed technical finesses with the flow of paint or the edges of tape that would have been unthinkable previously.

Helen Frankenthaler (1928-2011)   Morris Louis (1912-1962)
Al Held (1928-2005)   Ken Noland (1924-2010)
Jules Olitski (1922-2007)   Bridget Riley b.1931

NEO-EXPRESSIONISM 1980s

Was this 1980s flare-up of paint flinging the last hurrah of painting? Or was it a pastiche of much that preceded it, especially German Expressionism? Maybe or maybe not, but if you peruse the work of these and other painters of the decade, you cannot but be ravished by some of their glorious confections.

David Salle b.1952
Julian Schnabel b.1951
Jean-Michel Basquiat (1960-1988)

Georg Baselitz b.1938
Anselm Kiefer b.1945
Sandro Chia b.1946

TWENTIETH-CENTURY AND CONTEMPORARY SCULPTURE

Joseph Cornell (1903-1972)
Louise Bourgeois (1911-2011)
Christo (1935-2020)
H. C. Westermann (1922-1981)
Andy Goldsworthy b.1956
Kenneth Price (1935-2012)
Eva Hesse (1936-1970)
Lee Bontecou b.1931
Tom Otterness b.1952
Alice Aycock b.1946

David Smith (1906-1965)
Isamu Noguchi (1904-1988)
Anthony Caro (1924-2013)
Jeff Koons b.1955
Richard Serra b.1939
Martin Puryear b.1941
Judy Pfaff b.1946
Tony Cragg b.1949
Louise Nevelson (1889-1988)
Mel Kendrick b.1949

TWENTIETH-CENTURY AND CONTEMPORARY PAINTING AND MIXED MEDIA

Balthus (1908-2001)
Richard Diebenkorn (1922-1993)
Frank Stella b.1936
Lucas Samaras b.1936
Lucian Freud (1922-2011)
Gerhard Richter b.1932
Joseph Beuys (1921-1986)
Vito Acconci b.1940
Bill Jensen b.1945
Lari Pittman b.1952
Philip Taaffe b.1955
Carroll Dunham b.1949
Cecily Brown b.1969
Agnes Martin (1912-2004)
David Hockney b.1937
Sigmar Polke b.1941
Philip Pearlstein B.1924
Neo Rauch b.1960
Takashi Murakami b.1962
Bill Viola b.1951
Allan Kaprow (1927-2006)
Malcolm Morley (1931-2018)

R. B. Kitaj (1932-2007)
Elizabeth Murray (1940-2007)
Jim Dine b.1935
William T. Wiley (1937-2021)
Cy Twombley (1929-2011)
Bridget Riley b.1931
Bruce Nauman b.1941
Jennifer Bartlett b.1941
Eric Fischl b.1948
Terry Winters b.1949
Barbara Kruger b.1945
Matthew Ritchie b.1964
Sol LeWitt (1928-2007)
Francesco Clemente b.1952
Frank Auerbach b. 1931
George Condo b.1957
Howard Hodgkin (1932-2017)
Saul Steinberg (1914-1999)
Julie Mehretu b.1970
Richard Tuttle b.1941
Susan Rothenberg (1945-2020)
Nancy Graves (1939-1995)

TWENTIETH-CENTURY AND CONTEMPORARY PHOTOGRAPHY

Eugene Atget (1857-1927)
Walker Evans (1903-1975)
Henri Cartier-Bresson (1908-2004)
Andre Kertesz (1894-1985)
Cindy Sherman b.1954
John Baldesaari b.1931
Andreas Gursky b.1955
Sandy Skoglund b.1946

Alfred Stieglitz (1864-1946)
August Sander (1876-1964)
Man Ray (1890-1976)
Diane Arbus (1923-1971)
Lee Friedlander b.1934
William Eggleston b.1939
Gregory Crewdson b.1962

MODERN AFRICAN AMERICAN

African American artists have belatedly but deservedly gained wider attention in recent years as America considers how to rectify inequalities in our society. On the one hand, it seems arbitrary to list artists according to ethnicity. However, given past neglect and current change in attitudes, it is appropriate to recognize artists who have made outstanding contributions. These black artists span the modern era from the early twentieth century to the present. Each artist represents his or her own achievement without regard to style or chronology. Some artists are considered "outsiders," but so too are many artists of various ethnic backgrounds. The great length of this list is a testament to the depth of achievement black artists have made to the modern canon.

Bill Traylor 1854–1949
Horace Pippin 1888–1946
Alma Thomas 1891–1978
William Hawkins 1895–1990
William Johnson 1901–1970
Norman Lewis 1909–1979
Romare Bearden 1911–1988
Gordon Parks 1912–2006
Elizabeth Catlett 1915–2012
Jacob Lawrence 1917–2000
Robert Colescott 1925–2009
Thaddeus Mosley 1926–
Betye Saar 1926–
Thornton Dial 1928–2016
Faith Ringgold 1930–
Sam Gilliam 1933–
Al Loving 1935–2005
Emma Amos 1937–2020
Mel Edwards 1937–
Bob Thompson 1937–1966

William T. Williams 1942–
David Hammons 1943–
Purvis Young 1943–2016
El Anatsui b. 1944–
Harmony Hammond 1944–
Stanley Whitney 1946–
Bodys Isek Kingelez 1948–2015
Carrie Mae Weems 1953–
Kerry James Marshall 1955–
Nick Cave b. 1959
Jean-Michel Basquiat 1960–1988
Glen Ligon 1960–
Lorna Simpson 1960–
Mark Bradford 1961–
Kara Walker 1969–
Julie Mehretu 1970–
Mickalene Thomas 1971–
Wangechi Mutu 1972–
Theaster Gates 1973–
Amy Sherald 1973–

Jack Whitten 1939–2018
Beverly Buchanan 1940–2015
Martin Puryear 1941–

Trenton Doyle Hancock 1974–
Hank Willis Thomas 1976–
Kehinde Wiley 1977–

WOMEN ARTISTS

Opportunities for women in the arts have arrived late compared to the many centuries of art history. Extremely few female artists practiced with any recognition prior to modernism. The predominating culture with its values and traditions of a given period largely determined gender roles. Biases about women's role in society should not diminish the achievements of artists of the past. Fortunately, the modern era increasingly celebrates the accomplishments of all artists, regardless of gender, race, or creed. What emerging women students should appreciate is that they now practice art in the best of times.

The struggle for equal rights in America began in the early twentieth century with women's suffrage. The last fifty years have been a sea change for women in all spheres of life and in most professions and vocations. Feminism's demands ramped up to high volume in the 1970s and women artists finally began to receive their overdue recognition. Since then, women's contributions to contemporary art have been monumental. Art world plaudits are now nearly equally shared by both genders. In fact, data show that more women than men gain matriculating degrees and enroll in art programs at colleges and universities nationwide. Sociologists may offer rationales as to why that is the case, but the pent up need and desire from centuries of denial must play a role.

Women artists included in previous lists in this chapter are not repeated below. There are so many women modernists and contemporaries that it is only possible to enumerate a partial list. You will find many more women in the arts worthy of mention in your own research and in visits to galleries and museums. There is no attempt to categorize by style, medium, or historical time. Each artist represents her own unique contribution.

Artemisia Gentileschi 1593–1653
Berthe Morisot 1841–1895
Mary Cassatt 1844–1926
Susanne Valadon 1865–1938
Florine Stettheimer 1871–1944
Paula Moderson-Becker 1876–1907
Gabriele Munter 1877–1962
Natalia Goncharova 1881–1962
Agnes Pelton 1881–1961
Alexandra Exter 1882–1949
Sonia Delaunay 1885–1979
Hannah Hoch 1889–1978
Liubov Popova 1889–1924
Anne Ryan 1889–1954

Dorothea Rockburne b. 1932
Joan Semmel b. 1932
Paula Rego b. 1935
Ree Morton 1936–1977
Joan Brown 1938–1990
Janet Fish b. 1938
Nancy Holt 1938–2014
Sylvia Plimack Mangold b. 1938
Judy Chicago b. 1939
Mary Heilmann b. 1940
Joan Snyder b. 1940
Lynda Benglis b. 1941
Jackie Winsor b. 1941
Joyce Kozloff b. 1942

Sophie Tauber-Arp 1889–1943
Hilla von Rebay 1890–1967
Kay Sage 1898–1963
Alice Neel 1900–1984
Isabel Bishop 1902–1988
Barbara Hepworth 1903–1975
Frida Kahlo 1907–1954
Lee Krasner 1908–1984
Helen Lundeberg 1908–1999
Dorothea Tanning 1910–2012
Agnes Martin 1912–2004
Leonora Carrington 1917–2011
Louisa Matthiasdottir 1917–2000
Grace Hartigan 1922–2008
Miriam Schapiro 1923–2015
Nancy Spero 1926–2009
Lois Dodd b.1927
Ida Applebroog b. 1929
Yayoi Kusama b. 1929
Magdalena Abakanowicz b. 1930
Niki de Saint Phalle b. 1930
Marisol Escobar b. 1930
Deborah Remington 1930–2010
Audrey Flack b. 1931

Ursula von Rydingsvard b. 1942
Jan Groover 1943-2012
Annette Messager b. 1943
Mary Miss b. 1944
Valerie Jaudon b. 1945
Susan Rothenberg 1945–2020
Laurie Anderson b. 1947
Deborah Butterfield b. 1949
Jenny Holzer b.1950
Sue Coe b. 1951
Sally Mann b. 1951
Rosemarie Trockel b. 1952
Marlene Dumas b. 1953
Kiki Smith b. 1954
Amy Sillman b. 1955
Kathy Butterly b. 1963
Rachel Whiteread b. 1963
Nicole Eisenman b. 1965
Elizabeth Peyton b. 1965
Cecily Brown b. 1969
Tara Donovan b. 1969
Sarah Sze b. 1969
Jenny Saville b. 1970
Dana Schutz b. 1976

OUTSIDER ARTISTS

Outsider artists, defined as those who have not been formally trained in art, have assumed various, and often unsatisfying, categorical labels in the past. These include primitive art, folk art, naïve art, art brut, and visionary art. Outsider is the term of choice for the present. These artists work from an inner need to express their passions, often those that seem to have no other means of outlet. As a result, outsider art often explodes with an emotional mix of great exuberance, frenetic energy, and obsessive description.

Accepted art principles, traditional styles, and technical norms have little place in outsider art. Imagination for these artists knows no bounds. Their images and objects are often surreal in the best sense of the term. We "connected" artists can learn a great deal about the depths of creativity and the courage to make art on one's own terms from these remarkable art makers of necessity. As with all the lists in *Timeline*, there are many more deserving artists who can be identified than is possible here.

Charles Dellschau 1830–1923
Ferdinand Cheval 1836–1924
Bill Traylor 1854–1949
Adolf Wolfli 1864–1930
Heinrich Anton Muller 1869–1930
Morris Hirshfield 1872–1946
Simon Rodia 1879–1965
Madge Gill 1882–1961
Scottie Wilson 1888–1972
Horace Pippin 1888–1946
Joseph Yoakum 1890–1972
Henry Darger 1892–1973
Friedrich Schroder Sonnenstern 1892–1982
Philadelphia Wireman, name/dates unknown

Minnie Evans 1892–1987
Martin Ramirez 1895–1963
William L. Hawkins 1895–1990
William H. Johnson 1901–1970
Sam Doyle 1906–1985
Anna Zemakova 1908–1986
James Hampton 1909–1964
Gaston Chaissac 1910–1964
Eugene Von Bruenchen 1910–1983
Howard Finster 1916–2001
Thornton Dial 1928–2016
Judith Scott 1943–2005
Purvis Young 1943–2010
Susan Te Kahurangi King b. 1951

THE OUTER SPACE OF PICTORIAL ART

The standard model of Renaissance perspective reigned in painting for over five hundred years. The era saw humanity as the center of a universe filled with the abundance of nature and the growing ascendancy of human-made artifacts and architecture. Horizon level perspective, essentially what the eye sees when one is standing in the landscape, was mathematically based on the precise tenets of two Renaissance architects, Filippo Brunelleschi (1377–1446)) and Leon Battista Alberti (1404–1472). Thus, architects defined pictorial space for painters.

The illusion of deep space on a flat plane acquired a magical resonance for both artists and viewers. The "you are there" sensation put the viewer in seeming reality. That the Catholic Church defined that reality, that is, the persuasion that biblical scripture is historical fact, made perspective all the more significant. Later, with the emerging secular culture of the late Renaissance, perspective became a convincing illusion that pictorial space was a logical, objective equivalent of standing in and observing nature from the spectator's position. It gave visual form to our impressions and memories before the advent of photography.

The Renaissance concept of space became a powerful tool to describe the optical experience of narrative and storytelling. What the eye sees in Renaissance perspective is an implied imitation of nature. Despite its multiple centuries of dominance, perspective had inherent, severe limitations of what the human experience is and can be. Any emotional or expressive qualities had to come from the subject matter rather than from the manner of how it is seen. In other words, the expressive viewpoint of the artist was suppressed in favor of what the subject matter conveyed as content.

THE TRANSITION TO MODERN SPACE

The limitations in viewing the world through the lens of outward perception began to change in the modern period of the mid-nineteenth century. The rapid and proliferating innovations of industry and technology demanded new ways of perceiving and understanding the emerging world.

Furthermore, the accelerating pace of industrial development triggered massive migrations from the open, rural environments of farming to the congested, rapid construction of urban centers. One can enumerate a wide range of nouns to characterize this time: collision, fragmentation, dislocation, frenzy, stress, pollution, blight, poverty, and crime are just a few of the conditions that became more pronounced in the modern age.

Art had to reflect the consequences of proliferating change through a more emotionally responsive expression. Vision had to turn more inward to accommodate the modern sensibility of navigating the uncharted waters of urban industrial civilization. Art making in the nineteenth century was largely a fight between traditional academic rules and expectations and the need to break those rules to find appropriate responses to express the evolving circumstances of modern living. Individual expression became more important than adhering to the previously agreed upon principles of perspective.

THE AERIAL VIEWPOINT

Within a few decades, photography, cinema, flight, the automobile, the telephone, electricity, modern plumbing, and assembly line factories were invented, and Einstein published his theories of space and time. That signifies great cultural upheaval, a heady list of radical innovations, and only a partial list! One of the first artistic attempts to understand the new environment was seeing the world from above in a hot-air balloon or from a tall building, rather than the old tradition of standing firmly planted on the ground at eye level.

Photographers and painters began making pictures as if airborne, perhaps as a way to escape civilized madness or to see it anew. By looking at the world differently, it might be possible to see it that way, that is, distinct from the perspective of the old tradition. If living in modern conditions was already becoming a disorienting experience, why not see the world in its glorious disorientation?

THE ROAD TO FLATNESS

When you look down from a great height, the subject looks flatter and more abstract. In fact, some critics have coined this moment as the beginning of The Road to Flatness. In another way of experimenting with viewpoints, Edgar Degas displaced his subjects away from the center of attention and more toward the edges of the picture. This action led to a radical cropping of figures and objects, as if that physical displacement was also a psychological one. Instead of situating the horizon line at eye level, Degas and other artists tilted the landscape so far upward that the horizon was lifted nearly to the top of the picture or disappeared entirely with greater focus on the subject subsumed by the new flatness of space. In a conceptual sense, this brought the viewer not only closer to the subject but also acknowledged that the picture was a flat plane, now both an illusion and an object itself. This new way of viewing a picture as a flat plane became increasingly an expression of integrity. If the actual surface of a painting or drawing is flat, then it is honest to incorporate that awareness as part of the artistic experience.

JAPANESE PRINTS

In the mid-nineteenth century, Japanese woodblock prints became popular in Europe. They were cheap and were even used as packing material for imported goods. In a different way than European art, the resolute character of Japanese art was a flattening of the subject matter by means of limiting or eliminating the traditional gradations of light and dark values, of highlights and shadows. The woodblock artists also experimented with relating distant objects with foreground objects in a kind of optical acrobatics that brought them closer together as semiabstract forms. Changes in the perception of the modern world were developing in Asia, not just in the Western world. Of course, European artists were pleased to see their own innovations confirmed by other cultures.

PAUL CEZANNE, THE FATHER OF MODERN ART

The art of the great post-Impressionist Paul Cezanne played a key role in this new perception of flatness, of pushing space forward. The chisel-like brushstrokes of Cezanne's canvases strongly implied that the picture plane was itself part of the space of a painting. Since paint had begun to assume a greater materiality in the nineteenth century, coinciding with the invention of the paint tube, it seemed logical to reinforce that physicality on the canvas. Both the physical state of the canvas and the expressive texture of paint expanded the meaning of art. That sensuality of materials continues to broaden and enliven the art of today.

Paul Gauguin was another post-Impressionist to understand the potential of flatness in painting. In contrast to Cezanne, Gauguin emphasized line, contour, and shape. He diminished the effects of light and dark gradations, replacing that with bold, artificial color and well-defined edges between areas to dramatize his subjects. The strong color patterns in his paintings resonate with their spiritual and emotional overtones. Early in his career, Gauguin lamented the overcivilized culture in Europe and his travels to Tahiti put him in touch with both spiritual values and primitive art. He expressed these qualities in a wide variety of media in both two-dimensional (2D) and 3D works of art.

A generation later, Henri Matisse intensified color and pattern to theatrical heights. His deployment of expressive color and insistent patterns flattened space further and provoked a tantalizing ambiguity by designing his subjects in bold abstract forms. Matisse's late collages of painted papers expressed his subject matter as uniquely stylized, cutout shapes (with scissors) of great dramatic power.

CUBIST SPACE

The simplifying of the subject by means of Cezanne's planar strokes, and thus, rendering the subject in more abstract terms, became a rallying point for the Cubists. The fragmentation, repetition, speed, excess, and disorientation in modern life found its apotheosis in the structural inventions that Picasso and Georges Braque developed in Cubism starting in 1908. The Cubists felt that we walk around in our world rather than standing at a fixed point. Thus, a painting must reflect the sensation of moving around, that as you shift your eyes from one place to another on the picture, your viewpoint will also change location in relation to the subject.

The Cubists saw the world tumbling down into the viewer's space, making it more palpable, and thus, more real to experience. They thought of the world as a shallow box or a diorama, not a deep space culminating at the horizon. As a consequence, we might say metaphorically that pictures were now more like looking at walls rather than through windows or keyholes.

As objects were split into a patchwork of differing views with contour lines that did not enclose their forms, the objects began to "leak out" into the surrounding space. Thus, the space around an object and the object itself became more ambiguous and implied a sharing of space. The French called this phenomenon *passage*, that is, the same space passing through and into both objects and background, including near and distant forms. This sensation also reaffirmed the concept of flattening in order to bring subject matter closer to the viewer.

PRIMITVE ART

The Cubists found additional models in primitive art that reaffirmed and extended the concept of flattened forms and simplified planes. Picasso and other artists saw primitive art in the ethnographic displays at the Trocadero museum in Paris. This revelatory discovery prompted Picasso to collect African masks and sculpture. As with Japanese prints, primitive sculpture reaffirmed for artists that the new way of looking at artistic space was appropriate to their modern vision.

Tribal art, consisting mainly of figures and heads, was carved and fabricated with dramatically deformed and simplified facets and angles. These sculptures were not meant to be naturalistic but rather expressive of spiritual and otherworldly qualities. Although their formal means coincided nicely with Cubism's vision of shifting views and reduced description of subject matter, tribal art also appealed to the artists' antibourgeois insistence on realism and visual fact.

The Cubists and the artists who followed were enamored of the idea that one could cobble together fragments and pieces of their world to create new responses to modern culture. They could take what they knew and refashion it according to their imaginations. In short, primitive art inspired artists to tap into a realm of expression beyond traditional Western expectations.

FUTURISM

Around 1911 after a trip to Paris, the Futurists of Italy looked to Cubism to express opposition to the turgid history-laden heritage of their country. They looked to the new inventions of the automobile, racing cars, and the dynamic movement of industrial machines. The invention of the moving picture also inspired their preoccupation with speed. They deployed repetition and pattern to suggest rapid movement. A horse might have tens of legs instead of four, and a car might seem to be a continuous form across a painting with multitudes of tires and parts suggesting forward motion. These repeating lines and patterned devices are similar to the formal techniques rendered in comic strips.

CHAPTER 25

The overall effect of expressing speed through repetition made the object and background interchangeable. A speeding car or galloping horse seemed to sweep the surrounding space into itself. Thus, in a different way from the Cubists, the Futurists found a way to collapse space between near and far so that both seem to occupy the same planes. The Futurist painters found another way to express flatness and *passage*.

THE ARTIST AS SPACE INVADER

The reinvention of space in the modern era was not simply wrought by a host of exterior influences. The artist in his quest to reflect the relevance of his experience is the real driver. He must disregard convention and traditional expectations in order to respond to the constantly evolving conditions of modern civilization. He is an inventor as much as any industrialist or scientist. With little precedent for guidance in understanding the maddening pace of development in modern civilization, the artist must go out on a limb, experiment how to express what those changes mean. That path has a better chance of capturing his time and place.

Finally, the takeaway point is that space in picture making since the Renaissance has undergone radical innovation, enormous expansion, and has been portrayed with great richness of expression. Space is the place where art resides. This artistic revolution has been as complicated in its relentless growth and development as the last two hundred years of industrial and technological modernism have been.

The earlier description is by necessity only a brief summary of what the possibilities are for retooling space in pictures. Appreciate this artistic heritage. Get to know it by investigation and research. Then, apply what you know to what every art student and artist must do for themselves. Immerse yourself in understanding how art has changed the orientation of viewpoint, what the character of your time and place implies for art making, and how to express that in a personal and meaningful way.

SECTION VI

PUTTING IT ALTOGETHER
(OR, GETTING THE HANG OF IT)

chapter

THE PORTFOLIO

An art portfolio is a body of work completed during a given period of time, from a few weeks to several years. Depending on goals and purposes, individual works in the collection may be closely related, as in a series, or may represent a variety of subjects, styles, and media. An undergraduate portfolio should be a combination of variety and focus that reflects both the acquisition of skills and fundamentals and the development of ideas or themes into a series.

The number of works in a portfolio is somewhat arbitrary but should be ample enough to permit meaningful comparison and contrast among individual works. A student portfolio typically ranges from a minimum of ten to twenty or more art works. Ultimately, the number is determined by purpose and circumstances. These may include the course objectives of a college art program, the goals of an independent study, the requirements for submission to a college admissions process or employment interview, and that which best represents the artist in grant applications and in competitions.

One major concern in the first two years of college is constructing the best collection of work possible to prepare for the admissions process when the time is appropriate for transfer. If you are an entering student, you may not yet have had sufficient opportunity to develop a portfolio or you may have a portfolio from your high school art program or from your own previous initiatives. Whatever the case, you are likely to have made some work in the recent past that helped you decide to become an art major. What counts is the new work you make in your entry-level college art courses. Now you are in the major leagues. This time and effort will determine whether you have a future in an art career—in particular, whether you have the ability to sustain your interest and curiosity in the visual world.

A portfolio is always a work in progress, one that reflects the changes of past, present, and future accomplishments. This evolution is true for students and professionals alike. All artists believe (as they should) that their work will increase in quality with time and practice. This self-confidence is a necessary attribute that motivates the artist to produce work. With each success (and failure, because you learn so much from mistakes), you get smarter and more assertive. But making art is also humbling. What you produced last year or in the previous semester may have seemed impressive then, but what you are doing in the present is likely to exceed the merits of any past work. In fact, what you do now should be greater by leaps and bounds. Thus, the portfolio must be frequently updated to reflect new levels of skill and achievement.

However, here's a gentle admonition. I'd like to offer hindsight from my own experience as a student. Do not throw away any of your work regardless of how you or others value its quality! While the art does not change, your mind will, as you continuously gather new insights and develop greater sophistication. There is the considerable possibility that you may misjudge something as inferior when, in fact, it may be the opposite. Furthermore, flawed or problematic art may still represent a significant breakthrough or indicate a new direction—in which case the work is an important personal reference. Check with your professors before disposing of any masterpieces!

So, keep your mistakes—at least until you have had the perspective of time. They are important object lessons. You learn more from them than from your successes. There are any number of artworks I wish had saved from my student days or from the years shortly thereafter that were lost to carelessness or the judgment that they were undeserving.

WHAT MAKES A SUPERIOR PORTFOLIO?

A good undergraduate portfolio should include a range of important characteristics. These are criteria that I have developed through teaching and gleaned from what I know about other college art departments and from various art professionals. You may want to spread the contents of your portfolio on the floor or along a wall as you consider these points. Your work should demonstrate:
- Competence in the fundamentals of formalism and composition.
- The ability to render from life, as from directly observed still life, human model, and landscape. Include several examples from each category.
- Mastery of technical skills in various media. These include facility with the major drawing media of graphite, charcoal, pastel, ink, and watercolor, and with easel painting the traditional oils or acrylics.
- Evidence of creative problem solving and the development of originality. These core abilities reflect invention and imagination in the deployment of ideas, themes, and subjects.
- Versatility in the manipulation of materials, subjects, and styles.
- A willingness to experiment and take risks. Art is more proposal than proof.
- Commitment, diligence, and a capacity for work.
- In-depth investigation of form and content through a series or a sequence. The ability to find meaningful variations despite imposed limitations is the height of creativity.
- An awareness of art history, especially movements and tendencies in modern and contemporary art.
- Evidence of cultural, social, and historical relevance—that is, a connection to one's time and place.
- Expression of mood, feeling, tone, or atmosphere. Whatever the subject, your work should evoke the feeling you have for the art making process.
- Good craftsmanship. An object (whether a canvas, a sculpture, or a simple sheet of paper) should be well made and constructed with care. The worthiness of art often depends on the manner of how the work is put together. Good craft clarifies art content.
- Consistent competence across the entire production. Everyone has strengths and weaknesses, but you want to minimize the weaknesses so they do not distract.

- Evidence of work created outside class assignments. Some of your work should be self-initiated and reflect personal choices in style and content.
- The potential for further growth and development. This may be the most difficult criterion to evaluate because it suggests what is not there yet. However, diligent, inventive work of integrity usually provokes an informed viewer to imagine what rich possibilities or worthy directions might follow.

This is not an exhaustive list but covers the essentials you are likely to need for a successful collection of work. Daunting? Give yourself time to work and room to develop. When you are working on a project, you will not need to think about these criteria. When you are selecting and organizing your portfolio, when you stop to reflect on what you are doing, these guidelines will be helpful.

PRESENTATION: CLEANING HOUSE

In addition, the portfolio's physical organization matters greatly since its condition may either detract from or enhance the artworks contained. Since careless presentation should not overshadow the merits of your work, please observe these practical suggestions:

- Work should be clean and well maintained. Remove smudges and stray marks with an eraser. What cannot be removed with an eraser may be carefully covered with white paint that matches the color of the paper or ground—as long as the touching up is not more intrusive than the unwanted marks.
- Spray fixative to a sufficient degree to avoid smears and abrasions on all work containing charcoal, conte crayon, and pastel. Two or more coats are often required. Spot check after spraying by lightly passing a fingertip across key surfaces. If your finger picks up material, spray again.
- Do not include badly damaged works, such as those with prominent tears, folds, or pieces missing. Minor repairs to tears or small holes in works on paper can be made from the reverse side with carefully glued patches of the same or similar paper.
- Do not include unfinished art. The viewer's assumption may be that you tend not to follow through or lack the capacity to work.
- Do not wrap work in plastic, place in clear sleeves, or cover with glass and frames. The reflections from gloss and the extra material and weight are distracting and cumbersome.
- If possible, do not include works on newsprint, which damages easily, deteriorates quickly, and may imply an overly casual attitude.
- Matting is not recommended for portfolios unless specifically required by application guidelines. If you do mat your work, be sure mats are accurately cut and constructed in the professional manner of a window hinged to a mounting board. Mats must be only in white or off-white boards (no black or color). For more information, see Chapter 23, *Presentation: Mats and Frames.*
- *Do include* these works that are often overlooked: gesture drawings, sketchbooks, and preliminary studies. All of these formats reveal a desirable thinking process about your creative intentions. Sometimes, their freshness of execution and unpretentious quality can exceed a more finished work of art. Include a sketchbook if at least half or more of the pages are filled. Anything less looks like you were not sufficiently engaged.
- The portfolio cover, whether a deluxe embossed vinyl model with zippers and handles or the commonplace paper envelope, must be in good condition and free of extraneous debris, such as art supplies, blank paper pads, or drawing paper. However, an acceptable practice is to separate works with single sheets of

paper to keep the artworks clean and free from sticking to one another. If you do so, make all the sheets the same kind of paper that conform in size to each other and to the artworks to the extent possible. Too many variables in the contents can be annoying to handle.

Your portfolio is the measure of your success in art making at any given time. It represents the degree of your ambition, sophistication, and mastery of form, media, and content. At the same time, a good portfolio is a place to mine, a research center for assessing your potential for new possibilities and directions. If you are adept at "listening" to its cues, any of the contents of your portfolio can be the springboard for developing new art—and eventually a new body of work. Take advantage of your own resources!

As an important personal instrument, look at your art collection frequently. Pay attention to it. Live with your work. It will help you know where you want to go. The portfolio is your visual autobiography, and a peek at who you are likely to become as an artist.

chapter

PRESENTATION: MATS AND FRAMES

Presentation of art for display and exhibition is an art in itself. As the optimal platform for separating art from the surrounding world, presentation is crucial to a clear and satisfying viewing experience. A bad mat and frame can easily degrade an otherwise good work, but a good mat and frame cannot save a bad work of art. While it cannot improve quality, presentation can enhance whatever positive qualities a work has. If art is drama in form and content, then matting and framing is its opening curtain.

What are mats? A mat is a panel—usually rigid heavyweight paperboard designed for the purpose—that surrounds a two-dimensional artwork to make a border between the image and the outer frame, to protect the art from damage and to concentrate the viewer's observation by eliminating distractions. The idea is to provide a neutral, inconspicuous setting so that the art becomes the primary focus of attention. Mats may also serve the distinction of making the art seem more important, especially in the case of a small work of art in a large mat with generously wide borders. In short, enhancement without interference is the key.

Frames are molded strips of rigid, permanent material (usually wood or metal) that are placed directly around a canvas, painted panel, or matted artwork fitted with glass. Not all works of art need mats and frames, but a general rule of thumb is that works on paper installed for exhibition need to be in mats and under glass, fastened directly to the wall or held together by framing. Like mats, frames—especially those that are wide or elaborately decorative—can make smaller art works seem more important.

The aesthetics of framing tend to vary with the cultural values of the times. Look around in museums. Old master paintings from the Renaissance, Baroque, and nineteenth century periods tend to be housed in heavy and highly decorative frames—a little excessive and fussy for our modern tastes. By contrast, some contemporary paintings may require no framing or just a simple framing of strip lattice. Since the late twentieth century, most paintings are canvases that are stapled on the back, so that the edges are seen as clean and presentable. On the other hand, some artists today (myself included) place gilded or highly decorative frames on their works in order to create a deliberate formal interaction between frame and art. Or more extreme, they may design and execute the frame as part of the work of art so that frame and image become one. Logically, these are called artists' frames.

Thus, framing and presentation choices have a considerable degree of subjectivity due to differences of taste among historical periods, styles, and artists' intentions. Nonetheless, guidelines are useful in the contemporary world to help you make the best presentation for your work. The art, the mat, and the frame all have their own formal properties that must be taken into account and that relate to each other compositionally to make a coherent visual statement. For example, the mat's proportions to the work and the frame are critical variables. Borders that are too wide and excessive can make the art seem lost in its space, while narrow, stingy borders can make the art feel squeezed and awkward. Poorly chosen frames can diminish or overpower in similar ways. Therefore, some rules apply!

Mats and frames can be independent of each other—that is, one can function without the other. However, mats are a primary concern for us. First, any mat must be *neutral* to the artwork—especially with respect to color. It is more accurate and emphatic to say that colored mats are almost always bad. No good. Period. I am able to offer a definitive rule in art so rarely, but this is one. Yes, I know you may see colored mats across the spectrum in frame shops and local galleries. But general usage, whether to a greater or lesser degree, does not make it a good practice. In the best galleries, museums, and among artist professionals you do not see red, yellow, and blue mats—or green, purple, and black.

The rationale for using only white, off-white, or occasionally soft gray mats is that virtually all other colors interact with the colors and the light/dark values in the art. Why is this wrong? Because the color/value interactions between a colored mat and a work of art become active in the composition and a significant intrusion *not* intended by the artist. Colored mats effectively *change* the art *after* the artist has declared his work complete. Imagine a delicate pen line drawing of a still life or landscape executed with fine lines, marks, and textures in black India ink. The visibility and drama of these fragile lines depend on their high contrast to the white spaces left in the paper. A black mat with a 3-inch border surrounds the image. Suddenly the nuanced subtleties of the pen lines are drowned, overwhelmed by the heavy-handedness and foreboding darkness the mat imposes by its ocean of black surface area. It is like turning the lights out on the image. Instead of being hammered into submission by colors and forms that compete with it, the art must be quietly and clearly presented so that its aesthetic qualities can flourish on their own terms and without interference.

HOW TO MAKE A MAT

When you are ready to mat a picture, consider whether the image looks better against a white or off-white background. Mat boards are generally available whereby both sides are finished, one white, one off-white. You can place your art directly on a sheet of uncut mat board to make a judgment. The white side usually looks cool in temperature while the off-white looks creamy or warm. Decide which enhances your work more without diminishing its artistic qualities. See illustration at the end of this chapter regarding the following directions.

Next, take strips of white paper of varying widths that might approximate the width of your borders and place them around the image on all four sides. A rough guideline is that most images look appropriate in a mat of 3 inches in width. Greater or lesser borders can be considered with individual images and whether the work will be placed in a frame with glass. Usually any border less than 2 inches will look confining and skimpy. Some small images benefit by much wider borders of 5 or more inches. It is acceptable to make the bottom border wider than the sides or top, but never narrower. With experience, you will feel increasingly clear about your judgments of border proportions.

A mat is essentially a window with an inner edge that defines the rectangle of the opening for the art and an outer edge defining its overall size. You have two choices about how to relate the inner edges of the window to the art. If the art covers the entire surface of the sheet, you must "float" the paper so that there is 1/8 to 1/4 inch of space between it and the mat. Never overlap the art with the mat even by a fraction of an inch. When the mat crops the art, you are changing the composition. If the image stops from the edge of the paper, at least 1/4 of an inch, you can crop the mat over that margin—that is, conceal the untouched edge of the sheet with the mat. If the margin is a 1/2 inch or more, you can also choose to leave some of the untouched margin visible.

You will need some basic tools to proceed: a hard lead pencil in the H series (2H-9H are fine), a white vinyl block eraser, a metal straight edge of 36-48 inches in length, a razor knife (in the real world called a utility knife, in the art world a mat knife) with replaceable blades, a 90-degree drafting triangle (plastic or metal), a cutting mat (18 × 24 inches or larger), water-soluble white glue such as Elmer's Glue-All or wheat paste, brown paper craft tape (also called packing tape) 2 inches wide with water-soluble adhesive, white linen librarian's tape, mat board, and heavy gray or brown chipboard (cardboard without corrugation).

Always start with clean hands, tools, and work surfaces. Once you have decided on the size of the mat and the opening for the art, measure carefully the outer edges and the inner contours of the window to be cut by drawing *lightly* with an H pencil against the straight edge.

I emphasize lightly because pencil lines are difficult to completely erase on mat boards. Do not extend the lines beyond the corners of the window or anywhere where the lines may show. Use your triangle to check corners for 90-degree accuracy. Just eyeballing it is not acceptable. If off, measure and mark again. A carpenter's adage is appropriate here: Measure twice, cut once. Place your art over the drawn window to make sure the opening size seems right before cutting.

Before cutting a mat, practice, practice, practice. Making mistakes in measuring and cutting are costly. Mat board is expensive. Practice cutting clean, straight lines with your metal edge on scraps or on any cardboard of similar thickness. The goal is to be able to repeatedly cut perfect lines of 24 inches or so with no tears, burrs, wobbles, or multiple cuts along the edge. An absolute straight line identical with your straight edge is a must. Anything less is The Amateur Hour.

Do not bear down on the knife so hard that you intend to go through the material on the first stroke. That is when you make mistakes. Control, not muscle power, is what makes a good cut. Begin with light pressure and just score the top surface on the first stroke. Hold the straight edge firmly with one hand and apply successive light strokes with your knife until the board is cut all the way through. Professionals often use 6-8 strokes before cutting through. Each time you make a stroke you are making a groove—after about three passes, you can take away the straight edge and cut carefully into the groove.

When cutting the window, do not cut beyond the corners. Any cut marks will show on the mat and cannot be erased or filled. As you cut toward a corner, stop a fraction short. Finish the cut in the opposite direction by inserting the point of the knife exactly over the corner and applying pressure until the cut is through. Place your straight edge whenever possible over the part of the mat you want to protect. Should you cut off-line you will do so into a scrap area and not into the mat.

Cut the mounting board (gray chip board) the same size as the mat. Use the mat as a template to trace the size. You may cut the mounting a fraction smaller (1/16 to 1/8 inch) to ensure that it does not show from the front.

To hinge the mat to the mounting board, lay the mat upside down so that its top edge is adjacent and flush to the edge of the mounting board that is its same length. Line them up as perfectly as possible. Place weights, such as books, on both boards to prevent movement. The window will be hinged from the top and will open and close like a gate. Cut 3-inch strips of craft tape and place them so they are about 4 inches apart and positioned to overlap equally on both mat and mount. Place a minimum of two strips (more if the separation between the boards is longer than twelve inches) to make the connection. Moisten glue on tape with a watery sponge and apply with pressure. Wait a few minutes to dry. Close mat over mount so that the edges of both boards are aligned and press so that tape is permanently creased.

Place your artwork inside so it is centered under the window. If you are *floating* the art in the window, you may need to attach a sheet of opaque white paper on the mount first (larger than the window), and then hinge the art to the white paper so that the gray chipboard is not visible. Measure all four edges to be equally spaced within the opening. Put a heavy weight in the center of the work so it does not move. Lift the window back to avoid getting glue on its outer surface. Make small hinges (1/2- to 1-inch square) from librarian's tape or acid-free paper and fold at the center so the flaps are equal in size. Moisten tape or apply glue to paper tape and apply one to each upper corner at left and right—one half-glued to the art, the other half to the mount. Place the hinges a little away from the edges of the paper so they do not show from the front. If the work is not placed under glass, you may apply hinges to the bottom corners as well to prevent the sheet from swinging outward. Voila! Set your work against a wall and see how it looks.

Bevel cut edges are a more advanced skill in mat cutting and are often preferred by artists. First, master the straight 90-degree cut before attempting bevels. I like the simpler, stark look of the 90-degree cut for my own work. When ready, you can choose from a variety of bevel cutting tools.

You can make your own frames, but that requires some carpentry skills and additional tools that are impractical to describe here. Framing skills may be demonstrated in your fundamentals classes or you can ask your professor for assistance. In the meantime, you can buy ready-made frames in most art supply stores or you can have them custom made by a professional framer. Be sure when placing a mat in a frame that it is a loose fit to allow for expansion and contraction due to humidity changes. If the fit is too tight and humidity expands the boards, the mat will warp in waves and become impossible to flatten. Allow about 1/8 inch on all sides for expansion.

I recommend that you cut a sheet of heavy corrugated cardboard and place that over the mat and mount from the back to help ensure that the mat will remain flat in the frame. Close with glazier points or small brads driven every 3 inches or so into the back of the frame on all four sides. Set screw eyes on vertical, reverse sides of frame at appropriate height, connect eyes with braided picture wire, and hang on the wall.

CHAPTER 27

SAFETY

When using razor knives, safety is paramount. Whether sharp or dull, razors can slice flesh as easily as paper. Do not cut a mat or use a razor knife under any of these conditions:
- In dull or inadequate light.
- When talking or socializing with other people.
- When tired, sleepy, or otherwise distracted.
- When feeling hurried to complete a task or meet a deadline.
- Any other times when you do not feel fully alert.

Never attempt to make cuts if your control is compromised by the force exerted. In other words, lighten up. This bears repeating: Make several to many passes over a line you are cutting rather than fewer. Putting too much pressure into your mat knife threatens your ability to make accurate cuts, but worse, increases the risk that you may slip and cut yourself. Cutting is finesse, not muscle. I offer this advice from the battle scars of personal experience!

DO NO HARM

Since the mat is the part of presentation that has direct contact with the art, it is essential that glues, adhesives, and other materials that may damage the work be kept out of harm's way. Never use masking tape, duct tape, transparent tape, or any other self-adhesive tape as a way to attach the art to the mat. Paper art is easily punctured, so never mat a work without a mounting board behind for protection. Use mounts and tapes that are acid-free and colorless. Otherwise, dyes and acids will, in time, transfer to the art, leaving unsightly stains that are virtually impossible to remove.

Once the art is framed and ready for display, hang works on paper out of direct sunlight. Sun can bleach and fade colors in all media in short time, but especially photographs and collages made from printed matter. The effect of glass over a work can intensify, like a magnifying glass, the effects of fading. When storing art, do not assume that frame and glass provide all-purpose protection. Avoid storing art in basements or any other place where humidity levels can be high or where the threat of exposure to moisture is an ongoing possibility.

Though the guidelines for mats and frames may seem straightforward—compared to art!—there are many exceptions in how they are used by artists, galleries, and museums. In my own practice, I am partial to odd, sometimes beaten up period frames with rich textures, carving, staining, and other details. I am simultaneously cautious and enthusiastic about using them for my work. Frame and art are independent entities, but must be compatible in their interactions when put together. Finding the right found frame for an artwork is a delicate balancing act of trial and error and critical experience. I accept the risks I take when it does not work. But, when it does, the effect is indescribable and satisfying. Otherwise, when in doubt, the art is first and simpler is better.

Effective presentation of your art deserves your time and effort if you are to put it out in the world in its best light. In fact, you may find that you understand and appreciate your work better when you can see it in its optimum state of display. Then, you can also give your audience the same opportunity.

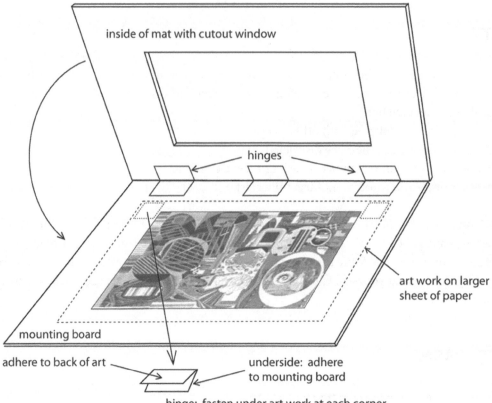

inside of mat with cutout window

hinges

art work on larger sheet of paper

mounting board

adhere to back of art

underside: adhere to mounting board

hinge: fasten under art work at each corner

MAT CONNECTED TO MOUNTING BOARD

MATTING ART WORK

MOUNTING OPTIONS

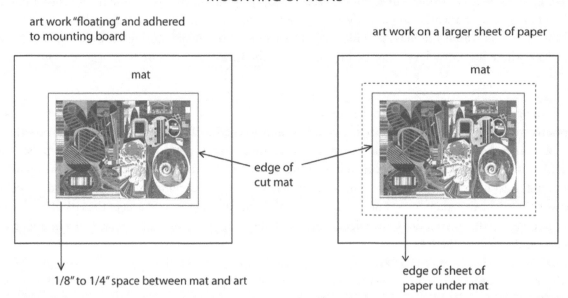

art work "floating" and adhered to mounting board

art work on a larger sheet of paper

mat

mat

edge of cut mat

1/8" to 1/4" space between mat and art

edge of sheet of paper under mat

Illustration contributed by Jerry Zinser. Copyright © Kendall Hunt Publishing Company

chapter 28

THE ARTIST'S STATEMENT

If you have been stopped in your tracks by a work of art in a gallery or museum, you may have wondered how the artist made his work. The artist's statement is meant to help fill that gap between viewer and object. As a written declaration of the artist's interests, sources, and goals, the statement can provide an enlightening context in which the viewer can find meaning and appreciation.

The artist's statement is a description of what drives the art to assume its particular subject, style, and material form. Consider its content metaphorically. The reader is guided behind the scenes into the artist's studio, often into his life, or into the nooks and crannies that are the links to his inspiration. It is a privileged moment to peer into the creative mind's diverse passions, preoccupations, and obsessions.

The statement should cast a spotlight on the artist's *hows* and *wheres*, but possibly less so on his *whys*. Art and its meanings often cannot be explained verbally. Look at the *art* for interpretation. Words can be illuminating and enriching, but they cannot give you a key to the city. The viewer still has to participate with the work to get the meaning.

If you have never written an artist's statement, now is a good time to start. Without the discipline of concentration and commitment to purpose, the creative mind can be a nebulous, diffused place of ill-defined urges and appetites. Writing a statement is an opportunity to focus your interests and intentions. Perhaps you have not yet attempted to identify them in concrete form. Making the effort to summarize what you want to do in art should be self-educating. You may understand more about yourself and your work, your motives and passions, because you wrote it down, nailed it into black and white reality.

There is no correct format for the artist's statement. Write in a prose style of coherent sentences that relate to one another in a series of organized paragraphs that highlight your interests, motivations, and purposes. In short, describe what you want to explore in art. Of course, your writing should be articulate, concise, grammatically accurate, and composed with good English usage.

As you write, be enthusiastic without bubbling over and be specific when possible, without larding on tedious detail. Above all, avoid clichés, platitudes, and preaching. Your statement should not be a political agenda or a social call to action. Your work may contain political or social commentary, but you do not need to convert readers to any political point of view. There are better venues if your objective is activism. The statement is about how you want viewers to direct their attention in viewing your art.

Do not be defensive. Your work is not on trial. Words do not define art, nor do they make or break its success. They are merely an introduction. The art has the responsibility of its success. Never think your words will cover a weakness or compensate for anything lacking. Art is not an illustration for captions. Instead, be positive and unapologetic. Remember to describe and not to explain.

How long should your statement be, you wonder? There is no rule about length, but generally statements are a page or two, more or less. Too little can prompt more questions than enlighten, too much can overwhelm the reader and become tedious. Strike a balance. Write as much as you feel the viewer should know without distracting him from the work and as much as satisfies your curiosity about what you are doing.

Consider these suggestions and questions when writing your artist's statement:
- Describe significant experiences (including those of childhood), influences, mentors, and interests that form the basis of your motivation to pursue art.
- Note unusual circumstances, living arrangements, travel, or situations outside your control that may have contributed to the choices you have made.
- Specify what subjects, ideas, and materials attract you and why.
- If there are styles, artists, and genres that are a special influence, describe how they affect your approach to art.
- Are there fields or disciplines outside the art world that inform your work? What and how?
- What do you want to accomplish in your art? What do you want to express?
- What do you want the viewer to experience?
- How do the goals in your current work relate to those in past work? How might those change in the near future?
- Does your general outlook and philosophy affect your art?
- Add whatever you think is relevant that has not been addressed here.

Besides its major purpose as an accompaniment to an exhibition, the artist's statement serves other practical purposes. When you transfer to a four-year college, a similar statement of purpose about academic and career goals is usually requested. You may have to revise your statement considerably to fit the requirements specified by the transfer institution. If you are preparing your statement to include in an application for transfer, consider these additional guidelines as other requirements permit:
- Describe where you think you are in your education and artistic development.
- Identify your strengths as well as areas you feel need work.
- What are your academic goals? Career goals?
- What attracts you to the institution to which you are applying?
- What do you hope to gain from that institution?
- What do you think you can contribute, especially to the department of your major?

After you write your statement, read it slowly and carefully. Read it again. Rewrite it.

Read and rewrite, revise, and correct until your statement is as faithful and clear a description of what you are trying to do in art as you are capable of writing. Nothing less is satisfactory. When you send it off or post it for others to read, that statement represents you.

Ask someone you trust to read your rough drafts and offer suggestions. If your reader knows you, he will be able to say whether your writing is a good reflection of your intentions. Think of the statement as a work of art in itself!

It may be helpful to read other artists' statements to get a sense of how artists think about their work. Be cautious. You do not want to imitate another artist's ideas and viewpoints. Your integrity and uniqueness are more important. Spend more time to find out what you think!

Should you ever face a creative block and not know what to do next in the studio, read your statement to get your bearings or to determine if you need to proceed in a new direction. As your art and your ideas change with time and circumstances, you will need to revise or completely rewrite your artist's statement. Synchronizing thinking and doing is a positive form of renewal to put your ideas and your work on the same track. Your words can guide your action, or your action can guide your words.

chapter

29

ARTIST'S STATEMENT
DENNIS LICK

The following are my artist's statements. They are not meant to serve as templates for others, nor do I present them here as typical examples of the form. In fact, there is no typical example since an artist's statement is as unique and personal as his work. I offer two here from somewhat different viewpoints. The first one is concise while broad in scope and perhaps more philosophical. The second is more specific with respect to the technique and content of collage making.

They may be read before or after viewing the portfolio of my work, not as explanations (art cannot be explained) but rather as testaments of my motivation and involvement in making art.

ARTIST'S STATEMENT I

To me everything in nature and civilization seems dense, contradictory, and complicated. What I do as an artist must reflect that.

My images operate outside universal laws. I can fragment perspective and defy gravity, float below the horizon, or fly above it. In my pictures time and space have no boundaries. Past, present, and future tenses can flow into their own narrative form like film, music, novels, and comic strips.

One of my ongoing pursuits is collecting objects and curiosities. My taste runs high and low, from elegant to trifling, from industrial to handmade, from eccentric to commonplace. My domestic and studio environments contain eye-dazzling arrays of "still lifes," the evidence of my acquisitive habits. The visual cacophony feeds my art.

The urban environment in which we all navigate and that has profound influence—especially in its juxtaposition with nature—is a baffling mash up of opposites, which explains how an individual can feel rage and ecstasy at the same time. It is the best of times; it is the worst of times. While I do not want to preach or illustrate, I make art to come to grips with these crucial issues. The environment, the planet, and the universe are never far from my thoughts. My interests are highly varied, extending especially to the sciences of astronomy, cosmology, and particle physics.

Art is my attempt to take a flawed, indifferent world and remake it into a utopian ideal, one where dreams, fantasies, and speculation about reality can blend and mix.

ARTIST'S STATEMENT II

The expansive and inclusive nature of collage with its endless varieties of forms and subjects fascinates me. I explore the world's abundance of printed matter to discover novel ways of cutting, mixing, and relating images. I make new images with found images. Though trained as a painter, I have also become a collagist.

The medium suits my preoccupation with the general glut in our culture, from indiscriminate consumption to the production of objects to satisfy every desire. Collage allows me to wander in the excess of Western overabundance, to see both the beauty and the brutality. I do not wish to moralize or politicize, but rather to manipulate cut images into new and rich environments.

I want to make work that is close to the way I think. My thoughts often jump from one topic to another, seemingly randomly or illogically. I am a daydreamer (despite a dependence on practicalities as well). The way the mind operates does not always rationally follow a prescribed pattern or direction. Psychologists call this mind of the eclectic, when thoughts come speedily and uncensored, "racing thoughts." My pictures often look like the concrete evidence of that process.

My collages (and works of art generally) should have an immediate impact. Getting it all at once, a "slam dunk", is an intuitive process that, ironically, must be followed by a slow burn. One should look long and lingeringly since the density of subject and material demands to be sorted out. The array of complicated parts may seem undisciplined, even chaotic, but that is a camouflage for the underlying structure. A glance followed by a prolonged analysis is one of the ways I understand my experiences. When anyone looks at my work, I want the sensation that encourages multiple viewings. Each time the art is viewed something new is revealed.

What is compelling to me is that I see my collages not only as complete works of art, but also as surrogates for drawing and painting. Since the cut outs in my collages are void of most of their original (prior) context, the collages can be re-imagined as if they were done in traditional art media such as paint or pastel. In another duality, representation and abstraction combine in both the content and shape of the cut outs in the collages. I like operating on the edges among all those mysterious and conflicting ambiguities and variables.

chapter 30

MY PORTFOLIO

The portfolio of collages on the following pages is deliberately executed in black and white. They are reproduced as they appear in reality. I am a colorist. Nonetheless, I am fascinated with how to make pictures when denied the strengths that have driven my art through the years. Color in all its rapturous glory has been a mainstay.

All artists attempt to understand what can be expressed when limitations are imposed. Restricted conditions are one of the ultimate challenges to creativity. How can I make more out of less? How can I stretch the muscles of my imagination?

I am reminded of Vincent van Gogh's ink drawings, denying him the rich color of his greatly revered paintings. How did he compensate? Van Gogh lavished rich patterns, textures, and energetic mark making in his drawings to express the drama and intensity he felt about his subjects. I have been inspired by that sensation. Black and white images can be as riveting and complex as any other medium.

John Chamberlain is a late twentieth century sculptor I admire for his unique method of making art with found materials. Chamberlain made sculptures with damaged auto bodies and car wrecks–found objects par excellence. He claimed that he was guided by how those broken objects wanted to fit together. Similar to an elaborate puzzle, he allowed the materials to suggest how they should be connected. The art materials themselves spoke to him.

With collage, I think along similar lines. How do my cut-out pieces want to interact? How to make them dovetail, collide, abut, and overlap in extravagant but compelling relationships? In collage, it is always about the contradiction of collision and connection. How do they maintain their visual power but still form a holistic image that is more important than as individual pieces?

If such unity of purpose can be accomplished, then all those singular, sundry pieces are melded as a magisterial event. I want that sensation of making something out of the debris of nothing.

Dennis Lick, *Campus*, acrylic and collage on paper, 12.5 x 8.5", 2019.

Dennis Lick, *The Nines Have It*, collage on paper, 11 x 9", 2020.

Dennis Lick, *Field Day,* graphite and collage on paper, 10.5 x 10", 2020.

Dennis Lick, *Water Carrier,* felt pen and collage on paper, 11 x 9", 2020.

Dennis Lick, *Fear,* ball point pen and collage on paper, 10.5 x 8", 2020.

Dennis Lick, *Supple Sticks,* ball point pen and collage on paper, 10.5 x 10", 2020.

Dennis Lick, *Time Machine*, collage on paper, 11 × 10", 2021.

Dennis Lick, *Ledger*, collage on paper, 10.5 × 10.5", 2020.

SECTION VII

ART MAKING WITH DIRECTION

chapter

INTRODUCTION TO STUDIO PROJECTS AND EXERCISES

The exercises described on the following pages are summaries of projects accomplished in class or suggestions for projects you can do independently. Required projects rely on classroom instruction since certain details and parameters in the written descriptions may change in a given semester.

Otherwise, a given summary is meant as a broad reminder of the structure of a project. When in doubt, ask questions, but know that making the best art you can is more important than following rules or guidelines.

Drawing Trees and Natural Objects in India Ink

When the weather is cooperative, take a hike in nature. Collect tree parts, branches, twigs, plant forms, rocks, and stones. If the weather is good, you can draw on site, as the Impressionists did. Otherwise, put your objects in a big bag and bring them home. You can stage your natural loot outside in your yard as a background or bring them indoors and set up your arrangement on the floor or a table. If you wish greater contrast, you can include a few manmade wood objects such as pieces of lumber, a chair, or a bench placed in your set up.

Trees and branches have remarkable linear qualities, often complex, winding, and convoluted. They also have rough, tactile textures in the way of bark and wood grain. Scale and size vary greatly too, from small, fragile twigs, to muscular limbs of thick branches, to trunks of bulging diameter. Tree ends that are broken or sawn or damaged often make striking effects. Take advantage of these contrasts to make your drawing dramatic in form, varied in expression, and forceful in execution.

Make a drawing of this subject in the India ink techniques of pen, brush, and washes.

First, do a practice drawing to get familiar with how to use these tools. The pen is a linear tool, especially good for hatching, cross-hatching, making crisp edges, and adding detail. The brush is a more blunt tool with thicker, wider lines and is good for emphasis, strength, and as a contrast to the more delicate pen line. When ready, do a full-sized 18" × 24" sustained drawing of your natural subjects in all three ink techniques, pen, brush, and washes. You must use good quality watercolor paper, three-ply Bristol paper, illustration board, or other sturdy papers designed for wet media.

Make washes by adding small amounts of ink to water. Mix ink and water in a tray with reservoirs made for the purpose. Never add water to your bottle of ink. Even a Styrofoam egg carton can serve as an impromptu mixing tray. Be aware that most washes look the same in the tray. You'll have to apply them to paper to see their lighter or darker values. Spreading these washes across paper can give you instant broad areas of grays of all values depending on the proportion of water to ink. It's especially beautiful to mix pen lines and washes on top of each other. They add depth and complexity to surfaces.

A lively technique with washes is to apply wet into wet. For example, a stroke of pen line run through a wet wash will create a "bleeding" effect in which the ink line and wash will run together in interesting and somewhat unpredictable patterns. You can also brush on plain water and run ink into those wet areas and see similar unpredictable "bleeds." You must experiment to know how to make the best use of these effects.

Ink is a dramatic medium and responsive to spontaneity. Be adventurous and creative in how you apply lines and washes. Since ink is not erasable, be flexible about little accidents, such as drips. Incorporate them as if they were on purpose. Keep your pen and brush handling lively and energetic as you apply ink to paper. If your lines seem stiff, hesitant, or otherwise uptight, your drawing will look awkward and overworked. We do not want to see your labor; we want to see your spirit as it sails around the drawing.

Drawing the Skeleton

The skeleton is the foundation of the human figure and a good primer for the drawer to begin to understand the highly varied anatomical components of the human body. The skeleton in a metaphoric sense is a bit like the timber frame structures of a house. The inner cores of those structures are often as beautiful and compelling as the outer skins. Observing the skeleton carefully will enable you to better understand the complexities of rendering the figure's external appearances, as when you draw directly before a live human model.

Notice the overlaps in space between various bony parts, especially in the torso region around the rib cage. Try to express which bones are where in that space and know that, as in all subjects in reality, light and dark, and highlights and shadows determine the ability to see these forms clearly. Notice the unique, organic contours and shapes of the bones. They are the opposite of the straight line or perfect circle shapes of the geometric objects we have drawn before in still lifes. To capture them in their multifaceted variety, look carefully and interpret your vision of them when you draw. Remember that seeing with understanding is the first step in drawing in a worthwhile and effective way.

Draw the entire skeleton that comprises all the major body parts, including head, torso, arms, and legs. You may crop parts of the head, arms, and legs, but the torso must be composed in its entirety since it is the center and lead player for all the anatomy. Everything else is an extension of the torso. Compose your drawing so that the sheet of paper is secondary and the subject matter predominates the composition. Consider the possibility of dividing your picture into multiple sections—diptych or triptych style—so as to include all the major parts , including torso, limbs, and head. This may mean including some background or not, depending on how you scale, section, and crop the skeleton in relation to the picture's rectangle.

Since color is largely irrelevant with this subject—which is more about structure and form—draw in any black and white medium we have used this semester. Choose from graphite, charcoal, conte crayon, or India ink. You may mix media as well. If you wish to draw with white charcoal or conte crayon, ask for gray or colored paper, otherwise white standard drawing paper is fine. Another suggestion is to divide your paper so that you can do two views of both skeletons (if two are present at the time) or include upper and lower halves on either side of the paper.

Plot your drawing with light strokes first and indicate all the parts of your skeleton and composition before darkening or adding details. With such a complicated subject matter, you will make mistakes, and lighter mistakes are always easier to correct. The best drawing is one in which you sense the whole subject and its arrangement on the paper first before starting lights, darks, and details. Recall from the drawing chapter how to block in essential forms in the first stage of the process.

Since you may not finish your drawing in class, you may come to the studio during open hours and request staff or faculty to set up the skeleton again. You may also take photos as needed and work from them outside of class workshop. Finally, remember that making good art is more important than adhering to rules. Now do the best skeleton drawing you have ever done!

The Eccentric Still Life

Search for unusual objects that may not seem "traditional" choices for a still life. Find at least 12 (more is always better) objects from the list below. You may interpret each word or description as you wish. In addition, look for objects that might be overlooked by others even if they might seem ordinary. These might be objects normally discarded or that you never imagined would be included in a still life. Do not be concerned about making choices according to a theme or unified idea. You will figure out how to relate them when you (1) arrange your still life, and (2) make artistic decisions about how you will compose and interpret you subjects.

Choose from these categories: rope, twine, wood scraps, box, tin can, cage, tool, tree branch or stump, rock, kitchen object, pair of shoes, pair of gloves, postcard, picture frame without the picture, mirror, something broken or incomplete, game board or game parts, playing cards, human figure statue, model of an anatomical part, a sign with words or symbols, multiples of an object (examples, many clothes pins, clamps, lights bulbs, paper cups) lamp shade, commercial package, anything architectural, and anything not on this list that you consider visually worthy, wacky, or unusual.

Bring your objects to class in a large plastic bag or cardboard box. During class, we will discuss the ways of putting your still life together in a portable construction and in a way that it can be transported between class and home in a reasonable manner. Some parts may not necessarily have to be permanently attached with glue or other fastening materials, so long as the still life parts can be accurately recreated each time it is moved to a different location.

Once arranged in a constructed format that you think is effective visually, begin making a painting of it from its most compelling viewpoint. At any time while painting, you may rearrange parts to reflect a better outcome or improved composition. As you paint, try to extract the visual essence from your subject matter. This attitude requires that you think abstractly about form and not just in response to an object's identity. Remember that a painting is not necessarily an eyeball imitation of reality. The objects you have chosen may suggest moods or feelings that go beyond their factual reality. Interpretation via imagination is what painting is about. Try to make your painting of the still life seem more special and mysterious than it may appear to the eye.

Your painting style and technique may be as eccentric as your choice of objects. Make an effort to use some techniques of paint application that you have not attempted before. Refer to Chapter 8, *Notes on Painting*. Use at least one tool (such as a palette knife) in addition to the usual brushes. Then, make the best picture you can with the possibilities and complexities suggested by your unconventional still life.

HOW TO MAKE A COLLAGE

Cubism changed pictorial space into a complex series of connected facets or planes. It shows us objects as if we are turning them over in our hands and from multiple viewpoints. This new sensation of seeing through experience rather than simple observation profoundly influenced all the visual arts. A major result is that it upset the 500-year-old invention of linear perspective that had dominated the pictorial arts since the Renaissance. Cubist space takes the premise that we do not experience our surroundings from a fixed viewpoint but rather move around in our world and see it simultaneously from many vantage points. With the old tradition of a picture, we are separate from its space, as if looking through a window into another world. In Cubist pictures, it is as if we have stepped *into* the space of subject. We move around in and participate in the painting. Cubism takes objects and figures apart and puts them back together in a way that we see more of its sides and surfaces.

Furthermore, Cubism put the world into a lively new fantasy—a Twilight Zone between representation and abstraction. As a result, abstraction has become a major branch of art making with its own subjects and styles. While greatly extending the boundaries and possibilities for art, Cubism makes us see and experience the world as never before. It's a whole new universe. Starting in 1908 with the bold experiments of Picasso and Georges Braque, art has never been the same.

The Cubist invention of collage in the early 1910s was a stunning intensification of the new pictorial space. With fragments of paper or fabric containing image, text, pattern, and texture, often combined with traditional drawing and painting, collages became a kaleidoscope of abrupt, shifting viewpoints and spatial anomalies. Suddenly, pictorial art could be simultaneously abstract and realistic—or entirely abstract. Illusionistic space can now defy the laws of physics and gravity when differing pieces of imagery are butted together or placed adjacent. Unlike the singular images of traditional art, collage is a new universe of multiple content.

As you make your mixed media collage, here are some suggestions about what strategies you can pursue. At the same time, invent your own way of developing ideas and approaches.

1. First cut into your photocopies and other collage sheets with your razor knife, making a variety of shapes and sizes that are sensitive to the shapes, forms, and subjects printed on their surfaces. Let the forms you see there help you decide how to cut them.
2. Reserve larger sections of some sheets to lay down a background for negative space. Consider how these spaces can suggest various levels of depth. It is desirable and natural to shift suddenly to advancing or receding space when two pieces are joined at the edge.
3. Move your cut shapes around on top of the background, looking for spatial and visual relationships as places to locate. Do a lot of shifting and moving around with a variety of pieces to get a feel for organization (composition) and the sensation eventually that the whole is more significant than the parts as it begins to express a mood or feeling beyond the material.
4. You can draw or paint on your collage sheets to change or enhance them. You may also draw or paint on separate sheets to create new collage material.
5. You can apply sandpaper and scratching tools to remove, blend, or otherwise change surfaces.

6. Look for additional kinds of printed matter in addition to photocopies and magazine pages, such as old posters, junk mail, wrapping paper, wallpaper, patterns printed on commercial products, etc. Printed fabrics and cloth are good sources for collages as well.

7. Work in the traditional square or rectangle, or consider doing a shaped picture in which the framing edge is an irregular shape considered "off the rectangle." Shaped pictures are more difficult because they can easily seem too casual or arbitrary in composition. Do some research first if you work outside the rectangle.

8. Most of all, when composing your picture look at it from a distance frequently during the working process—not just from a tabletop where you are too close to judge compositional effects and visual relationships. Put it on the floor and stand in front as you look down. Your distance of height will give you a better impression. You can also attach pieces temporarily by spot gluing with a glue-stick and putting the work on the wall as meant to be seen. You can break glue-stick easily with a razor or palette knife before doing the permanent gluing with acrylic gel.

9. When you are ready to glue up your collage, take a photograph of it. This document will serve as an important record to guide you in the successive layers of knowing where to glue various pieces with compositional accuracy.

10. Apply glue to the entire area of the piece to be put on the mount. You may also apply glue to the area of the mount where the piece will be placed. To ensure no air bubbles develop, apply glue to both piece and mount.

Consult Chapter 10, Collage and Mixed Media for additional advice about collage making.

DRAWING FROM COLLAGES

Instead of three-dimensional reality as the subject, your collage is the model for a drawing. Although the absence of the third dimension of space may, at first, seem like a disadvantage, the collage has several advantages that nature does not. First, its two-dimensional form as a picture shares many similarities to drawing, so mapping the formal relationships between collage and drawing may actually be easier in many ways. In addition, the convenience of looking directly at your collage and placing it adjacent to your working area is useful in the way it should effectively encourage you to look at its forms intently and with understanding. If you imagine many of the photographic and printed details of your collage translated to drawing by hand, you are already on your way to making the drawing a grand interpretation of your printed subject matter. It is then a matter of visual problem solving: how to make the equivalent drawn version of this or that area as it appears in the collage.

You may interpret the entire composition of your collage, or crop it with strips of paper and recompose a smaller section. A third choice is to make a new composition by combining the best parts of multiple collages you have done. You may also divide your drawing into diptych or triptych sections as we have done in several previous drawings.

Your goal should be to make your drawing *better* than your collage. In that interest, you may wish to make changes from the original collage, that is, improvements in composition, form, color, and details as the drawing develops. You may add, subtract, simplify, or complicate as the occasion merits in the rendering of your image.

An important issue is whether you wish your drawing to retain the illusion of collage. The hard-edged contours resulting from razor or scissor cuts may be significant to your way of thinking about the subject matter. These crisp, sharp edges may contribute clarity, contrast, and beauty to the overall effects of the drawing. However, if that is not the case, you may prefer to express the cut edges in a softer, more blended, less linear style to enhance the integration and unity of different passages.

However you decide to execute your drawing, take advantage of the abundance of detail that this kind of photography-based collage imagery provides. You have so much visual information in your collages that you should have no difficulty discovering lively and energetic forms to include and interpret. Remember that the mind's eye hungers for detail—that it is better to draw more rather than less.

Draw in a medium that best approximates the color, texture, and surface qualities of your collage or how you want to interpret it. Choose from pastel, watercolor, colored pencil, India ink, or mixed media. As always, draw with generosity of spirit and draw as if you mean it.

Mixed Media Artists

Picasso and Georges Braque began the mixed media revolution more than one hundred years ago when their reinvention of pictorial space—Cubism—led them to additional innovations with collage, assemblage, and found materials and objects. Ever since, artists have championed their material inclusiveness and greatly expanded the horizons of what art and painting can be.

The following artists have incorporated found materials, that is, art supplies outside tradition, in their work. To understand these artists, you will need to look at bodies of work, since most of them have also produced art without found materials.

Many of these artists defy categorization, making art that is neither exclusively painting nor sculpture. It may be more meaningful to think of mixed media art as hybrids of the various genres. Thus, names and labels seem trivial and fussy. After all, the range of creativity and artistic insight among these artists is far more compelling than idle definitions. Look in art books and on the Internet for these especially inventive painters. This list may be expanded with additional artists who mix materials in their works.

Kurt Schwitters
Robert Rauschenberg
Jasper Johns
Jim Dine
Lucas Samaras
Sigmar Polke
Anselm Kiefer
Judy Pfaff
Julian Schnabel

Bruce Conner
David Salle

Richard Hamilton
Hannah Hoch
John Heartfield
Alfonso Ossorio

Jessica Stockholder
Frank Stella
Richard Tuttle
Terence La Noue
Mark Bradford
Robert Motherwell—the early collages
Jess
Elizabeth Murray
Joan Miro
Max Ernst

Lance Letscher
Bruce Helander
Lee Krasner
Eduardo Paolozzi

Romare Bearden

Mixed Media Painting

Picasso said that to make a painting you must start with something, regardless of how abstract it may become. So,

Take something from reality—figures, objects, landscape, or any mixture of the three.

Document it with a photograph, either found or one you shoot.

Transform—change, add, or subtract—this photograph into an abstract image.

Do a black and white drawing derived from the altered photograph that emphasizes abstract forms, freely mixes representations of figures or objects with abstraction, or otherwise transforms the subject matter of the image.

Interpret your drawing as a painting with approximately equal measures of paint and collage, including found objects. This is called mixed media. You can glue or otherwise attach several of the following materials into your painting:

Part of a map	Newspaper
A piece of printed fabric	Additional found materials
Several scraps of wood or objects you choose	
String or rope or wire	
Printed letters or numbers	Combine the above with easel paint

Artists to consult: Look at the modern greats. A little research will expand your understanding of what's possible and suggest ideas for getting started. The following artists are essential for their contributions to mixed media: Picasso, Georges Braque, the Cubists, Kurt Schwitters, Robert Rauschenberg, Jasper Johns, Robert Motherwell, Alfonso Ossorio, Frank Stella, Julian Schnabel, Elizabeth Murray, and David Salle.

Advice: Be creative, adventurous, exploratory, experimental, and open minded to the outlandish. Take risks. Paint as if it's the last artwork that you'll make. This is the artist as Alchemist.

If you're not sure, do it. Don't like it? Try something else. If you think you don't know what you're doing, then pretend that you do know. Picasso didn't know he would invent Cubism and change the art world. Columbus didn't know he would discover America. This is the artist as Actor and Pioneer.

What you paint, what you make will be how you interpret these directions. Once you start painting, don't worry about how far you may be departing from your photograph or drawing. The painting and what it needs as art is more important now. Take my advice or, if you have a better way, ignore it. You are limited only by your imagination.

ART MAKING WITH TEMPLATES AND STENCILS

Shapes, lines, and what happens at the edges between adjacent areas are fundamental to the description of images in art. These include photographs, drawings, paintings, prints, and all manner of surface design. Shapes, as representations of both figural and abstract forms, are at the very core of the formal elements of art making. A shape, and therefore any figure or object, is rendered in art by means of a contour line that encloses an area of space. To help raise your line and shape consciousness, you will design, draw, and cut out with razor knife from heavy paper 10 or more templates and stencils.

As shown in class, a template or stencil is a flat, sturdy card-like surface cut into a specific form that becomes a tool to trace or guide the drawing of shapes and lines that can eventually create an image. Here's a simple distinction between template and stencil. A template is the positive form of a shape—the substance of the card itself—while a stencil is the negative space of the shape's cutout area. Think of a stencil as the hole in the donut.

Look around you. Shapes abound in nature, manmade structures, and in the art of the masters. Design and cut at least 10 templates and stencils altogether, but design at least one each in the following ways: (1) as a representational object or figure, (2) derived from a shape found in a photograph or master painting, (3) whose form is geometric, (4) whose form is organic, and (5) as an object that represents a three-dimensional illusion. The rest of your designs may come from any other sources, including your imagination. For example, Leonardo da Vinci could see significant forms in coffee rings spills, and splashes. As you develop your collection, put your designs side by side and aim for variety and contrast in type, character, and size.

When you have a variety of drawings for your stencils and templates, transfer their outlines in pencil or pen to sheets of thick paper. You can also mount your drawings directly to the cardboard to be cut with glue or tape. Proceed to cut your forms out of cardboard, mat board, illustration board, or heavy Bristol paper with a razor knife. Hold you knife to the drawn outline and score over that line as you move along it. Do not try to cut through on the first stroke, but cut deep enough that you can retrace that cut line by scoring over it repeatedly until cut all the way through. Using too much pressure in cutting initially will cause mistakes, strain, and possibly injury by cutting your hand. Always be careful when cutting with razor knives. Patience and careful attention to the task are essential. If you do not have a cutting mat, ordinary sheets of scrap cardboard or thick sheets of newspaper will protect tables or furniture on which you are working.

Now, to start a picture draw in light pencil a grid of blocks parallel to the picture frame, each block of equal dimensions, as small as 3 inches square and up to 6 inches square. Use a straight edge and measure out the dimensions before drawing. After the grid of squares is established, draw a number of diagonal lines at 45 degrees by lining up the straight edge through the corners of the squares. Be sure all the lines are visible but light enough to be erased later or covered easily by subsequent drawing. Think of this grid as a convenient scaffold or clothesline, to use metaphors, to hang your lines and shapes as you draw and locate their places in the space of your picture. This predetermined structure will provide a kind of road map for developing the design of your composition and for guiding the eye of the viewer. The grid will help inform your decisions about line and shape placement, the overlapping of forms, and the description or pictorial space. However, do not allow it to dictate those choices or hinder creativity. Whenever it seems desirable to break the grid for the purpose of variety, contrast, evoking movement or rhythm, or changing the nature of the image, do so! The grid is a guide to foster suggestibility and possibility, not a cage for confinement.

In this project, make a picture in which the design, spatial complexity, and the rhythms of patterns are the subject matter of your image. You may be immediately reminded of wallpaper or wrapping paper. But do not be limited in your thinking by these often simply designed surfaces that usually serve as unobtrusive backgrounds or temporal decoration. Pictures are meant to be food for thought. They should bite a little; evoke mood, tension, and feeling; —and have a visual presence that is substantive and commanding in the mind's eye.

To make a pattern requires one or more (often many) motifs or design shapes repeated in rows, columns, or other organizing configurations. Do not be afraid to get complicated. You will not be able to do much with just one motif running in a single direction. Use many, overlap, run them in several directions, let them change course or form for complexity and surprise. Try to incorporate at least once all of your templates and stencils. Shapes and patterns might collide, crash, and otherwise interact with each other. Seek possibilities of how pattern might change to something else, metamorphose, or change its "stripes" altogether. In short, while pattern implies a certain arrangement of predictability, it is really the job of the artist to contradict expectations, to upset the conventional apple cart. What happens if I try this, or that? It is the key question to a creative mind making a fresh discovery. So during the working process, there may come a time to break the pattern or break out of the grid as artistic expression and your intuition demands.

As demonstrated in class, you can make many different shapes and lines from just one template. Some templates may be used to make multiple contours—instead of shapes—in which certain lines are repeated very close to one another in a kind of hatching and cross-hatching effect. Templates can also be used as a guide to cut out shapes on printed or colored paper and then inserted into a picture as collage. Stencils may be used the same way, but, in addition, their forms can be "printed" by painting through the openings. The range of technical possibilities of how to use them as mixed media tools in picture making are vast, and they are limited only by one's imagination and courage to take artistic risks.

Do not be limited to using only your templates and stencils to make your image. At any time, you may include free-hand drawing and other kinds of invented graphic mark making to enhance your art. You may want to describe something that cannot be done with a template or stencil. Of course, the artistic result should still speak to the subject of patterns, rhythms, and pictorial space. There are several kinds of space we have discussed, including positive and negative space, lateral or decorative space, and the illusionistic space of depth made by overlapping, diminishing sizes, and the effect of the diagonal lines of perspective.

Modern artists who have used the principles of pattern making in their work include Jasper Johns, Frank Stella, Kim McConnell, Robert Kushner, Miriam Shapiro, Jennifer Bartlett, Sean Scully, Roy Lichtenstein, Andy Warhol, James Rosenquist, Philip Taaffe, and the grandfather of them all, Henri Matisse. Google any of these names or look them up in the library's art books and see a sea of inspiration in this wide-ranging art principle.

Please understand that this written description of the project is neither inclusive nor complete. It does not replace the directions, demonstrations, visual aids, and guidance given during classes. This paper and the chapters you have been given from *Art Start* serve as supplements to help provide encouragement and enhancement to your creative process. Nonetheless, when in doubt, worry less about specific requirements and more about making art.

Finally, a project to follow may be titled *The Anti-Pattern*, an artistic antidote to this one. In the meantime, work up your own artistic storm to make the best pattern picture you can.

Steps for Construction of a Paper Relief

- Plan ahead to the extent possible. It's the best way to ensure that your labor will be doable and productive. Make a drawing as a plan of your 3D intentions. When you're satisfied with your drawing, you may use it as a template to cut the platform, which is the first form to be made to start the relief. See specific directions below. Otherwise, you may draw freehand onto the paperboard to be cut out.

- Cut out the platform first. On the back, draw in pencil with a straight edge a diagram of where you will glue the support structure that will hold everything together and serve also as a device to hang on the wall. With one-inch or wider strips, "outline" this diagram by gluing down the strips so they connect to the platform and to each other—like the studs and rafters in building a house.

- Guided by your template drawing, draw with a pencil directly onto your platform (the side opposite the support structure) the composition of your 3D pieces. Then, you can more easily see the whole arrangement as you fit individual cut pieces into the drawing and plan in a more efficient way the order of construction.

- Reinforce and overbuild whenever possible on all structures. It can be surprising and dismaying when forms warp and ruin an otherwise beautiful structure. Your construction must be sturdy and reinforced where needed to accommodate the rigors of display, transport, handling, and storage. Painting the surface of the relief will also warp weakened areas. Think like an engineer as well as an artist. In fact, in manufacturing where paper is the medium, such as with pop-up books, designers are also called paper engineers.

- Make sure the 3D structures of your composition carry the art. The surface may become important later, but it is secondary to the third dimension. If you paint, draw, or collage onto the relief surfaces, make sure that those embellishments do not disrupt the clarity and unity of the 3D structures.

- Remember that craft in 3D art is as important as the quality of the art content. Craft allows the art to become visible in its best presentation. Viewers will immediately notice the manner and quality of your relief's construction, whether edges meet where they should and gluing appears to secure its structures.

- Think about working some forms at angles that are counter to the traditional picture frame (that remains a reference despite the relief format) and wall, which are both strongly oriented along perpendicular and parallel angles.

- Develop detail in designing your forms and look to contrast and variety to dramatize your construction. Refer to the chapter on *Formalism* for more ideas.

- When attempting to match a cut form to your drawing to then glue into your relief, it is useful to make a mock version out of regular paper first to test its appearance, fit, and accuracy. Then, use that mock cutout as a template to trace and cut into board.

- During the working process, be sure to frequently hang your relief on a wall to judge its progress. Working horizontally on a table is a great distortion of how your art will look. It is important to stop, look, and listen to your art in between work sessions to understand what you are doing and what the work needs next. Cultivate the habit that the art will tell you what it needs if you take the time and thought to look at it in its proper presentation.

DRAWING FROM PAPER SCULPTURE

This dual project enlivens awareness of the contrasting attributes of both sculptural form and pictorial space. The art process is divided into two parts. You will first make a paper sculpture and second, render a sustained drawing from the sculpture.

- Gather various sheets of paper. Include lightweight drawing paper or computer paper and heavyweight paper such as Bristol paper, mat board, illustration board, watercolor paper, compressed cardboard, and commercial packaging such as corrugated cardboard. Most papers for your sculpture should be white or off-white to maximize the contrasts of light and dark values under a light source. A few colored papers and brown cardboard are fine for contrast.

- With razor knife, scissors, and white glue create numerous three-dimensional (3D) "objects." These might include cubes, boxes, cylinders, cones, and other primary forms. The simplest can be a long ribbon of paper or a strip folded "accordion" style. Some should be more complicated in their formal structure.

- Construct at least ten or more of these paper sculptures. Invest good effort in making your objects. Variety and contrast are desirable. Take pride in making them aesthetic, unique, and well crafted. The more compelling and original your 3D forms, the more likely your drawing will be too.

- An artwork composed of many pieces or modules is often called installation art. Attention is spread over a wider area than a single object. Find a suitable horizontal surface that will not be disturbed during the working process. This can be a table, chair, large box, other appropriate furniture, or an area on the floor. Arrange your constructed paper forms on this surface as a unified and beautiful installation. Whatever you choose, consider that the height of the installation will affect the viewpoint, the level at which you see its perspective.

- You may also think of this as an abstract still life. Make some objects touch, overlap, stack atop each other, and otherwise physically interact with one another. The feeling of action, stability, instability, or the suggestion of an impending event will enhance both the drawer's and the viewer's participation.

- Make sure the still life/installation has sufficient length, width, and height. Height may be the most crucial, also called elevation (especially by architects). Elevation will give the forms visual impact and that will serve you well when making a drawing.

- Place a single directed light at the subject, such as a table lamp with shade, clip-on light, or a floor lamp. Avoid ceiling light if possible. Direct lighting intensifies the drama of light and dark, whereas overhead lighting tends to dilute contrasts.

- Once the arrangement is established, consider the best angles for viewing. Each view reveals different relationships among the objects. Then, start drawing thumbnails from several of the best views. Plan your composition with a viewfinder. Decide whether you want more or less of the subject matter, a close-up of selected objects or a more distant view of the whole. Whatever you choose as a viewpoint, fill the space of the paper in a way that carries the eye to all areas, including top, bottom, sides, corners, and middle.

- Read or reread Chapter 6, How to Make Good Two Dimensional Art and Chapter 7, Drawing on Necessity for practical tips and advice about good drawing practices. Use the appropriate medium assigned in class, or if this is an independent project, you can choose any medium, wet or dry, black and white or color. A sustained drawing or a painting should be 18 × 24 inches or larger.

- Make your goal to draw a more dramatic, compelling, and beautiful image of the subject matter than the reality of your arrangement. In short, you want your art to be better than its source.

Drawing and Painting Drapery

Drapery as a subject matter in art has been represented in painting and sculpture since the ancients. Think of those long, glowing tunic robes in Greek and Roman art. Though costume fashions have changed constantly in the course of subsequent centuries, portrayal of drapery continues to be represented in contemporary art. In addition, drapery, fabric, and cloth of various and contrasting forms have always adorned living environments. Naturally, these subjects appear in art as well: in figurative subjects of clothing and costume, in still life table linens, as drapery to frame images, and even as symbolic wrappings suggestive of textile folds and creases in abstract art. If you look for the words "clothing" and "drapery" in a thesaurus, you will find a vast multitude of synonyms that describe their pervasiveness in our lives.

The endless range of colors and patterns that appear in all types of ornamental drapery are a beacon for the exploits of artists seeking to enliven their images. The great twentieth-century French painter Henri Matisse collected elegant, highly decorative textiles that he set up in still lifes and around models to enhance the festive spirit of his paintings. Since the 1970s, the Pattern and Decoration movement has focused on colorful ornamentation as the central theme of their artworks.

ARRANGE THE FABRIC AND OBJECTS

With the inspiration of viewing a rich variety of drapery traditions in art available via museums, books, and the Internet, make a drawing or a painting in which the forms and expanses of cloth and fabric play a major role.

*   Begin by choosing among the various fabrics available in your household. These may include garments, table cloths, bed linens, quilts, curtains, upholstery fabrics, towels, and even rags and tarps.
*   Arrange them as a still life on a tabletop, chair seat, or other horizontal surface. Twist and turn them in ways that create compelling lines, shapes, edges, folds, and creases.
*   As you do so, combine your cloths with at least two more contrasting objects. These might have hard surfaces such as wood, metal, glass, plastic, or cardboard. Play with the relationship between cloth and objects, either concealing or partially revealing the forms.
*   Continue manipulating all these materials until their arrangement appeals to your visual sense of beauty and order.

DRAW WITH THE CONCEPT OF DRAPERY ANATOMY

A few basics about how to interpret the complexity of the folds, lights, and darks in cloth will aid in representing its essence without the tedium of excessive detail. First, prioritize. Focus on the largest and most important lines and shapes, that is, those that are necessary for the overall three-dimensional illusion of the fabric. Sketch them (as in Stage I of drawing and painting) by representing the lines and edges that the fabrics make as shapes. Know that some minor folds may be eliminated from your composition if they are not essential to the overall quality of your image. Focusing primarily on the forms that matter will keep your subject fresh and free of the tedium of overworking.

Perceiving the most important lines and shapes, the forms that matter, can be simplified by applying a concept that I call *Drapery Anatomy*. See the illustration on the next page. Every fold, large or small, has just three components. A landscape metaphor will describe each one. A fold at its high point is a crest, like the top of a mountain, as it advances outward toward the light. Immediately, the fold slants downward as slopes at each of its two sides. The slopes finally end in flat planes or valleys. The next fold at the end of either of the valleys will begin to rise upward as a new slope toward another fold's crest. This simple formal pattern repeats constantly until the entire cloth is revealed. If you can see each fold individually this way, then you will understand that the entire cloth is an accumulation of many folds closely related and dependent on each other.

RENDER THE GRADATIONS OF LIGHT AND DARK

After you have defined the linear forms of the cloth, begin blocking in the light and dark patterns (Stage II) within the three parts of each fold. The crests tend to be in highlight because they advance in space, whereas the slopes are shaded as they turn away from the light. The valleys may be in the deepest shadow if there are two adjacent folds extremely close together, or somewhat lighter or even highlighted if the folds are much farther apart. Of course, these guidelines on light and shadow can change based on how each part of the cloth faces toward or away from the light.

Since cloth is yielding and flexible by nature, the surfaces curve in space and change direction, creating gradual and varied shifts between light and dark. See carefully how the crests, slopes, and valleys have gradations in how and where they reach the light or not. Rendering those gradations is crucial to representing a convincing illusion of three-dimensional form.

In all other ways, draw or paint with your best awareness of formalism, light and dark values, and composition. Remember that you are not imitating your subject, but interpreting it so that you sense both its essence and uniqueness.

DRAPERY ANATOMY AS LANDSCAPE METAPHOR

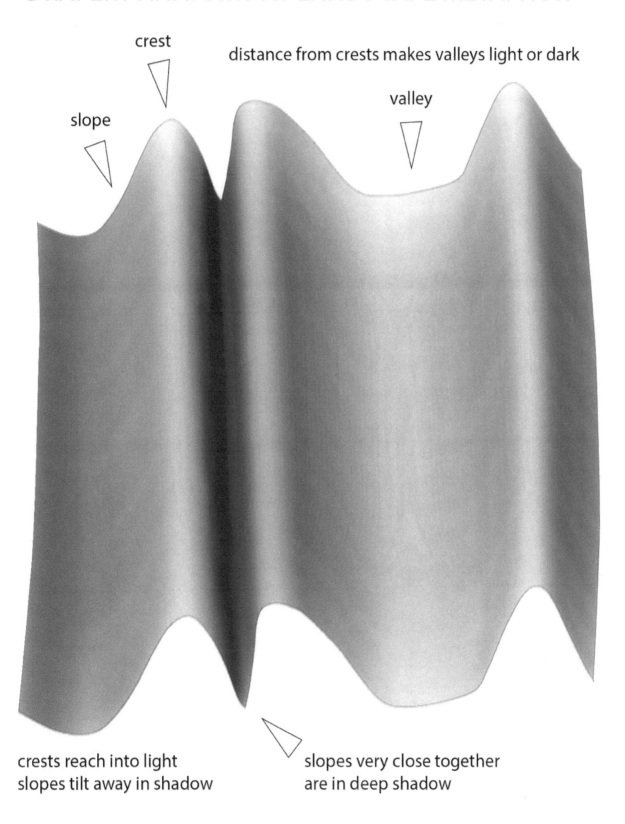

crest

distance from crests makes valleys light or dark

slope

valley

crests reach into light
slopes tilt away in shadow

slopes very close together
are in deep shadow

Grid and Pattern Composition

A grid is the division of a surface into multiple perpendicular blocks. The Cubists adapted the grid into an innovative pictorial structure. In early Cubism, the subject matter often nearly disappeared amid a flurry of shifting viewpoints, reduced descriptive details, and increasing abstract symbols replacing realistic imitation. The grid became a structural device to "contain" the subject, as if it were a readymade clothesline on which to hang objects and figures. The grid as an organizing principle for all manner of subjects and styles has become a standard of modern and contemporary practice.

You can assume that the "block" grid is the simplest pattern, that is, if pattern is a motif repeated throughout the expanse of a surface. Ultimately, dividing space into beautiful, interactive configurations is what art is about. Add to that light and dark values, color, texture, and additional details, and voila, that is the appeal of pattern. We see color and pattern everywhere in our domestic environments. Look around. The garments you wear, the cloths on your walls and tabletops, what you see in media images, and notice in nature's structures are an abundance of forms dependent on repeating motifs.

To take advantage of the expansive richness inherent in the post-Cubist grid system, you will make a mixed media drawing collage featuring the imaginative design of patterns organized into a unifying grid composition.

- Select a good quality heavyweight 18 × 24 inches (or larger) sheet of paper suitable for both wet and dry media. Divide the sheet into blocks with a straight edge by drawing a grid with a hard pencil (No. 2 or any "H" series, not the "B" soft pencils), measuring carefully squares that are no larger than 4 inch and no smaller than 2 inch. You can make all the blocks the same size or incorporate different-sized square blocks within the stated size range.
- Following your pencil lines carefully cut the grid out with a sharp razor knife guided against a straight edge. It is essential that your cuts are perfectly straight lines, as exact as the straight edge. Remember to always stand when you cut with a razor knife, for both safety and precision. Accurate cutting is described in more detail in the collage chapter.
- Now that the blocks are cut you will have 25 or more perfect squares 2 to 4 inches in size. Retain any end blocks that are not square (since 18 divided by 4 results in some 2 × 4 inches rectangles), since they will become part of your art.
- To enliven and expand your awareness of the vast range of pattern design consult books, magazines, the Internet, and your household surroundings. Pattern is literally everywhere. Pattern is not generally patented, so you can "steal" all you can find. What any artist actually does is redesign and adapt what he discovers to suit his aesthetic purposes. Anything you apply from your research is creative interpretation.
- Think of each block as a minidrawing. Begin each block with a light pencil drawing of a pattern. Render the patterns in all the blocks that way. Some patterns may be repeated or varied from block to block. But, you can change pattern designs at any point. Wide variety or variety within limited means is your choice.
- Embellish each of your blocks with color, texture, and details that describe the surfaces of your designs. You can render in any drawing or painting medium, except charcoal and pastel. Those media do not hold up well to the considerable handling that these blocks will undergo. Be careful not to leave too many areas of untouched paper. Too much white paper will tend to overwhelm your drawing and weaken its visual impact.

- You can draw each block separately or occasionally you can group two, three, or more blocks adjacent to each other so connections are made across the cut edges to bridge a continuation of lines and shapes. Since the blocks will eventually be placed side by side, that is, butted together as one seamless composition, consider how the cuts of the grid and their drawn "crossovers" create an intriguing blend of sharp collisions and defined connections.
- When all the blocks are drawn and embellished completely, arrange them onto a heavy paper mount into a pictorial rectangular whole by placing the blocks side by side, adjacent with edges touching so that no space on the mount is visible. Shift the blocks around frequently to different placements until they relate in an organized, harmonious, and beautiful way. This process is somewhat akin to solving a puzzle, except here the possibilities for constructing an image are far greater. Among the appropriate mounts are 3- or 4-ply Bristol paper, mat board, or illustration board.
- Look critically at your arrangement placed on the floor to get a better sense of how viewing distance affects the overall design and composition.
- When you have determined the best composition, take a photograph as a guide to gluing it to the mount. Otherwise, you will likely forget the order. You may choose to have a border or you can run your composition all the way to the four edges of the mount. Limit a border to no less than one-half an inch and no larger than one inch.
- Draw a light grid with pencil on the heavy paper mount, measured carefully with a straight edge, according to the location of the drawn blocks. Be accurate so that the perpendicular structures are all 90 degrees to the mount. You can start gluing blocks anywhere on your grid: middle, top, bottom, or at the sides. Apply glue with a brush to the entire reverse side of each block and to the area on the mount where the block is placed. Do not spot glue! Align the block carefully to your penciled grid and apply pressure. For proper glue mounting directions see the appropriate section in Chapter 10, Collage and Mixed Media.
- If you have odd areas to fill that are not square that must fill out the space of the picture's rectangle, cut any remaining squares measured to that space and glue in place accordingly. If you run out of drawn blocks, it is back to the drawing board!

This project has a wonderful appeal combining opposite approaches to the creative process. On the one hand, you are deliberate in planning how to design on each block. On the other hand, when you begin to place them all together as one composition, you will be spontaneous as you discover compelling relationships among all the parts. This latter process you would not have foreseen. Planning combined with discovery is the heart and soul of art making. Know that is the road to an exciting and satisfying visual experience.

Diptych to Polyptych

A picture divided is a picture that invites contemplation between its differing halves or panels. The concept of pictures within pictures began in ancient times and has continued in varying formats into contemporary practice. The vocabulary for this type of picture making is a diptych is a picture divided into two images that remain as one composition, whereas a triptych is three images and a polyptych is many.

In the Renaissance, as well as in the many centuries before most of the public became literate, sequential picture making was a way to inform and tell stories. One frame describes an incident that progresses into the next frame, repeated until the story or information is complete. In great splendor and profusion, the effect of combining images is everywhere in art history: Egyptian painting and stone reliefs, medieval manuscript illumination, Renaissance altarpieces and fresco murals, modern and contemporary art, comic strips, and graphic novels.

Drawers, painters, printmakers, photographers, and graphic designers continue to practice in the divided picture format even though most of the public can now read. The compelling nature of the polyptych is that the viewer experiences the fourth dimension, the passage of time. In each panel, the artist describes a different time and place. The viewer is persuaded to consider the connections (or seeming lack of) and the relationships among the panels. It is a brand of magisterial artistry to see the double effect of each panel for itself and for its differences and similarities next to other adjoining panels. In other words, the divided picture dramatizes both itself and its references to all the panels portrayed.

You will make a multipanel drawing or painting, that is, a diptych or polyptych. It will be derived from photographs you shoot, which have been cropped to form a composition composed of two images placed adjacent to one another if a diptych, or more than two images placed adjacent if it is a polyptych.

To understand the vast range of possibilities in working with the polyptych concept, begin by researching in books and on the Internet this list of artists past and present: Piero della Francesca, Michelangelo, Robert Rauschenberg, Jasper Johns, Jennifer Bartlett, Eric Fischl, James Rosenquist, Andy Warhol, Roy Lichtenstein, George Condo, Frank Stella, Jean-Michel Basquiat, Joan Mitchell, William Kentridge, Saul Steinberg, Chris Ware, and any number of comic strip artists, including George Herriman for *Krazy Kat* and Winsor McCay for *Little Nemo in Slumberland*. Most of these artists also worked in singular panels so do enough looking to see a variety of images.

- To start your project you need to determine the subject matter. Shoot many photographs in a range of various subjects seen indoors and outdoors, human-made and natural. These photographs may be of the same subject but with contrasting views or of different subjects that contrast or complement one another. Mix your shots from different perspectives, including close-ups and distant views.
- Look through your collection of images carefully. Select the best ones and those that you think may work well when mixed into the same composition. Print the selected images on good computer paper.
- Cut your prints with a razor knife into individual panels by eliminating the white borders that surround the images. Now each image is one potential panel for your composition. Begin to experiment by tentatively arranging the panels into polyptych formations. Explore as many combinations as possible, since some will be compelling, some indifferent or ineffective. Look for ways the panels relate to each other by shape, continuation of line or contour, color, or by similarity and contrast.

- The panels may run horizontally (laterally) or vertically (stacked atop each other). The cut panels may touch edges, that is, be placed adjacent, or there may be borders of space separating them. Keep borders at a fraction of an inch, up to one inch maximum. Borders too wide will not visually connect your panels as one composition.
- The panels may be equal in shape and size or not. If you choose to make them unequal, the composition can be irregular in its overall shape, that is, it does not have to conform to a standard rectangle. Whatever their sizes, shapes, or placement, the panels should suggest energy, impending change, or visual drama because of their proximity to each other.
- Once the best composition is established, glue the arrangement onto a heavy paper mount. This is essentially a collage. Reread Chapter 10, Collage and Mixed Media for technical information about cutting, gluing, and mounting. This collage is your model for making a drawing or painting in the diptych or polyptych format. The overall size must be at least 18×24 inches. The length and width may vary from those dimensions as long as the total of the two dimensions is 42 inches or greater. For example, the composition might be 20×22 inches because the total is 42 inches.
- Reread Chapter 9 if you are working on a canvas or Chapter 7 if you are working in any medium on paper. Your drawing or painting can be done on a single sheet or canvas with divisions between images marked by a hand-drawn contour line or a line drawn with a straight edge or template. These divisions do not have to conform to straight lines. Curved lines and irregular contours may divide your polyptych if it suits the purpose of your composition.
- With these types of more organic contours you may also choose to have your individual panels abut adjacently or separate from one another by use of a border of a fraction of an inch. Remember that the panels will not connect visually as one composition if the border is more than 1 inch wide. However, you decide to separate your images, the composition may be done on one sheet of paper or one canvas surface or you may execute each of your panels individually, that is, as physically independent but installed on the wall as one composition.
- As you draw or paint you may follow faithfully your photo collage composition, or if you discover better possibilities, you can crop, eliminate, add, or change details from your original plan.
- Whatever you do, always attempt to make your art better than your model.

The Micro- and Macro- Perspective Picture

We mostly see reality at eye level from a distance of inches or feet in order to navigate our surroundings or respond to the environment. However, there are other realities different in appearance from those we experience in daily life. For example, if you get extremely close to a subject you will see details of form and color not visible otherwise. Such a radical viewpoint will alter the perception of the subject. At that range, it may be seen as if something else entirely. In fact, getting especially close, as seen through a microscope, the subject matter is likely to be unrecognizable and more abstract than real.

At the opposite end of extremely close perspective is the perspective from a great distance away. Subjects photographed from the air via airplane, helicopter, or high altitude will include so much more visual information as the subject's area is vastly expanded. The image of that subject matter becomes multiple rather than singular. The absolute opposite of the microscope view is the image shot from a satellite. Perhaps the most startling change in perspective in the modern era is the shot of Earth as seen from the Moon landing in 1969.

The compelling contradiction with micro- and macro-viewpoints is that as you get increasingly closer or farther away, the subject will appear more abstract, often mysteriously unrecognizable. The lesson here is that realism and abstraction are really kissing cousins. One cannot exist without the other and both are human-made concepts in art. As one nineteenth-century painter noted, before a horse is a horse, it is first a shape and a color. This concept should persuade the viewer that neither realistic subject matter nor abstract forms are superior. Both share the same space.

- With that conceptual background in mind, collect photographs of both micro- and macro-subjects. You can find them from many sources: magazines, books, the Internet, or from your own photographs. Your subjects may be human-made or natural. Once you have ten or more worthy images, consider which ones have the best characteristics to interpret into a drawing or a painting. You must have several of the best images printed on paper to proceed.
- If multiple photographs contain desirable forms, you can mix parts of those photos into a single composition. You can also mix passages from both micro- and macro-photos. A good method for mixing images is to cut out areas from your prints and create a collage as your composition. You can also do that "mentally," that is, create a synthesis of those areas by designing them into a drawing plan.
- Whatever your approach, proceed by making numerous rough sketches (thumbnail size is fine) to explore the possibilities. Choose the image that seems to be the best composition.
- Begin interpreting your sketch into a sustained drawing or painting. Imagine how the lines, shapes, textures, patterns, and colors in your subject matter will translate to your chosen medium. Develop your composition according to the stages of drawing or painting as you have practiced before. Remember, manually made pictures are always about mark making (the tracks made by your tools) and the materiality of the medium. Consider how a particular technique may best interpret certain passages in your image. Feel free to change techniques in different parts of your picture according to need.
- You are never a slave to your sources. Nonetheless, look carefully at your photographs, collages, and preparatory drawings to guide your aesthetic decisions. Add, subtract, or change from your plan to develop the best art.

- Reality does not care whether it can be identified by name, label, or convenient word. Your drawing or painting should reflect the dualities of realism and abstraction. Chances are that abstract form will dominate the picture even as it may tantalizingly suggest figure, landscape, or object in symbolic terms.

Your completed art will likely have the ring of mystery and intrigue because of the extreme viewpoints represented by micro- and macro-distances. Take advantage of escorting viewers on a trip to a place they have never seen before.

MAKING ART WITH MAPS

Maps of all kinds have a beauty of their own. The myriad details of roads, cities, boundaries, bodies of water, mountains, and other descriptive terrain are all represented by the formal elements of line, shape, color, texture, and pattern. Maps are works of art, carefully designed by a range of professionals, including cartographers, engineers, surveyors, geographers, and graphic artists.

The most common maps are country, state, and city maps. These also appear in road atlases. There are many different kinds of maps with a richness of detail and imagery. A partial list includes topographic maps, aeronautical maps, blueprint maps, foreign country or world maps, weather maps, and mass transit maps (subway). Spend time to discover them. A little research is a way to expand your awareness of creative possibilities.

- You will make an artwork using maps as a foundation, a starting point for constructing a more exciting and compelling pictorial statement. Collect all the maps you can find. You may also print maps found in books, the Internet, or directly from maps themselves. If you do not want to physically alter a map, printing its image is a valid method to gather art material.
- Consider your maps as found materials, to be used along with the traditional media of drawing and painting. You can begin in various ways. Glue your map onto a heavy-mounted paper if you plan to make a drawing or onto a canvas or panel if you plan to make a painting. You can glue one or more maps whole or cut one or several maps into sections or fragments and attach to your mount in a variety of smaller pieces. Cover all or most of the surface with map material.
- Think of this map mounting as the beginning, as the background for your composition. Then, draw, paint, or collage onto the maps' surface. In other words, transform the context of the map material by altering it creatively.
- Be sensitive to what is already printed on the maps. Those existing lines, shapes, and colors may suggest interesting possibilities to add, subtract, enhance, or otherwise alter the printed forms. You can simultaneously pay tribute to the maps by emphasizing or enhancing what is already there, or you can violate their surfaces by changing, covering, or contrasting the maps with more of your own assertive drawing and painting.
- Another option is to start drawing or painting first and attach map cutouts later. You can alternate between applying map materials and traditional art media as often as needed.
- Build your surfaces until your image seems to be more your statement than the maps'. At the same time, be sure the maps play a prominent role in the composition. If there is too little map visibility that defeats the concept. Think of the map imagery as a kind of silent actor, one that will participate in the drama while you direct how its role will be played.
- Take heart in the fact that you will be starting with beautiful and complex forms that somebody else provided for your artistic benefit. Then, with your personal vision, enhance to a greater extent all the glory of its intricate and dense physical properties. Embellish with your chosen media until the image is your interpretation of how maps can be transformed into beautiful art.

- Finally, the texts in maps, that is, the words, numbers, and symbols that explain its details may contribute something positive to your composition. Artists have incorporated texts in their art since the Cubists first glued newspaper into their collages. The visual and the verbal combined can sometimes add interesting content to art. On the other hand, you can choose to eliminate text if it does not suit your purpose by drawing or painting over it.

What you choose to retain, add, or eliminate is part of the creative problem-solving process. Know that you have a lot of artistic latitude. The choices are yours, so revel in the prospects as you make your art.

THE BOX AS AN ART FORM

The box or container as a visual form has a rich history in both domestic design and fine arts. The box is a unique hybrid between utility in life and aesthetic beauty as sculptural art.

The spatial conditions of boxes are compelling in their great variety of form and shape. Consider that a box has essentially four visual areas for artistic intervention: (1) the exterior form of the box, (2) its interior space, (3) the contents that occupy its interior, and (4) the finish on the box's outer and inner surfaces. These formal areas are an opportunity for the artist to invent or reinvent the box.

- Your project is to create a box as art and sculptural form. Practical function is optional. Whatever choices you make as to its utilitarian accessibility, your box sculpture must transform the domestic suppositions of the myriad ordinary containers that do not reflect artistic intention. For example, a box that cannot be opened but which amplifies in dramatic terms only its exterior form may be tantalizing for what it both reveals and hides. As you mull ideas for the design of your box, focus at first on which of the four visual areas described earlier you want to emphasize. But, you must address at least the two areas of the sculpture's exterior and its surface finish, while the interior and any contents are optional choices.
- Choose your construction materials according to the requirements of the assignment or freely choose if you are making an independent project. These may include wood, cardboard, mat board, metal, plastic, or other malleable materials for which you have tools and experience in handling.
- Too often we assume that boxes are cubes with four walls set at 90 degrees with a bottom for support and a lid to close. Not necessarily so. A box (think of the broader implications of the term "container") can take on any shape: curved, oval, circular, irregular, or multiple shapes that extend in various directions in space. It can have numerous interior spaces, like rooms in a house, and have special compartments such as drawers, doors, or hidden nooks and crannies. Angles comprising these parts may be 90 degrees or not. A box may stand on its own or be attached to another box or nonbox form. The range of possible formal structures is countless and only limited by the maker's imagination.
- Start by drawing. Drawing stimulates your ability to be expansive in your structural considerations. Planning in two dimensions frees you from having to be concerned with the how of construction. At the same time, you will need to be cognizant of your abilities with tools and materials.
- Before or during the planning of your box, you need to research with books or the Internet the important artists who have mastered the art of the box. The following artists are must sees for appreciating and understanding the enormous range of expression possible: Lucas Samaras, H. C. Westermann, Louise Nevelson, Joseph Cornell, and Donald Judd. These artists have made other kinds of art in addition, so make a thorough search.
- Once ready with your best drawing plan, begin the construction. Consider this a mixed media project. You may include in your box sculpture any found materials or found objects that enhance the art of your box. Consider the direction of how you want the viewer to understand your box and where on the box you want to focus the visual attention of the viewer. Remember that you are departing from ordinary experience and discovering new ways of what a box can be and what it may contain. The "shock" or surprise of upsetting expectations in order to express new possibilities is what any art making is about.
- NOTE: A variation of this project is to start with a found box or other existing container, one that already had a context in reality. For example, a jewelry box, wood crate, cigar box, toolbox, birdcage, or other existing container can be a starting point. The challenge is to transform the found container so that the viewer is more concerned with your invented expression than with its former function.

THE ARTIST INTERVIEW

Write a fictitious interview with a favorite artist who is deceased. Make it convincing and plausible despite the differences of past and present times. Write the questions and the answers, as if the artist is speaking when he responds to your questions. Compose the interview in the traditional format. You ask, then, he/she answers.

You will need to do some research to understand that historical period and to be able to ask questions that address the artist's concerns and interests. You can assume that you live in the time of the artist. Imagine yourself in that environment.

The alternative interview is to assume the artist is "reborn" into the present time. How the artist might react in such a time warp might be both wise and humorous. For example, what would Picasso think of contemporary artists working in digital media or making images unheard of in his time, that is before his death in 1973. Would van Gogh as a gifted colorist approve of the color revolution expressed in Matisse's Fauvism movement? What would Paul Cezanne think of Cubism?

The more you know about the artist and his influence on succeeding generations, the more likely your questions and answers will be informed and compelling. Spend some time reading and researching the artist's work and the time in which he lived. If you can find actual interviews the artist gave, that is a valuable source of reference. If you can visit a museum where the artist's work is in the permanent collections, visit. That is a gold mine to see the art in person. New York City's great museums, The Metropolitan, the Guggenheim, the Whitney, and the Museum of Modern Art, are the best in-the-flesh bets.

If you do your homework, research the artist, understand the temper of the times, and write questions that reflect that understanding, you and your readers will have a new set of insights about the art and life of a different era and how it compares to our own.

Write in Response to *Art Start*

Reading and writing about art enhances your understanding of what you are doing in the studio and offer insights into new possibilities to explore. Reflection has always been a hallmark of the artist's mission to reinvent tradition and convention, to transform what we already know into new experience and creative visual forms.

What you have practiced in class and interpreted from the reading of *Art Start* should guide you to identify the key points that have aided your development. These should include both mistakes and successes in your art making and what that has taught you. Read the following prompts to identify the most important attitudes and abilities you have acquired. Write in response to as many of these cues and questions as are relevant to your experience.

1. What have you learned that has enhanced your awareness of and appreciation of art? Cite the relevant chapters, passages, or sentences.
2. The book emphasizes both practical strategies for art making and philosophical viewpoints that result from art experiences. Identify at least one of each that you have gained from the course and the book.
3. Do the three art history chapters help you locate yourself in reference to your own time and place? Describe the benefit to your art making that historical or contemporary art practice provides.
4. Is there anything in the book that is especially surprising (but still meaningful) that you did not realize beforehand? Explain.
5. Was it of value to read passages that confirmed what you have already experienced, or that caused you to understand in a new or different way?
6. Are the chapters on Studio and Independent Projects helpful to your understanding of how to do those projects?
7. Which chapter(s) is most helpful to your art making and why?
8. Is there anything you did not understand? Be specific.
9. Are the illustrations helpful? How about the art history "family tree" diagrams?
10. In Chapter 34, Quotations: Portable Ponderables, identify a quotation (or several quotations if you can be expansive) that has strong meaning for you. Describe why and what you think the quote means.
11. In Chapter 24, Art History Timeline choose two artists or styles, one from the past and one that is contemporary. Use the Internet to look at many images of the art involved and read a few passages to understand the style or the artist. How do you respond to the art and how does it relate to your own art inclinations?
12. Do the three modern art diagrams (see pages 136–138) help you to see the Big Picture of the art world in a clear and condensed way? Does it help in navigating the complexities of the numerous styles that modernism represents? Explain.
13. If you are an art major, do you think you have what it takes to become an artist? Consult Chapter 5, Character of the Artist. What are your strengths and your weaknesses? Are there additional attributes you think necessary that are not mentioned in the chapter?
14. If you are not an art major, can you identify the qualities or principles you can take from the experience of art making that will have a lasting influence on your life?

15. Abstraction may be the most confounding content in art to understand and appreciate. Have Chapter 15, Abstraction, Representation, and Reality and Chapter 16, How to Evaluate the Quality of Abstract Art as well as what we have done in class helped to dispel the ambivalence and uncertainty about abstract art? Explain.
16. Would you like to see anything added to the book in the next edition?
17. Would you recommend *ART START* to others who may have an interest in art? Explain.
18. Did you respond in any additional way to reading *ART START* that is relevant to you but not previously suggested?

TOPICS FOR DISCUSSION

1. How has university training in the fine arts influenced artists? What are the advantages and disadvantages for artists in acquiring baccalaureate and graduate degrees in art? What processes of learning and training are gained in college art programs that are not available otherwise?

2. Degree programs in art train students to become artists. Yet, the vast majority of art graduates earn their living outside the art professions. What qualities of a college education benefit students in pursuing careers that may be outside or only tangentially related to their majors?

3. The contrasts between the fine arts and the applied arts (graphic design, commercial art, and industrial design) are considerable relative to purpose, temperament, and cultural values. What personal qualities and attitudes must be considered in choosing a career in either of these disciplines? How are the skills and understanding of artistic principles similar and different in each area?

4. Pluralism began in the 1970s when art became more diverse in media, subject matter, and content. Art no longer flowed from a dominant style or movement, but rather from a cross-disciplinary mix of political, social, and cultural references. As pluralism replaced the once prevailing art movements of modernism (1850–1970), it became known as postmodernism (1970–present). Although everything seems possible in which no stone is left unturned, one contention is that pluralism is really modeled on and derived from past innovations. What seems new is not really new at all, but rather a variation of or homage to what has already transpired. Whether this argument seems true or not, how does that change how we understand modern art compared to postmodern art? Describe a list of the similarities and contrasts that characterize the qualities of art in these two periods, modern and postmodern.

5. Film, video, photography, installation art, performance art, conceptual art, and mixed media all existed before postmodernism. Digital technology greatly expanded or enhanced these traditions. Is digital technology more about new tools for the artist, or has digitally driven art become as innovative as the great movements in modernism?

6. Is the creation of beauty still a major artistic skill? Is it an assumed given that art works should be beautiful? What is the relationship between beauty and ugliness? Can an ugly, repugnant, or otherwise grotesque subject matter become aesthetic when expressed by an artist? Can less offensive subjects that are awkward, ungainly, mundane, dull, or unpopular be made into meaningful art? Explain your viewpoint with specific examples.

7. Popular culture and fine arts often seem at odds. Does pop culture tend to emphasize the familiar in order to be easily understood and reach the largest audience? Does the overexposure of pop icons result in clichés that diminish their cultural worth? How does cuteness play a role in attracting audiences? How does cuteness affect art content?

8. Some observers consider fine arts to be elitist, meant only for the highly educated and the affluent. Does understanding and appreciating modern art require some degree of predisposition and learning? Should art give the viewer pause for thought, reflection, and a reconsideration of norms and expectations in art and culture? Can art be accessible for anyone who wants to participate?

9. Sometimes, objects or images, regardless of whether they were intended as art or not, are so bad they're good. It may be an unexpected quality of strangeness, obsession, eccentricity, uniqueness, mystery, extremeness, or otherwise unique character that makes one realize its worth as something of value to view and contemplate. Can you identify and describe any examples in your experience? Can objects so-bad-they're-good be useful thought experiments to extend the imagination? Can these kinds of objects give inspiration for artists to push the boundaries in developing their art?

10. While art refers to content, craft (or craftsmanship) refers to the quality of how something is made. Sometimes, art and craft can be confused. Where one stops and the other begins can be difficult to know. When craft or the techniques of applying materials dominate content, the resulting object may be called craft. Yet, all art is crafted to a greater or lesser degree. What purpose does craftsmanship serve in the making of and viewing of art? Can art be made with deliberately "bad" craftsmanship and be effective artistically? Can art be diminished by poor craftsmanship?

chapter

INDEPENDENT PROJECTS

1. **The eccentric surface:** Draw or paint on an unfamiliar, nonart surface, or found object. You can make art on envelopes, paper bags, commercial packaging, old calendars, etc. Open the envelope, bag, or carton to reveal its odd, irregular shape. You can now make a "shaped" drawing or painting, using the unusual contours of your object as the shape of its composition. If possible, incorporate into your picture any text or image that may be printed on the material. Be creative. Alter, deface, or add elements to any of the found printed matter so those elements become part of your statement. Whatever you do, don't be intimidated by any of the given printing or folded qualities of your chosen material. Work it up until it feels like your own expression rather than something found.

2. **The upside-down drawing:** Clip a black and white photograph, preferably one that is a little out of focus such as from a newspaper. Turn it upside down and look at it *only* that way—eventually *forgetting* what it represents. Keep it upside down as you look at it to make a drawing. When done, turn it over to see if it still resembles the subject matter. You may prefer to view it upside down as the right way to see as art!

3. **The symbolic self-portrait:** Draw or paint yourself without your face or figure in the image. The subject matter you include in the composition can be highly subjective and intuitive. However you interpret the concept, gather objects and items that have personal meaning for you. Avoid anything that may smack of cliché or cuteness to an observer. You can also think of this as a Self-Portrait as Still Life.

4. **The power of words:** Look for a word in the dictionary that conjures up a strong image or visual impression. Verbs, nouns, and adjectives are all appropriate. Draw the quality or sensation that the word suggests by allowing your forms to become abstract and associative, but not literal and blatant. Variations to a single word might include choosing a line from a poem, an axiom or adage, a paragraph from a novel or short story, a children's story or fable that you reinterpret, a commercial jingle on which you put a new twist, an automatic sentence you write spontaneously (a Surrealist technique), a line from a news story, etc. Don't try to illustrate the word or phrase, but rather capture its feeling or essence as a visual expression. Get carried away. If you're too rigid in your thinking, you'll likely be too obvious or literal in what you do.

5. **Color *à la* Matisse:** Spend a day or so painting sheets of plain white paper (any types or sizes) in a variety of colors with acrylics or tempera. Do some that are color wheel vivid,

some tints, shades, tones, and other mixtures that are more subdued. This is raw material to make a collage. Cut up with scissors or razor knives, thinking of these tools as if they're drawing instruments—fashioning elaborate contours, shapes, some flat, some 3D, some representational, some abstract. When you have a robust inventory, assemble into a collage. Cover the mount first with large areas of color, then superimpose the smaller, positive shapes, objects, and figures. You can stay all figurative, abstract, or mix it up.

6. **On-site drawing:** Take a hike (when weather permits) into the landscape of the less familiar. Find environments different from the ones you normally frequent or inhabit. Carry a folding bench, some paper, and art supplies. Draw or paint on the spot, that is, on site, just as scores of artists have done since the Impressionists. Make studies you can work up later in the studio or assume the challenge to make a finished work there in the moment. Nature is the best teacher (and artist), but man-made structures are fine subjects too.

7. **The accidental still life:** Have a junk drawer bursting at the seams? Take the drawer out of its cabinet and draw as is—or spill its contents out onto the floor or tabletop. Don't try to arrange "nicely" or consciously. Instead, try to avoid the staged look of many traditional still lifes and accept how the objects look in their happenstance state. Alternatives include a cluttered closet, a box of random objects from the attic, an overstuffed toolbox from the garage, a heap of unwashed laundry ... or just spill the contents of a wastebasket on the floor. Challenge: Draw this chaos into an organized composition.

8. **Letters and text:** Look for them in magazines, packaging, old posters, calendars, wherever you can cut them out. Search for a variety in sizes, shapes, styles, colors, and proportions. Don't be concerned with messages or meanings. In fact, cut many of them so they are no longer legible as words. The purpose is to make visual art out of these raw fonts and types whose original purpose you are violating. Think of letters as mysterious abstract forms or a language that cannot be read. Work up into a collage in which the letters and text assume a new state as texture, pattern, color, and shape—with the tantalizing prospect of at first appearing to look readable, but actually becoming illegible and abstract. If your forms are too obviously verbal and readable, then you end up with worn-out slogans, tiresome essays, or didactic messages. This is the pleasure of form, not the preaching of gospel.

9. **Larger than life drawing:** Take a magnifying glass and hold it over a subject in such a way that it looks strange or unrecognizable. Make a drawing by looking through the lens of the glass. Try to capture the distorted and magnified qualities of the subject matter.

10. **Big deal doodle:** Start a drawing (or painting) with a random line, mark, or shape anywhere on the surface. Don't think about things, objects or figures. Make lines, marks, and tones that are impulsive in the moment. After a time, let the previous mark, that is, what's already there on the surface, suggest what to do next ... and next. Allow the process to "mushroom" until the picture plane seems saturated with forms and or feels complete as an image. Change color or media whenever you have the urge. Don't "judge" elements as you work, but take pleasure in your spontaneity and trust in the prospect that as the density of line and form builds your picture will become substantial and expressive. See artists such as Jackson Pollock, Arshile Gorky, Mark Tobey, Picasso's pen and ink drawings, and Joan Miro's oils and watercolors to understand how seeming random spontaneity can be made into artistic purpose.

11. **Image by reflection:** Find a mirror at least a foot square, the larger the better. Tilt it at an angle to your vision, 30-45 degrees or thereabouts and so it reflects a visually engaging subject. Notice how the shape of the mirror is thrown into perspective as the lines of its frame are slanted in space. Fit this irregular frame of the mirror within the rectangle of your composition so that you can see both the reflection and the negative space between the outer edges of the mirror and the edges of your picture. Draw or paint

both positive (reflection) and negative (outside the mirror) spaces of your composition. Pay particular attention to how the shape of the mirror relates to the rectangle of your work.

12. **Room with a view:** Find a room with interesting forms and objects, specifically, in a corner. Frame your composition so that parts of two walls, the ceiling, and the floor are visible. It is as if you are standing on the bottom of a box and facing one of the four corners. Use a viewfinder to help see cropping and perspective. Make a drawing from this viewpoint by including as much spatial depth and description of the room's details as you can. You can do the same view in an attic, garage, basement, or public building. You may want to take a few photos to see how the perspective affects the pictorial rectangle. Drawings and photographs can provide studies for a more sustained painting later.

13. **Pattern as picture:** Create a proposal for a wallpaper or textile design. Many artists did commercial work of this kind in addition to studio work. Look at the wallpaper of Charles Burchfield (twentieth century, American), Rauol Dufy (twentieth century, French), and the fashion designs of Sonia Delaunay (twentieth century, French). Some artists brought this subject into their studio work, such as the Pattern and Decoration Painting of the 1970s. This project should not resemble the banal designs of the local painting and decorating store. Be creative and make compositions that are more related to your studio work.

14. **Write your own proposal as I've done in the previous examples.** Then execute a work of art according to your own game plan!

chapter

33

HOW TO TAKE BETTER PHOTOGRAPHS

Photography is a major tool for the artist, a brand of "note taking" to document the wonders of the visual world. Photographs can be an important source for stimulating the imagination—serving as models for deriving images in drawing and painting or as plans for making sculpture. If truth is stranger than fiction, then photographs are a useful record for understanding the surprising complexities of the visible environment. Below are suggestions to make your photographs of better quality and more relevant to art making.

1. **Light is always your subject in photography.** Carefully deployed highlight and shadow intensify, dramatize, and clarify. Consider the time of day and the weather when shooting outdoors and how those conditions influence your subjects. Light is often especially effective when expressed in black and white photography. Look at photographs of the modern masters and the black and white movies of the early and mid-twentieth century.

2. **When in doubt, snap the shutter.** Sometimes an image seen through your camera will seem unimpressive, but shoot anyway. When you import your photos and see them in greater size and detail and properly edited, those lesser images can suddenly and pleasantly surprise. Besides, good photographers take many more photos than they keep. More choices increase your artistic possibilities.

3. **Avoid clichés, such as postcard and calendar stereotypes.** Remember that art is about taking us somewhere new to experience what we *don't* know. So, change your point of view. Look for subjects that have been neglected or overlooked by others.

4. **Use your LCD screen or viewfinder to frame your subject to its best advantage.** Look for the qualities that make good composition, that is, with the formalist principles of order, rhythm, contrast, variety, and description.

5. **Turn off the flash.** It tends to wash out areas or destroy clarity and detail with glare. It is better to improve an imperfect photograph later by editing its flaws.

6. **Patterns versus unique forms often comingle in subject matter.** Patterns and textures are compelling since they appeal to the sense of touch and set up rhythms that keep the eye moving. To establish focal points, look for ways to break up those repetitions with single objects or larger forms. These breaks in continuity can help to avoid monotony and consequently offer a visual surprise or curiosity.

7. **Lines that lead the eye.** Watch for long contours that characterize some subjects. A fence, a stream, a tree's contour, or a road or meandering path may provide a way to zip the eye around your image. Long lines can enhance perspective, and become a road map to navigate the image, especially if they're slanted or diagonal.

8. **Consider your distance from the subject.** Moving closer or using your zoom can greatly change the character and impact of your image. To crop or not to crop, and precisely how much, is always an important factor in composition. Take several shots from different distances and vantage points. Later, you can compare the qualities among those varied shots. A common mistake is shooting the subject from too great a distance with critical loss of detail and engaging description.

9. **Rarely is the world of objects found in an already aesthetic order.** When shooting objects, as in still life, move them around if possible to improve their arrangement.

10. **Space it out.** All pictures based on illusion have foreground, middle ground, and background. Try to find engaging forms in all those areas of an image. Consider how objects touch, overlap, and position themselves in receding and advancing space.

11. **Do take photographs of reflections on water, glass, mirrors, and glossy metallic surfaces.** These are often overlooked, but they provide a fresh way to reexperience reality through a secondary "window."

12. **The found frame.** Sometimes a window, doorway, architectural structure, or some other grid-like object may present a readymade opportunity for composition. Take advantage when possible to allow the subject to help you compose your image.

13. **Use a good editing app.** The wonder of digital photography is how you can convert a flawed photo with poor light and imperfect focus into an image that is clear and resolved.

14. **Print your photographs.** Well, not all of them, but printing makes photos more "real" and tangible. The concrete quality of a print will correspond more closely to how you may utilize the photo in making your art, as in a model for a drawing or painting. Think of your photo archive as another form of sketchbook. Refer to it often, and your images can stimulate impulses and ideas for art making.

SECTION VIII

SPEAKING OF ART:
THE VERBAL AND THE VISUAL

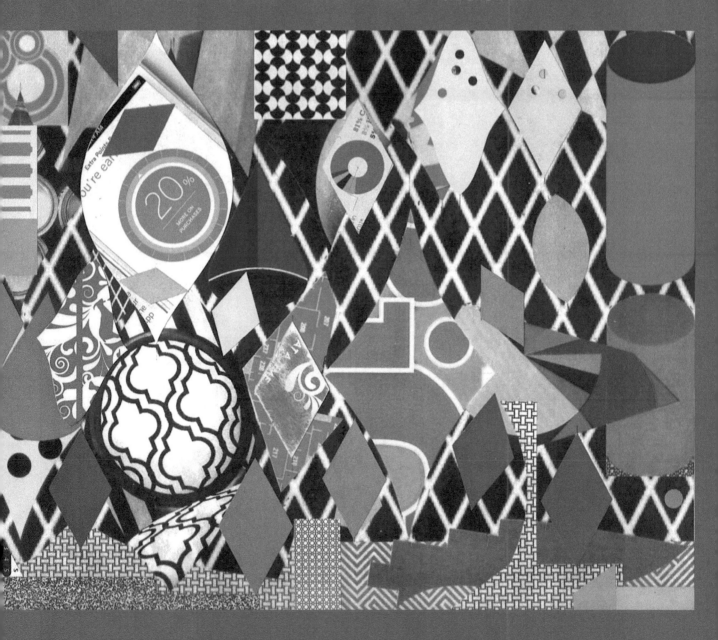

QUOTATIONS: PORTABLE PONDERABLES

I am not sure how or when my interest in quotations started. Reading has always been akin to a treasure hunt: surely around the next corner, by turning the page, there will be the key to the mystery, the answer to any number of questions that have rattled around in the attic of my mind. Maybe quotations are a shortcut to bolster our senses and sensibilities in a world wracked with insensitivities and insensibilities. If I am not sure what to think, it helps to know what the best thinkers can offer.

It seems fitting to include in this book a collection of the best thoughts by the most distinguished personalities from the ancients to our own contemporaries. Whether credited to a fourth century B.C. Greek philosopher or an American Pop artist, the ideas expressed in these quotes all have modern relevance. The external forms of culture change with trends and fashions, but human nature does not.

A few gifted people have the ability to pack a wallop by the least means possible, to describe Big Thoughts with the fewest words. Poets do this supremely well. In prose, so do a variety of artists, composers, writers, scientists, philosophers, and public figures. What these quotations may lack in poetry is surely compensated for in poignancy and insight.

Good quotations are not sound bites that soon vaporize but are little mental firecrackers that linger in the mind. You might agree or disagree with any given example, depending on your experience and disposition, but your response is the handle by which to either embrace or wrestle with its idea. Pondering how someone else's verbal proposal might relate to your own life is a large part of the appeal. In some cases, you can appreciate the new way an idea confirms your own viewpoint. On the other hand, if the insight is unfamiliar, it may challenge your thinking or extend your frame of reference. Either way you gain.

This collection is my own, gathered from the pleasant task of perusing all manner of books, documents, and electronic media. The process is not unlike strolling on a beach and discovering the most striking shells or sea-washed stones. While filling my basket with the best specimens, I have made no attempt to represent all professions or give balance to opposing viewpoints. These quotes have no unifying thesis, no ideology, no chronological order, and some admittedly address subjects beyond the parameters of art.

My criteria for including a quote is its relevance for art students and the bearing its message has on art making and life-long learning. Yes, messy life gets mixed in too. No artist would deny that the boundaries where art ends and life begins are all but imperceptible. Issues in society, politics, popular culture, science, and the various humanities all resonate in the efforts and thinking of creative people.

While brevity tends to be a dominant feature of quotations—they rely on concise formats for their dramatic impact—their length was not a criterion for selection. At the risk of shortchanging their contexts, a few statements are paragraphs selected from larger treatises but their messages still pack meaning despite their briefer forms.

Some authors may seem to contradict others, but in those cases the reader can decide how to reconcile their contrasts. I believe that art and life are filled with tantalizing questions of mystery and ambiguity—that little of either can be neatly reduced to black and white absolutes. Irony, opposites, and contradictions are the ways of the world in its glorious and unsettled complexity. In fact, the ability to simultaneously hold two opposing viewpoints in mind is a crucial skill in the powers of reasoning for all who would be educated.

Since it is the thoughts that count, I have not attempted to track the sources of writing or speech from which these quotes originate. The message is the medium. Of course, you can find information about virtually all of these speakers and writers whose insights have caught public attention because of their achievements.

Some notes about the contents: Since Picasso's art has played a gargantuan role in modernism, I have included a collection of his provocative speeches in its own group. While Picasso wrote very little, his quotes come to us from a variety of witnesses during the span of his life and career.

If this collection seems unwieldy or protracted, know that you do not have to read in the order arranged or at one sitting. In fact, the process is better as a dipping exercise, as in a bowl of chips. This is fast food for the brain. But I bet you cannot eat just one! Anyway, read a few. See what you think. If just a handful of these quotations resonate with a handful of students, my task will have been well spent. Pass the peanuts.

> While I recognize the necessity for a basis of observed reality … true art lies in a reality that is felt.—Odilon Redon (1840-1916)
>
> All knowledge has its origins in our perceptions.—Leonardo da Vinci (1452-1519)
>
> A man paints with his brains and not with his hands.—Michelangelo (1475-1564)
>
> The aim of art is to represent not the outward appearance of things, but their inward significance.—Aristotle (384-322 B.C.)
>
> Any work of art that can be understood is the product of journalism.—Tristan Tzara (1896-1963)
>
> A subject that is beautiful in itself gives no suggestion to the artist. It lacks imperfection.—Oscar Wilde (1854-1900)

Art hath an enemy called Ignorance.—Ben Jonson (1572?-1637)

Painting is silent poetry, and poetry is painting that speaks.—Simonides (sixth-fifth century B.C.)

For the mystic what is how. For the craftsman how is what. For the artist what and how are one.—William McElcheran (1927-1999)

Without art, the crudeness of reality would make the world unbearable.—George Bernard Shaw (1856-1950)

Because a work of art does not aim at reproducing natural appearances, it is not, therefore, an escape from life … but an expression of the significance of life, a stimulation to greater effort in living.—Henry Moore (1898-1986)

All great art is by its very essence in conflict with the society with which it coexists. It expresses the truth about existence regardless of whether this truth serves or hinders the survival purpose of a given society. All great art is revolutionary because it touches upon the reality of man and questions the reality of the various transitory forms of human society.—Erich Fromm (1900-1980)

Artists who seek perfection in everything are those who cannot attain it in anything.—Eugene Delacroix (1798-1863)

Illusions are art, for the feeling person, and it is by art that you live, if you do.—Elizabeth Bowen (1899-1973)

It is well to remember that a picture—before being a battle horse, a nude woman, or some anecdote—is essentially a plane surface covered with colors assembled in a certain order.—Maurice Denis (1870-1943)

Art is nature seen through a temperament.—Emile Zola (1840-1902)

The form is the outer expression of the inner content.—Vasily Kandinsky (1866-1944)

Expression to my way of thinking does not consist of the passion mirrored upon a human face or betrayed by a violent gesture. The whole arrangement of my picture is expressive. The place occupied by figures or objects, the empty spaces around them, the proportions, everything plays a part. Composition is the art of arranging in a decorative manner the various elements at the painter's disposal for the expression of his feelings. In a picture every part will be visible and will play the role conferred upon it, be it principal or secondary. All that is not useful in the picture is detrimental. A work of art must be harmonious in its entirety; for superfluous details would, in the mind of the beholder, encroach upon the essential elements.—Henri Matisse (1869-1954)

I know perfectly well that only in happy instants am I lucky enough to lose myself in my work. But this thought produces a feeling in me that is quite the opposite of what others imagine. Since I have now become one with my conscience, the statement that coldness is more necessary in the conquest of art than blind devotion or untrammeled passion seems right to me.—Carlo Carra (1881-1966)

The aim of art, so far as one can speak of an aim at all, has always been the same; the blending of experience gained in life with the natural qualities of the art medium.

Visual experience cannot be based on feeling or perception alone. Feelings and perceptions, which are not sublimated by the essence of things, lose themselves in the sentimental.—Hans Hofmann (1880-1966)

I must impress upon myself that I know nothing at all, for it is the only way to progress.

A picture is something that requires as much trickery, malice, and vice as the perpetration of crime.—Edgar Degas (1834-1917)

… To us art is an adventure into an unknown world, which can be explored only by those willing to take the risks. … It is our function as artists to make the spectator see the world our way— not his. …—Adolph Gottlieb (1903-1973) and Mark Rothko (1903-1970)

At a certain moment [post-World War II ca. 1945] the canvas began to appear to one American painter after another as an arena in which to act— rather than as a space in which to reproduce, re-design, analyze, or "express" an object, actual or imagined. What was to go on the canvas was not a picture but an event.

The painter no longer approached his easel with an image in his mind; he went up to it with material in his hand to do something to that other piece of material in front of him. The image would be the result of this encounter.—Harold Rosenberg (1906-1978)

Art is I … science is we.—Claude Bernard (1813-1878)

A picture is finished when I stop looking at it, and it starts looking back.—Paul Klee (1879-1940)

There are things known, and things unknown: in between are the doors.—William Blake (1757-1827)

Anyone who does not want to be an apprentice will never be a master.—Jan Tschichold (1902-1974)

Art must take reality by surprise.—Francoise Sagan (1935-2004)

The more distant and distinct the relationship between the two realities that are brought together, the more powerful the image.—Pierre Reverdy (1889-1960)

If you ask me what I came to do in this world, I, an artist, I will answer you: I am here to live out loud.—Emile Zola (1840-1902)

Chance favors the prepared mind.—Louis Pasteur (1822-1895)

If you look at certain walls covered with stains and built of mingled stones … you will … discern provinces with their mountains, their rivers, rocks, trees, plains, great valleys, hills in many aspects … battles and the swift movement of faces and singular expressions, clothes and innumerable other things.—Leonardo da Vinci (1452-1519)

The man who can't visualize a horse galloping on a tomato is an idiot.—Andre Breton (1896-1966)

Among a hundred men there is one who can think, but only one among a thousand who can see.—John Ruskin (1819-1900)

The entire course of our life depends on our senses, of which sight is the most universal and noble.—Rene Descartes (1596-1650)

The problem about art is not finding more freedom, it's about finding obstacles.—Richard Rogers (b. 1933)

To hear is to forget, to see is to remember, to do is to understand.—Chinese proverb

True artists are almost the only men who do their work with pleasure.—Auguste Rodin (1840-1917)

I like to make an image that's so simple you can't avoid it, and so complicated you can't figure it out.—Alex Katz (b. 1927)

What we want to make is something that utterly fills the sight.—Sam Francis (1923-1994)

I try to apply colors like words that shape poems, like notes that shape music.—Joan Miro (1893-1983)

Flesh was the reason why oil painting was invented.—Willem de Kooning (1904-1997)

If one could only reproduce nature, and always with less beauty than the original, why paint at all? Georgia O'Keeffe (1887-1986)

I have been forced to contradict myself in order to avoid conforming to my own taste.—Marcel Duchamp (1887-1968)

A drawing must bring life to the space which surrounds it.—Henri Matisse (1869-1954)

My brushwork is quite unsystematic. I slam the paint on in all sorts of ways and leave each result to take care of itself.—Vincent van Gogh (1853-1890)

In the brush doing what it's doing, it will stumble on what one couldn't do by oneself. Any art is academic by definition if you know what the result is going to be before you start. Robert Motherwell (1915-1991)

Any art communicates what you're in the mood to receive.—Larry Rivers (1923-2002)

The concern of the artist is with the discrepancy between physical fact and psychic effect.—Josef Albers (1888-1976)

Fine art is that in which the hand, the head, and the heart of man go together.—John Ruskin (1819-1900)

QUOTES BY PABLO PICASSO (1881-1973)

Everyone wants to understand art. Why not try to understand the songs of a bird? Why does one love the night, flowers, everything around one, without trying to understand them? But in the case of a painting people have to understand. If only they would realize above all that an artist works of necessity, that he himself is only a trifling bit of the world, and that no more importance should be attached to him than to plenty of other things which please us in the world, though we can't explain them.

Art is the lie that enables us to realize the truth.

Painting isn't an aesthetic operation; it's a form of magic designed as a mediator between this strange, hostile world and us, a way of seizing the power by giving form to our terrors as well as our desires.

If you know exactly what you are going to do, what's the good of doing it? There's no interest in something you know already. It's much better to do something else.

Freedom is something you have to be very careful about. Whatever you do you find yourself in chains. The freedom not to do something means that you're absolutely bound to do something else. And there are your chains.

When I paint my object is to show what I have found and not what I am looking for. In art intentions are not sufficient and, as we say in Spanish: love must be proved by facts and not by reasons. What one does is what counts and not what one had the intention of doing.

When there's anything to steal, I steal.

Forcing yourself to use restricted means is the sort of restraint that liberates invention. It obliges you to make a kind of progress that you can't even imagine in advance.

I'm always saying to myself: "That's not right yet. You can do better." It's rare when I can prevent myself from taking a thing up again … x number of times, the same thing. Sometimes, it becomes an absolute obsession. But for that matter, why would anyone work, if not for that? To express the same thing, but express it better. It's always necessary to seek for perfection. Obviously, for us, this word no longer has the same meaning. To me, it means: from one canvas to the next, always go further, further …

Painting is stronger than I am. It makes me do what it wants.

The artist is a receptacle for emotions that come from all over the place: from the sky, from the earth, from a scrap of paper, from a passing shape, from a spider's web. That is why we must not discriminate between things. Where things are concerned there are no class distinctions. We must pick out what is good for us where we can find it— except from our own works.

Anything new, anything worth doing, can't be recognized.

We work not only to produce but to give value to time.—Eugene Delacroix (1798-1863)

To avoid situations in which you might make mistakes may be the biggest mistake of all.—Peter McWilliams (1949-2000)

Education's purpose is to replace an empty mind with an open one.—Malcolm Forbes (1919-1990)

Since we cannot know all there is to be known about anything, we ought to know a little about everything.—Blaise Pascal (1623-1662)

Study without desire spoils the memory, and it retains nothing that it takes in.—Leonardo da Vinci (1452-1519)

To define is to destroy, to suggest is to create.—Stephane Mallarme (1842-1898)

I believe that education is a process of living and not a preparation for future living.—John Dewey (1859-1952)

Every man is worth just so much as the things are worth about which he busies himself.—Marcus Aurelius (121-180)

Action and faith enslave thought, both of them in order not to be troubled or inconvenienced by reflection, criticism and doubt.—Henri Frederic Amiel (1821-1881)

You have learned something. That always feels at first as if you had lost something.—H. G. Wells (1866-1946)

Creative activity could be described as a type of learning process where teacher and pupil are located in the same individual.—Arthur Koestler (1905-1983)

Mistakes are the portals of discovery.—James Joyce (1882-1941)

Whether one has natural talent or not, any learning period requires the willingness to suffer uncertainty and embarrassment.—Gail Sheehy (b. 1937)

You must understand the whole of life, not just one little part of it. That is why you must read, this is why you must look at the skies, that is why you must sing and dance, and write poems, and suffer, and understand, for all that is life.—Jiddu Krishnamurti (1895-1986)

When we feel stuck, going nowhere— even starting to slip backward— we may actually be backing up to get a running start.—Dan Millman (b. 1946)

You must either modify your dreams or magnify your skills.—Jim Rohn (b. 1930)

We only do well the things we like doing.—Colette (1873-1954)

The world can only be grasped by action, not by contemplation. The hand is the cutting edge of the mind.

The thing that's important to know is that you never know. You're always sort of feeling your way.—Diane Arbus (1923-1971)

A whisper can be stronger, as an atom is stronger, than a whole mountain.

I think most artists create out of despair. The very nature of creation is not a performing glory on the outside, it's a painful, difficult search within.—Louise Nevelson (1899-1988)

The object of art is not to reproduce reality, but to create a reality of the same intensity.—Alberto Giacometti (1901-1966)

The quality of American life is an insult to the possibilities of human growth.

Making social comment is an artificial place for an artist to start from. If an artist is touched by some social condition, what the artist creates will reflect that, but you can't force it.

The life of the creative man is lead, directed and controlled by boredom. Avoiding boredom is one of our most important purposes.

A photograph is not only an image (as a painting is an image), an interpretation of the real; it is also a trace, something directly stenciled off the real, like a footprint or a death mask.—Susan Sontag (1933-2004)

Life is either always a tightrope or a feather bed. Give me the tightrope.—Edith Wharton (1862-1937)

I have been absolutely terrified every moment of my life— and I've never let it keep me from doing a single thing I wanted to do.—Georgia O'Keeffe (1887-1986)

Hard work, dedication, and desire don't guarantee you a thing, but without them you don't stand a chance.—Pat Riley (b. 1945)

Go to the edge of the cliff and jump off. Build your wings on the way down.—Ray Bradbury (b. 1920)

Nothing is particularly hard if you divide it into small jobs.—Henry Ford (1863-1947)

Any great work of art revives and re-adapts time and space, and the measure of its success is the extent to which it makes you an inhabitant of that world— the extent to which it invites you in and lets you breathe its strange, special air.—Leonard Bernstein (1918-1990)

Creativity requires the courage to let go of certainties.—Erich Fromm (1900-1980)

Creativity is more than just being different. Anybody can play weird— that's easy. What's hard is to be as simple as Bach. Making the simple complicated is commonplace— making the complicated simple, awesomely simple— that's creativity.—Charles Mingus (1922-1979)

Sometimes the majority only means that all the fools are on the same side.—Anonymous

The chief cause of human errors is to be found in the prejudices picked up in childhood.—Rene Descartes (1596-1650)

I suggest that the only books that influence us are those for which we are ready, and which have gone a little further down our particular path than we have gone ourselves.—E. M. Forster (1879-1970)

The key to everything is patience. You get the chicken by hatching the egg— not by smashing it.—Ellen Glasgow (1873-1945)

An idea can turn to dust or magic, depending on the talent that rubs against it.—Bill Bernbach (1911-1982)

The greatest revolution of our generation is the discovery that human beings, by changing the inner attitudes of their minds can change the outer aspects of their lives.—William James (1842-1910)

You live your life between your ears.—Bebe Moore Campbell (1950-2006)

Stupidity consists in wanting to reach conclusions. We are a thread, and we want to know the whole cloth.—Gustave Flaubert (1821-1880)

Opposites are not contradictory but complementary.—Niels Bohr (1885-1962)

A long habit of not thinking a thing wrong gives it a superficial appearance of being right.—Thomas Paine (1737-1809)

An artist can show things that other people are terrified of showing.—Louise Bourgeois (b. 1911)

I'm interested in what would normally be considered the worst aspects of commercial art. I think it's the tension between what seems to be so rigid and clichéd and the fact that art really can't be this way.—Roy Lichtenstein (1923-1997)

Most artwork comes out of someplace you can just tap into, and make that so obvious. And then other people can look at it and say, "I know that place too, that craving."—Judy Pfaff (b. 1946)

One teacher is better than two books.—German proverb

chapter 35

ART, EDUCATION, AND LIFE THEREAFTER

I have been guided by my experiences first as a student and then as an artist and a professor to know what to include in this book. My college art education was an earth-shattering, life-changing revelation. Students of my generation came of age during one of the most politically charged and socially tumultuous periods in our history. Several important political assassinations, the civil rights riots, women's liberation, the Vietnam War, the Watergate scandal, and the alternative lifestyles of the counterculture all occurred in the short span of a decade between the mid-1960s and mid-1970s. All were profound influences.

However, I do not think you must live through great political and social upheaval (one can debate whether that is the case now!) to gain from your art education positive internal transformation and personal insight. In fact, if you do not come away from your education with the sense that your philosophical outlook and intellectual capacity has been profoundly enhanced as a result, then I fear you have missed one of life's great journeys. You should consider, from opening day as a freshman, how a college education can enhance your prospects for the future. Of course, I am referring less to career and more to developing how art stimulates new ways of thinking, doing, and living. Your experience will be unique, so expect surprises, detours, and unexpected opportunities.

WHY BECOME AN ARTIST?

The first healthy test of your academic goals might be to identify your reasons for pursuing art. Is art something you must have in your life? What influences in your childhood may have helped you decide that? I have compiled a list for myself that has been relevant since my student days. However, I admit that I'm not sure how conscious I was of these factors then. In any case, it surely follows that the more aware you are the better. So I offer my reasons for making art. I encourage you to make your own list, but feel free to overlap with any of mine.

- Art makes me feel more alive. Since humans cannot achieve immortality, this will have to do.

- Art satisfies my curiosity. This is not entirely accurate: As soon as I finish an artwork, my curiosity is aroused again as I consider the next one. Art satisfies my continuous visual appetite may be a better description.
- Art provides the opportunity for discovery. If much in life is about maintenance—you know, duty and responsibility, repetition and predictability, cleaning up and repairing—then a creative channel for exploring uncharted territory is appealing and probably necessary for well-being.
- Art is a way to travel in my head, to go to dreams, fantasies, and fictional places.
- Art can communicate what cannot be said in any other medium. Making art gives me another way to express what I think is significant.
- Art gives me a way to exercise my skills and capabilities. The challenge and satisfaction of doing a job well is its own reward.
- Art makes me feel connected to the larger social network that is the history and tradition of all artists. I relish the feeling of camaraderie with my predecessors and contemporaries.
- Art is a basis from which to understand the rest of the world. Because all my subjects come from my experiences in the larger world, I can feel a greater unity between what I do and what I think, between art and life.
- Art provides me with an aesthetic sensibility that extends to all matters in the larger world, including an appreciation of nature, social experiences, and the environment.
- Art allows me to leave a concrete legacy of my existence. My work will become a part of culture's posterity, in greater or lesser forms, whether in museum collections or in the private domains of ordinary citizens.

THE ART DEGREE AS CAREER PREPARATION

What can you expect from a college art education in practical terms, as preparation for a career? You may already know that the answer to this question is less than glowing. It is no secret that the arts are admired in our society but poorly supported economically. The reasons for this diminished status relative to other professions are a topic for debate in another time and place. Instead it may be more productive to focus on what is possible.

If you are a visual arts major pursuing a bachelor of fine arts or a bachelor of arts degree you are essentially in the big pack that emerges from a four-year education with a liberal arts degree. There is no stigma attached to this since liberal arts graduates dominate the college educated and the professional marketplace. The twist is that you must be willing to consider work in fields outside the arts. The difficulty is maintaining a productive studio outside the prime time of performing in a job unrelated to art making. This requires that you split your life into two distinctly different careers. While it can be done, in the long term it requires more discipline and commitment than most people have.

Nonetheless, you may want to consider this dual path, at least initially, as a way to earn a paycheck and make art at the same. Most jobs begin as on-the-job training since liberal arts degrees provide an essential foundation but not the specific tools for performing in the business world. The single most important ability you bring from your college education to the marketplace are highly developed verbal skills. Period. Employers demand sophisticated verbal abilities for their best positions because articulate thinking and communications skills are the basis by which all manner of transactions are accomplished. Simply put, ideas that are not clear and concise never see the light of day.

On resumes and especially during interviews, the initial impression you deliver to a prospective employer is the quality of your communication—how you answer questions, present ideas, and outline goals and objectives. Since effective verbal communication is the backbone of any interview, people get hired or not largely on that basis.

So how do you compete with the herds of liberal arts graduates once you are in the job market? You may not like the sound of my advice. Take more than the required English Composition I and II courses during your college years. Be sure to include courses in speech, communications, and English electives in creative writing and literature. Of course, effective verbal skills also enhance your abilities in art. These skills of analysis and clear thinking will help you understand where you are in your work, where the world has been by comparison, and where you want to go from there.

FINE ARTS VERSUS COMMERCIAL ART

Every entering art major faces this choice. I did when my professors told me my work was facile and had commercial qualities. But commercial work was not my interest, so I had to relearn everything about materials and techniques. For a while I felt caught in the crossfire between the two. Although it can be argued that fine art and commercial art share the common language of composition and formalism, what they do not have in common makes for a stark choice.

In commercial work, the art, the subjects, the media, and their purposes in the marketplace are determined by the needs of business clients, not the artist. While commercial artists are valued and rewarded, they are not permitted the free range of self-expression of the fine artist. The artist in the business environment must act within a defined system of requirements, limitations, and deadlines. By contrast, the fine artist acts independently and according to his own internal creative needs and desires. The great risk for the fine artist is that no one else may be interested in what he has to offer. He assumes a considerable responsibility in finding a relevant subject matter and a way of representing it that arouses both him and an audience.

So how do you decide? If serving the business community and tailoring your creativity to its specific purposes seems agreeable, you may want to opt for the career possibilities that commercial art can offer. If you are independent and value the individuality of your art, you may want to preserve the parameters of self-expression by pursuing one of the specialties in the fine arts. The differences in these two visual worlds suggest a huge philosophical divide that only the aspiring artist can evaluate. These distinctions are matters of personal ethics, values, and perceptions about contemporary art, the business world, society, the environment, and the individual's role in all of them. Whatever you decide, you will make the best choice based on knowing who you are.

THE ARTIST AS TEACHER

A practical career choice is to major in art education to prepare for teaching K-12 grades in public or private schools. Teaching is a realistic alternative to the uncertainties of a career in the fine arts and to the business pressures of commercial art. Verbal skills are immensely helpful at all levels of teaching since classroom motivation is so closely linked with the instructor's powers of persuasion. As an instructor, you get to use the same expertise in the classroom that it takes to make art in the studio. This is an important continuity between the necessary day job and the role of the artist, avoiding the psychological fragmentation that can so easily silence that role when the day job is in an unrelated field. Another benefit of teaching is that an academic calendar allows time to produce your own work.

As a student, the trade-off is that you will not be able to register for as many of the fine arts courses that are available to majors. Instead you will be required to take education courses for teacher preparation. It means you will be less prepared as an artist. But you can have your cake and eat it too! I did. Stay in college an extra year and do a double major in art education and fine arts. Voila! You have more career options than your single major peers when you graduate, and you have not sacrificed developing your skills in making art.

I know from the experience of teaching elementary art that teachers need reams of patience and a healthy appreciation of children in large groups and the culture that comes with it. Since art making by definition often calls upon the artist to tap into the resources of his own childhood, the connection to children's experiences should seem natural to the classroom art teacher.

GRADUATE SCHOOL

Is graduate school too early to think about while still an undergraduate? If you are committed to completing an undergraduate degree in art, it is useful to consider the main reasons for pursuing graduate work: (1) if you want to teach on the college level, you must complete the Master of Fine Arts (MFA) degree; (2) if you want to pursue more specialized areas inadequately covered in undergraduate programs, such as art history or museum and curatorial studies, you will need an advanced degree; and (3) the two years of postgraduate concentration in your chosen studio specialty will help develop (and possibly hasten) a mature body of work that can begin to represent you in the art gallery world.

Any graduate school application requires competitive screening for admission. (Screening is not generally required in undergraduate programs.) Juried work at this level will mean that you will need to produce a superior portfolio during your undergraduate years. It may be wise to take a couple years off after earning a baccalaureate degree to concentrate on building a focused and unified body of work that will increase the quality of your portfolio for application to graduate programs. When you are ready, apply to three or more schools to insure your acceptance to one of them.

ART SCHOOL OR UNIVERSITY

A frequent question I am asked by students is whether they should transfer to an art school or university. My response nearly always is go to university! Since the advent of modernism 200 years ago, art has become so much about itself, art for art's sake, that it is now too separated from general culture and a mainstream audience. This dilemma is the likely cause of the breakdown between art and the public and why there is so much misunderstanding about art in our society. There is recent evidence in the gallery world that artists are beginning to attempt to bridge the gaps by endowing art with more social, political, and worldly content relevant to the times.

Art schools are especially inbred with limited course offerings outside the arts and strong emphases on art specialties and career development. You have less wiggle room in art academy environments. The best art schools have academic requirements in the humanities, but none can match the range and depth of universities. Since life after higher education has a way of changing course, perhaps several times during adulthood, why needlessly limit your options?

Universities have the mission to offer students, regardless of department majors, the opportunity to sample courses from a spectrum of subjects and disciplines, from the humanities to the sciences. In fact, should you decide that art is not for you after all, you can change majors to any number of other departments without the hassle of changing institutions.

Since the subject matter of art derives from the world at large and universities best represent the vastness of that range, selecting which university becomes your greater problem.

WHO IS THE TEACHER?

Speaking of education, an underappreciated quality of artists is that much of what they do is self-taught. More often than not, the specialty you choose as an undergraduate is not the art you will practice years later. It was true in my case. I had a double major in painting and printmaking, but my practice has gradually evolved into mixed media and collage. I am not sure why this seems to be a common tendency. Perhaps what is exciting to the novice artist is not necessarily of sustaining interest for the mature artist. Since invention or innovation is the nature of art making, the need to change tracks from time to time is not surprising.

The point is that if you did not learn about a material or a technique in college but now feel inclined to do so, you will find a way to work in new directions if you have the curiosity and willingness to experiment. If an unfamiliar way of working is exciting, that provides the motivation to figure it out, to find how to make that material or method work on your own terms. Be patient enough to practice and do the research necessary to master a new medium. You are teacher and artist rolled into one.

THE ARTIST AS CITIZEN GENERAL

If you are not yet convinced of the merits of the university, maybe this topic will help. You will understand, sooner rather than later, that art making is more than clocking time in the studio. Since inspiration comes from life experiences, the richer and deeper you know the world, the better the possibilities for choosing subject matter and content—and ultimately the better the quality of the art. The relevance of your work, how its meanings connect to an audience, is made possible by how you as an artist understand the issues of the day. What are its most timely and pressing interests and concerns? How is it possible to harness those interests to art?

The most significant artists know the temper of their times. The artist who "speaks" to his time senses "something in the air," as if his mind and senses are attuned like radar to what is happening in society and culture. These sensitive qualities are seen in the movements and stylistic changes throughout the history of art and into the present day. For example, the Cubist vision that shattered the 500-year-old tradition of Renaissance perspective was an appropriate response to the social unrest and cultural fragmentation triggered by the abundant and rapid innovations of the Industrial Revolution. In our own time, the breaking down of mainstream culture into myriad subcultures has been hastened by new forms of electronic media and is reflected in the lack of focus or dominant forms of expression in the contemporary art world.

How do you deal with it all? Stay informed, cultivate a wide range of interests, keep your eye on the horizon, and make your work in that context—that is, in the world you live in as you understand it.

ART AND POPULAR CULTURE

The topic of popular culture in relation to art may be a third rail. Most of my students know that I am critical of American mainstream culture. It is not sacrilege to suggest that its mass appeal is generally aimed at the lowest common denominator. Pop culture is not meant to sustain thinking or express profound truths. I think most of it is generated by the excesses of American consumerism and sustained by the indiscriminate pursuit of redundant profit. Yes, this complaint may be the rant of a cranky professor. However, I hasten to say (1) I have held these opinions since my student days, and (2) there are remarkable multitudes of thoughtful people who agree.

With that shocker as a preface, let me get to the point. One of the ways you must operate as an artist is to distinguish the good from the bad. You want to make good art rather than, well, the other kind. This means training yourself to become a cultural critic by knowing what is shallow, superficial, banal, clichéd, indifferent, and irrelevant. This does not mean you must embrace only perfection or that what is meaningful must be elitist. A discriminating mind is one that can evaluate fairly and accurately the culture, society, and politics of given time and place, particularly the present time and place.

I do not think you must turn your back on popular culture. Experiences have value as long as you understand them in their contexts. Hold on to your hat. I observe and partake in pop culture. I want to know what is going on in the world and how that culture may affect my thinking and that of other people. Sometimes my attention is held by how bad something is. In a few cases, a form or a given subject is *so bad* it is good! An object can occasionally be so crass, crude, or blatant that it carries its own fascination. Then I am challenged to figure out why. The pondering of its "mystery" may be its merit, whether or not I can explain it in any rational terms. Confused by what may seem to be contradictory assessments? Remember the gray areas in art and life. It is possible to love the object we hate and vice versa.

In fact, many artists pay close attention to selected areas of popular culture because they are interested in how to adapt it as subject matter for their art. The Pop artists of the 1960s are prime examples. Andy Warhol's provocations with coke bottles, Campbell's soup cans, and Brillo boxes made us see our consumer habits in a new way, while Roy Lichtenstein's adaptation of the comic strip as visual melodrama on a grand scale was cunning and ingenious. These artists expanded the way we see both art and popular culture.

The irony of adapting forms from popular culture for art making is that you can set aside your judgment— it is possible to alter the context of these forms so that it does not matter that they are bad, clichéd, or indifferent—as long as you redefine and transform the material knowingly. Naïve or indiscriminate adoption of pop culture subjects will invariably backfire. We count on the artist to know the difference.

THE ARTIST AS SOLITARY FIGURE

Creative disciplines require so much internal effort that making art requires prolonged periods laboring in solitude. (Theater, dance, film, and some of the applied arts may be exceptions.) Distractions are anathema to the practice of art. If you are not comfortable in your own skin, art may not be for you. The need for solitary effort does not mean the artist must be a social misfit or misanthrope. Most artists, like other members of society, seek a balance between the singular enterprise of the studio and the supporting society of family and friends. What is significant is to understand your own social and creative rhythms and adjust them to your needs.

IN A WORD, WHAT DO WE WANT FROM ART?

The following is a list of words that suggests the scope of what we might want when looking at or making art. Note that many of these descriptive nouns and phrases seem polarized. Dualities, opposites, and contradictions are often the content in art—expanding its mysteries, tensions, and dynamic confrontations. The words are arranged in loose groups that suggest their possible interactions. Art may be about any, all, or none of them as seen through the eye of the beholder. This is just a start. You can make your own list and find yourself in it.

- Skill, method, spontaneity, gesture.
- Beauty, order, artlessness, unaesthetic form (ugliness).
- Intellect, intuition.
- Reality, truth, fantasy, dream, fiction, propaganda.
- Trend, fashion, tradition.
- Work, purpose, play, whim.
- Revolution, insurrection, stability, familiarity.
- Challenge, originality.
- Society, public, self, privacy.
- Clashing juxtaposition, classic form.
- Appearance, inner vision, proclamation.
- Description, elaboration, complexity, reduction, simplicity.
- Quality, taste, bias, connoisseurship.
- Mystery, explanation, clarity.
- Travel, transformation, transcendence.

Enough wordplay. Get visual. Start your art.

chapter

36

BIBLIOGRAPHY: SUGGESTIONS FOR READING AND LOOKING

Reading is an art in itself—and knowing what is worth reading is part of that process. The abundance of books in American life is a cultural wonder alongside the various technological forms that would seem to replace it. Perhaps books endure because they do not have to be plugged in or lighted up—and they can be taken to any quiet, comfortable spot to read and contemplate.

I confess to a bias. I am an eclectic bibliophile. I am drawn to books both for their content and for their physical properties as objects. Their various bindings, papers, typefaces, and general design all appeal to me. A new book smells as good as the inside of a new car (though both are the product of chemicals, of course). Leafing through an art book with profuse reproductions and illustrations is a wonderfully idle but stimulating pleasure. Depending on what the art is about (or where it may be located as a collection), you can be transported to another time and place. It is the ultimate armchair traveling. And yes, a picture is worth a thousand words.

The greatest value books provide is the privilege of reading about other people's experiences and insights. As I turn the pages of a book, there is the anticipation that the author's words will suddenly answer some conundrum I have not been able to resolve on my own or reveal some secret truth I have been yearning to uncover but only vaguely sensed. Fortunately, that is sometimes the case! It has always felt worth the effort to find ideas in reading that resonate with my own inclinations or, more dramatically, introduce new viewpoints and information that expand my awareness of a subject.

Artists realize that the subject matter and the content of their work come from sources *outside* the art world. The best shortcut to getting to know those subjects is to read. You do not have to be a rocket scientist to read about jet propulsion or a brain surgeon to read about the latest discoveries in human consciousness. Also, you do not have to understand everything you read to extract from it a general framework of what the subject is about. The important function for artists is that reading stimulates the imagination—and that is what our business is about. For many artists, visual and verbal acuity seem to go together.

The books I have chosen to recommend are all selections from my personal library. Many I have read cover to cover, a few more than once, while others I have dipped into many times for reference. Close reading, skimming, or occasional referring are all valid ways of getting sustenance from the printed word. These lists are in no way inclusive and are by necessity a reflection of my interests and biases as an artist. I have tried to choose according to what I imagine would be of interest to art students. In fact, a few of these books I read as a student myself, and have been retained as a continuing influence on my thinking. In other respects, I trust that what I think is significant and compelling to read may also be to others. After all, an artist never stops being a student.

I do not know if all the books listed here are still in print. I do know that most of the older copies I own have been reprinted in newer editions. Many older books are now classics in the field and should not be difficult to find.

The absence of a list of art history survey books is deliberate. Most are massive tomes that few read verbatim, save those you will be required to read in your art history courses. The only art history survey I think is as readable as a novel is Robert Hughes' engaging summary of modernism called *The Shock of the New*.

The reading suggestions are divided into separate categories of subject for easier reference. I am especially fond of *Artists' Writings and Interviews* since I believe artists speak best about their art and the art of their peers. I think we can all appreciate hearing from the horses' mouths. That list is the longest and the one with the most annotated descriptions. I have added annotations wherever I thought they would be useful to know, and of course, to motivate the reader. If any of these books uncovers worthy advice or helpful insights to those who search, then my effort will have been rewarded.

ART FUNDAMENTALS/FOUNDATION

These books offer great variety. Many are lavishly illustrated and can be good reads when the text is connected to the art works represented. All are meant to supplement studio practice in the foundation courses.
- Barrett, Terry, *Making Art: Form and Meaning*, McGraw Hill, 2011.
- Bevlin, Marjorie Elliott, *Design Through Discovery*, Holt, Rinehart and Winston, 1985.
- Dantzic, Cynthia Maris, Design Dimensions, Prentice Hall, 1990.
- Fichner-Rathus, Lois, *Foundations of Art and Design*, Thomson Wadsworth, 2008.
- Goldstein, Nathan, *Design and Composition*, Prentice-Hall Inc., 1989.
- Itten, Johannes, *Design and Form*, John Wiley & Sons, 2003.
- Knobler, Nathan, *The Visual Dialogue*, Holt, Rinehart and Winston, 1980.
- Lauer, David A., and Stephen Pentak, *Design Basics*, Thomson Wadsworth, 2008.
- Luecking, Stephen, *Principles of Three-Dimensional Design*, Prentice Hall, 2002.
- Poore, Henry Rankin, *Composition in Art*, Dover Publications, Inc., 1976.
- Stewart, Mary, *Launching the Imagination: A Comprehensive Guide to Basic Design*, McGraw Hill, 2008. This book is also printed in two volumes, one for 2D and one for 3D.
- Taylor, Joshua C., *Learning to Look*, University of Chicago Press, 1963.
- Wong, Wucious, *Principles of Form and Design*, Van Nostrand Reinhold, 1993.
- Zelanski, Paul and Mary Pat Fisher, *Design: Principles and Problems*, Holt, Rinehart and Winston, 1984.
- Zelanski, Paul and Mary Pat Fisher, *Shaping Space*, Thomson Wadsworth, 2007.

DRAWING

Drawing textbooks vary greatly in quality and scope. While these are the best ones I have seen, I am sure there are many others in print worthy of attention. Of course, books cannot teach you how to draw, but they can provide substance from conceptual insights to practical tips.

- Brooke, Sandy, *Drawing as Expression*, Pearson Prentice Hall, 2007.
- Chaet, Bernard, *The Art of Drawing*, Holt, Rinehart and Winston, 1978.
- Dantzic, Cynthia Maris, *Drawing Dimensions*, Prentice Hall, 1999.
- Drury, Fritz and Joanne Stryker, *Drawing: Structure and Vision*, Pearson Prentice Hall, 2009.
- Edwards, Betty, *Drawing on the Right Side of the Brain*, J. P. Tarcher, Inc., 1979.
- Enstice, Wayne and Melody Peters, *Drawing: Space, Form, and Expression*, Pearson Prentice Hall, 2003.
- Mendelowitz, Daniel, David L. Faber, and Duane A. Wakeham, *A Guide to Drawing*, Thomson Wadsworth, 2007.
- Sale, Teel and Claudia Betti, *Drawing: A Contemporary Approach*, Thomson Wadsworth, 2008. This book is highly recommended.
- Verbell, Victoria, *Exploring the Basics of Drawing*, Thomson Delmar Learning, 2005.

FIGURE DRAWING

These books focus on the human form as the subject matter of drawing.

- Bridgman, George B., *Bridgman's Life Drawing*, Dover Publications, Inc., 1971. This is a short, concise classic in which illustrations of the drawn figure play the major role.
- Brown, Clint and Cheryl McLean, *Drawing From Life*, Thomson Wadsworth, 2004.
- Flint, Tom, Consultant/Editor, *Anatomy for the Artist*, Barnes & Noble Books, 2004. Clear drawings illustrate anatomical structures.
- Goldstein, Nathan, *Figure Drawing*, Pearson Prentice Hall, 2011. This book is highly recommended.
- Nicolaides, Kimon, *The Natural Way to Draw*, Houghton Mifflin co., 1975. As one of the earliest popular texts on drawing (first published in 1941), this book has influenced many others since, including those on this list.

COLLAGE

Aside from artist monographs—that is, books about artists who specifically work in collage—there are few good books on the subject. I heartily recommend Taylor for its descriptive text and beautiful illustrations. The Larbalestier is excellent for exploring a wide range of materials and techniques.

- Ades, Dawn, *Photomontage*, Thames and Hudson, 1986.
- Lavin, Maud et al., *Montage and Modern Life* 1919-1942, MIT Press, 1992.
- Larbalestier, Simon, *The Art and Craft of Collage*, Chronicle Books, 1995.
- Taylor, Brandon, *Collage: The Making of Modern Art*, Thames & Hudson, 2004.

COLOR

Josef Albers' compact book is the modern bible on color since its publication in 1963. It has been reprinted many times, and deservedly so for its clear and concise descriptions of color behavior. Those by Johannes Itten, who taught at the famed Bauhaus School in Germany between the wars, are excellent guides as well.

- Albers, Josef, *Interaction of Color*, Yale University Press, 1976.
- Birren, Faber, *Color: A Survey in Words and Pictures*, Citadel Press, 1963.
- Burner, Alan Shijo McManus, *Dynasty of Light: Foundational Studies and Discourses on Color Theory*, Thomson, 2006. Aided by many illustrations, the author explores everything about color, including in architecture and in music.
- Itten, Johannes, *The Elements of Color*, John Wiley & Sons, Inc., 2003. A smaller, concise version of the one below.
- Itten, Johannes, *The Art of Color*, John Wiley & Sons, Inc., 2002. A coffee table book with vivid illustrations in an extra-large format.
- Pentak, Stephen and Richard Roth, *Color Basics*, Thomson Wadsworth, 2004.
- Zelanski, Paul and Mary Pat Fisher, *Color*, Pearson Prentice Hall, 2006.

MATERIALS AND TECHNIQUES OF STUDIO PRACTICE

Many of these books address the various media of painting, including oil, encaustic, acrylic, tempera, gouache, and watercolor. These are useful guides as references to materials and technical procedures. Although painting no longer dominates the visual arts, it did so for centuries and remains today a major player. The bible for painters is Mayer's thick tome, a virtual encyclopedia of what is possible in paint. It has been in print since 1940.

- Chaet, Bernard, *An Artist's Notebook: Techniques and Materials*, Holt, Rinehart and Winston, 1979. This concise book is excellent for the new painter.
- Colquhoun, Norman, *Painting: A Creative Approach*, Dover Publications, Inc., 1969.
- Goldstein, Nathan, *Painting: Visual and Technical Fundamentals*, Prentice-Hall, 1979.
- Kay, Reed, *The Painter's Companion*, Webb Books Inc., 1961.
- Mayer, Ralph, *The Artist's Handbook of Materials and Techniques*, Viking, 1985.
- Robertson, Jean and Craig McDaniel, *Painting as a Language*, Wadsworth Thomson Learning, 2000. The subtitle, *Material, Technique, Form, Content*, lives up to its promise. This is the most thorough coverage on the practice of painting I have seen.
- Verhelst, Wilbert, *Sculpture: Tools, Materials, and Techniques*, Prentice-Hall Inc., 1973.

ARTISTS' WRITINGS AND INTERVIEWS

Who should know more about art than artists? The great masters, who have had significant influence on subsequent generations, have told us much about how they make their art and how they view the world outside their studios.

- Bayles, David and Ted Orland, *Art & Fear*, Image Continuum Press, 2005.

- Berger, John, *Ways of Seeing*, BBC and Penguin Books, 1983. Primarily a novelist, Berger's uncanny eye understood the hidden messages in our culture glut of images and the dialogues between the fine arts and popular culture.
- Cabanne, Pierre, *Dialogues with Marcel Duchamp*, the Viking Press, 1971. Duchamp had an enormous impact on mid-twentieth century art by greatly expanding the definition of art. His work sets the stage for Pop Art, conceptual art, and installation. His responses in this interview make the reader think about the basis and purposes of art making.
- Close, Chuck, *The Portraits Speak: Chuck Close in Conversation with 27 of his Subjects*. Art Resources Transfer, Inc., 1997. Interviews with contemporary artists the painter has depicted make this thick tome a wonderful read about ideas in postmodernism.
- Flam, Jack, *Matisse on Art*, University of California Press, 1995. What Matisse had to say is good advice—and no one has said as much again quite his way.
- Fletcher, Alan, *The Art of Looking Sideways*, Phaidon, 2001. This huge volume (534 pages) is a delightful treasure of facts, ideas, stories, quotes, and illustrations relating to visual phenomena of all kinds. Its entertaining and eclectic style allows you to drop in on any page and find a nugget of fact or fancy relating to the visual world.
- Gabo, Naum, *Of Divers Arts*, Princeton University Press, 1962.
- Henri, Robert, *The Art Spirit*, Harper & Row, 1984. Henri may have been a better teacher than an artist. This book, first published in 1923, is a cogent memoir of his ideas expressed in the classroom. He espoused spontaneity in art making and embraced the many connections between art and life.
- Hickey, Dave (introduction) and Lucinda Barnes, editor, *Between Artists*, ART Press, 1996. Here artists interview artists—a good combination.
- Hockney, David, *Hockney on "Art"*, Little, Brown, 2002. Brilliant observations about art making and its connections to both old and modern masters.
- Hockney, David, *Secret Knowledge*, Viking Studio, 2001. Hockney proposes that the old masters used a variety of technical devices, from special lenses to camera obscuras, to make their paintings remarkably illusionistic.
- Kandinsky, Wassily, *Concerning the Spiritual in Art*, MFA Publications, 2006. This short, lyrical treatise of 1911 is the seminal work on the development of abstract art. The feeling of search and experiment expressed by Kandinsky has the effect of "you are there" at the "eureka" moment of discovery.
- Kuh, Katharine, *The Artist's Voice*, Da Capo Press, 1990. The voices are revealing and engaging interviews with 17 modern masters.
- Leger, Fernand, *Functions of Painting*, The Viking Press, 1973. Leger was a pioneering Cubist and later an influential teacher whose writing style is concise, direct, and powerful—much like his paintings.
- Miro, Joan, *Selected Writing and Interviews*, edited by Margit Rowell, Da Capo Press, 1992. The other Spanish Surrealist offers his insights on a wide range of topics.
- Nesbett, Peter and Shelly Bancroft, Sarah Andress, editors, *Letters to a Young Artist*, Darte Publishing, LLC, 2006. Twenty-three established artists respond poignantly with useful advice to a letter from a young, struggling artist. Rilke's book below was its inspiration.
- Orland, Ted, *The View From the Studio Door*, Image Continuum Press, 2006. This book and *Art & Fear* offer useful advice to students and artists about coping with the current climate of career survival, cultural change, shifting values, and worldly concerns.
- Rilke, Rainer Maria, *Letters to a Young Poet*, W. W. Norton & Co., 1962. The poet is an artist; see Nesbett's book above.

- Salle, David, *How to See*, W. W. Norton & Co., 2016. Salle is a master of both art and words. He manages to communicate complicated insights about art via plain language.
- Shahn, Ben, *The Shape of Content*, Vintage Books, 1957. Shahn speaks directly to the student and emerging artist. He argues for understanding the difference between form and content.
- Sloan, John, *Gist of Art*, Dover Publications, Inc., 1977. Another great teacher sums up his thoughts about art.
- Sontag, Susan, *On Photography*, Dell Publishing Co., Inc., 1977. Though not exactly a fit in this category, the artist (novelist) has uncovered and redefined how we see photographs of all kinds.
- Truitt, Ann, *Daybook*, Penguin Books, 1982. This is the journal of an artist who thought deeply about art, life, teaching, and students. Two other journals have been published as well with the titles, *Turn* (Viking) and *Prospect* (Scribner).
- Wilkinson, Alan, editor, *Henry Moore: Writings and Conversations*, University of California Press, 2002.

CRITICISM, THEORY, AND GENERAL TOPICS

These selections do not fit neatly into the other categories, but each offers something distinctive and valuable to an art education.
- Anderson, Kimberly, and Carson, Jenny, *Understanding Visual Artforms in Our World*. Kendal Hunt Publishing, 2017. This book is not an art history text. Its rich and expansive descriptions of all manner of visual forms, styles, and artifacts are beautifully supported by prolific color illustrations. Dip into any page or chapter as a ready reference.
- Buster, Kendall and Paula Crawford, *The Critique Handbook*, Prentice Hall, 2010. This compact paperback describes how to get the most out of critiques in and out of the classroom.
- Chipp, Herschel B., *Theories of Modern Art*, University of California Press, 1968. The great documents of art since postimpressionism is here, and most are in the words of the artists themselves.
- Cooper, Douglas, *The Cubist Epoch*, Phaidon Publishers, 1971. This lively narrative is a primer of modern art with good illustrations.
- Goleman, Daniel, Paul Kaufman, and Michael Ray, *The Creative Spirit*, Dutton, 1992. Find out how and where creativity originates and how to put it to work.
- Hughes, Robert, *The Shock of the New*, McGraw Hill, 1991. For three decades, Hughes was the art critic for *Time* magazine. The book is a compilation of modernism's highlights that was first a TV series aired by Public Televisions in the 1980s. Hughes' incisive and highly descriptive language makes this classic hard to resist.
- Hughes, Robert, *Nothing if not Critical*, Penguin Books, 1990. Less sweeping than *The Shock*, this small paperback offers concise summaries of individual modern and contemporary masters.
- Lazzari, Margaret R., *The Practical Handbook for the Emerging Artist*, Wadsworth Thomson Learning, 2002. With lots of practical advice for the new artist, you may want to read this offering to know what you may be about to confront in the real world.
- Maizels, John, *Raw Creation: Outsider Art and Beyond*. Phaidon Press Limited, 1996. A concise text and excellent illustrations make this large format book a good source for appreciating the enormous range of styles in outsider art.
- Sayre, Henry M., *Writing About Art*, Prentice Hall, 1995. Here is evidence that improving your verbal expression improves your visual understanding.

- Varnedoe, Kirk, *A Fine Disregard: What Makes Modern Art Modern.* Harry N. Abrams, 1990. The author contends that great changes in the perceptions of space distinguish modern art from the art of centuries past. While cultural influences play a role, Varnedoe argues that artists reinvent primarily through their imaginations.
- Watson, John, and Horner, Brian, *Living the Dream: The Morning after the Dream.* Kendall Hunt Publishing, 1917. When your formal art education is complete, what then? This short, concise book offers sound, practical advice about how to live and work as an artist.
- Whitford, Frank, *Understanding Abstract Art*, E. P. Dutton, 1987. Despite the fact that abstract art is one hundred years old, there is still a lot of misunderstanding about it. This may clear up some of the mystery and enhance your appreciation.